PRAISE FOR
SELLING SATURDAYS

"When I was putting together championship football teams at Oklahoma, I knew it was all about the players. I recruited the best of the best, the guys every team in America wanted. Winning in that environment required great selling skills, exactly the stuff Jeff Beals talks about in this book. I recommend it highly."

— Barry Switzer
Hall of Fame coach of the Oklahoma Sooners
and championship coach of the Dallas Cowboys

"For years, I have delivered motivational speeches to organizations and corporations around the world. When I talk about leadership, I borrow heavily from the world of sports. In this book, Jeff Beals inspires sales professionals using thought-provoking stories from college football recruiting. His colorful writing style makes you feel like you're right there alongside Hall-of-Fame coaches racing to outsell the competition in a high-stakes battle for the nation's best athletes. Whether you're a rookie or veteran sales professional, Jeff's advice is relevant and ready to implement."

— Pat Williams
Orlando Magic senior vice president
and author of *Leadership Excellence*

"I liked this book so much I recommended it to both my sons. *Selling Saturdays* is great for all coaches, managers and CEOs. There are years of experience represented in this book by some of the best salesmen/leaders there ever has been."

— R.C. Slocum
Hall of Fame former coach of the Texas A&M Aggies

"Recruiting is the life blood of college football and Jeff's book gives insight like never seen before."

— Sean Callahan
Rivals.com and publisher of Huskeronline.com

"As someone who has lived in both the corporate and football worlds, I can attest that similar skills and competencies are required for success on the field and in the boardroom. In *Selling Saturdays*, Jeff Beals does an outstanding job of portraying how football coaches become such effective marketers and dealmakers. Apply the strategies and techniques described in this book and watch your business soar."

— **Joe Moglia**
head coach of Coastal Carolina University
and chairman of TD Ameritrade

"How about this! A sales book that is so readable and entertaining, you turn the pages like a good novel. Jeff Beals gives sales people a real pre-game pep talk...alternating from doable 'Blue Chip Tips' to great stories of college football players and coaches...to important reminders about branding, commitment, relationships, and trust. If you love college football – if you love selling – this is the book for you!"

— **Lou Heckler**
motivational speaker and business essayist
on the PBS television program, *Nightly Business Report*

"Jeff Beals has thoroughly captured the passion, compet-itiveness and daily life of a college football coach. While it may seem extreme to those on the outside of college football, it is the norm for individuals and families who choose to live and work in that environment. Jeff uses this setting as a model for creativeness, hard work and perseverance. He has compiled experiences that are amusing, insightful and applicable to those who live in a competitive world. Great job, Jeff!"

— **Gary Barnett**
former coach of the Colorado Buffaloes and Northwestern Wildcats
and college football color analyst, *Sports USA*

"The recruiting world is quite the roller-coaster ride, and it's only gotten that much more frenetic in recent years. Jeff Beals really hustled to detail how the sales pitch works—and doesn't—through the experiences of several top college football coaches in *Selling Saturdays*. Football fans will be as intrigued as sales people, who like these coaches are looking for every edge."

— **Bruce Feldman**
New York Times Bestselling author of
Swing Your Sword and Meat Market:
Inside the Smashmouth World of College Football Recruiting

"Jeff Beals hits another homerun in his second book on sales and marketing. The book is not only entertaining through Jeff's storytelling, but provides an incredible amount of take-a-ways for anyone aspiring to have a winning career."

— **Jane Schulte**
author of *Work Smart, Not Hard!*

"While *Selling Saturdays* uses stories from football recruiting, it's an outstanding resource for collegiate coaches of all sports. Reading how so many legendary football coaches sold their programs to elite athletes gave me ideas I can use to help build by program."

— **Amanda Lehotak**
head softball coach, University of Texas at San Antonio

"*Selling Saturdays* is a highly innovative and engaging book. It's well written, tightly edited, and brimming with action, suspense, and fascinating stories. Jeff brings it all together with his very practical Blue Chip Tips. It's a winning formula for boosting sales and marketing effectiveness."

— **Jim Clemmer**
practical leadership author,
workshop facilitator and team developer

"Brilliant! *Selling Saturdays* explores the marketing and selling of college football as a resource for career sales people like myself. I especially like the Blue Chip Tips after every chapter. You have given me some great ideas to implement in my own career. Thank you!"

— **Van Deeb**
national real estate speaker & author

"*Selling Saturdays: Blue Chip Sales & Marketing Tips from College Football* is perfect for football fans who look at a sales career as the ultimate competition. Put your helmet on and fasten your chin strap, because this book will give you the knowledge and skill you need to tackle any competition."

— **Brian Sullivan**
author of *20 Days to the Top*

"Everyone sells every day of their lives, and Jeff's original and in-depth, behind-the-scenes review of college football proves this. A great analogy of sales, marketing, branding and persuasion."

— **Samara Pope**
author of *The Sales Psychologist*

"Mind-boggling stories and deep insight! Jeff Beals takes you behind the scenes of one of America's most beloved spectator sports in order that you may be more successful in whatever you do. If you're looking for a book that inspires you to step out of your comfort zone, this is it."

— **Pam Lontos**
Pam Lontos Consulting and author of
I See Your Name Everywhere: Leverage the Power of
the Media to Grow your Fame, Wealth and Success

"If you want to succeed in ANY business today, Jeff Beals' *Selling Saturdays* is a must-read for you. In today's information-overloaded society, you have to work harder than ever to make yourself stand out. *Selling Saturdays* teaches the critical principles of selling that you need to know in today's hyper-competitive marketplace. From 'Everyone on the team must sell' to 'Prospecting is a never-ending activity,' Jeff magically delivers a full buffet of money-making nuggets in an easy-to-digest way that makes it impossible to put this book down. Five out of five stars!"

— **Glenn Shepard**
president of Glenn Shepard Seminars, Nashville, TN

"In *Selling Saturdays*, Jeff Beals scores tremendous insight from the legends of the gridiron that translates into universal advice on selling and marketing. This book will help you win in any walk of life."

— **J.P. Hansen**
best-selling and award-winning author of *The Bliss List*

"Jeff Beals does a wonderful job taking you into the heads of some of the finest football coaches in history and relates their thoughts and actions to today's sales dynamics. He has made this book a wonderful read and makes us think differently about who we are, what we do, what we strive for and how to carry it through to completion with a high level of integrity! Jeff parlayed a wonderful mix of Knute Rockne to Tom Osborne and many in between, all in the hopes of helping us to be the best that we can be! Thanks Jeff for you artistry!"

— **Ron "Gus" Gustafson,**
author of *Fully Armed*

"Rarely is the topic of football recruiting tied to success in sales and marketing in business, but Beals does a fantastic job of blending the two seamlessly. This is a must-read for anyone who's a football fan—and trying to get ahead in the business world."

— **Adam Gorney**
West analyst, Rivals.com

"If you're in sales or leadership, this book is a must-read even if you have little use for the game of football. The lessons this book teaches go far beyond football. Jeff shares how coaches, when they're recruiting, are actually selling confidence and trust to high school students and their parents. The strategies necessary for coaches to be successful are the same strategies salespersons need if they intend to be leaders. *Selling Saturdays* will become your playbook. You'll read it, study it, make notes in it and then go out and apply it."

— **Mark Hunter**
author of *High-Profit Selling*

"Jeff Beals uses examples and anecdotes from the world of college football recruiting to illustrate the key tenets of effective sales and brilliant marketing. He offers sound advice on marketing plans, branding, identifying new prospects, building trust, and closing the deal. If you love football, you'll love the book. If you don't love football, and don't even know anything about football, don't let that hold you back. If you're keen to improve your sales and marketing skills, this book is packed with good lessons."

— **Joshua Waldman**
author of *Job Searching with Social Media For Dummies*
and blogger at CareerEnlightenment.com

"*Selling Saturdays* is chockfull of practical and productive tips to dramatically increase sales and marketing results. Jeff's use of real-life college football examples really drives home his points with amazing and exciting impact. Even non-football fans (like me) will benefit from the way Jeff marries his football passion and exhaustive research with his sales and marketing insights and expertise. This book will not only motivate you, it will give you the tools to improve your career, your business or your life. Get it today!"

— **Michael Hughes**
North America's Networking Guru

"For those who can't stand to read a dry 'how-to' sales book, this is the one for you. Jeff has combined principles from the worlds of sports and sales seamlessly."

— **April Kelly**
former LinkedIn executive and author of *Spaghetti on the Wall:*
Branding and Networking Methods that Stick!

SELLING
Saturdays

Blue-chip sales tips from college football

SELLING
Saturdays

KEYNOTE O
PUBLISHING
OMAHA, NEBRASKA

JEFF BEALS

Library of Congress Control Number: 2012948364

Paperback ISBN: 978-0-9797438-2-5
Cataloging in Publication Data on file with Publisher
Kindle ISBN: 978-0-9797438-3-2
E-book ISBN: 978-0-9797438-4-9

Marketing and Publicity: Concierge Marketing Inc.
Cover and Interior Design: TLCGraphics
Editorial services: Sandra Wendel, Write On, Inc.

KEYNOTE PUBLISHING, LLC
PO Box 540663
Omaha, NE 68154
www.JeffBeals.com

Printed in the United States of America.
10 9 8 7 6 5 4 3 2 1

To my beautiful daughter, Madeline Nicole Beals.

May you grow up to be as lovely a woman and as big a college football fan as your mother.

CONTENTS

PREFACE

Our contemporary marketplace is full of opportunity yet fraught with peril.

To succeed as a marketer or salesperson in today's hyper-charged economy, it pays to borrow generously from other professions. You need new ideas and techniques to master the ancient art of deal-making in the twenty-first century. You must beat the competition and build relationships with prospects in order to close deals. Learn from the best—those sales professionals who succeed at the highest levels despite bearing the burden of unfathomable competitive pressure.

I can't think of a more brutally competitive selling environment than the one inhabited by highly competitive, highly compensated and highly pressured college football coaches.

To win games and thereby keep their fat paychecks, college football coaches need talent. The only problem is that blue-chip talent is extraordinarily rare. In any given year, only a couple hundred high school seniors are available who have the potential to be game-changers in college.

College football coaches pursue the greatest high school players with relentless, unflagging intensity. In order to seal a deal with a star player, coaches must fight off high-powered competitors with huge marketing budgets and a willingness to do whatever it takes to win (sometimes even illegal acts). Coaches must recruit year round even during the football season. They regularly work sixteen-hour days, and selling the team to prospective players takes up a big portion of those hours.

If you study the gridiron's greatest salesmen, and imitate their strategies and tactics, you will become a better marketer or salesperson yourself regardless of your profession or industry. And make no mistake about it: football coaches are salesmen. In the world of college football, the effort to attract talented players is known as "recruiting," but football is not like the human resources recruiting you would see in a typical company. College football recruiting is marketing and sales in its purest and most competitive form.

What's more, college football coaches sell the intangible just as so many of us do in the modern service economy. Coaches take the high school stars of Friday night football and sell them on the glory of Saturday afternoons inside huge stadiums on picturesque college campuses. Learn to sell the way a coach sells, and you'll be able to sell just about anything.

Successful college coaches bring great intensity to their sales work. Despite common beliefs to the contrary, those coaches whose careers persist for decades don't cut corners by cheating or lying. Nor do they rush the recruiting process and trick prospects into signing. The great ones do it right and dedicate the appropriate time, attention and resources at each step until the deal is signed, sealed and delivered.

That's what this book is all about—developing marketing plans, branding organizations, identifying prospects, building trusting relationships and closing deals. I wrote this book to show you new ways to approach marketing and sales while inspiring and emboldening you to reach new heights.

My hope is that you will want to draft new marketing strategies, pick up the phone or hit the streets when you are finished reading.

As an author and speaker, I enjoy helping people and organizations become better at sales and marketing, but I have no interest in writing in "textbook" style. Instead I wanted to give you easy-to-implement sales and marketing techniques in a fascinating format that will stretch your imagination and pulse your desire to accomplish more than you ever thought possible.

I believe in learning through analogies and compelling stories. I constantly seek ideas and inspiration from other disciplines, adapting the material to my work. What's more, I believe learning should be entertaining and enjoyable.

What better way is there to improve your sales and marketing abilities than by using a sport that millions and millions of people so thoroughly enjoy? As a sales process, college football is dramatic, downright riveting. At times the poignant, personal stories in this book will feel like a soap opera. At other times, you'll think you're reading a mystery novel. In other instances, it may be more akin to an action-packed suspense movie.

College football is the second most popular major sport in America behind only the National Football League. Millions of people find fulfillment in following their favorite teams. While I assume most readers are at least casually interested in football, being a card-carrying member of the fandom is certainly not a requirement for you to get the key points here.

While writing this book, I delivered a handful of trial speeches based upon this concept of sales and marketing as a way to test the ideas and the stories. I considered these speeches to be my own little focus groups. After each one of those presentations, at least one person came up to me and said, "I'm not even a football fan, but I loved it!"

To assemble the material, I personally interviewed current college coaches, players going through the recruiting process, high school coaches, national recruiting experts, and perhaps most importantly, several legendary former coaches—guys such as Barry Switzer, Tom Osborne, Phillip Fulmer, Gary Barnett, John Cooper, Hayden Fry, R.C. Slocum and Jim Donnan. I worked for three years on this book, diligently researching and conducting hours and hours of interviews.

For experienced sales and marketing professionals, this book is intended to give you fresh ideas with a perspective you probably haven't viewed before and motivation designed to give you a kick start in your new sales ventures or renew energy for an established career. For new professionals, it will make the marketing and sales process come alive with captivating stories from a cut-throat profession.

As you read each story, picture yourself in the situation. Then imagine how the situation relates to the marketing and sales work you do or would like to do. Constantly be thinking about how you can transfer these strategies and tactics to your work. The football characters and their stories are entertaining and thought-provoking, but the purpose of this book is to help you be more effective as a marketer/ salesperson while motivating you to do more.

This book traces the marketing process from branding to the follow-up after a sale is closed, but the first couple chapters will explain how football recruiting/selling actually works. Once you have a thorough understanding of that, it will be time to roll up your sleeves and prepare to emulate how the gridiron's greatest salesmen beat the competition and bring in highly rated classes of blue-chip players.

At the end of each chapter, you will find "Blue-Chip Tips," which are a summary of important take-aways you can apply to your marketing and sales work.

I don't normally use only male pronouns. And I do not wish to slight female readers. But football is male dominated and only men are coaches and players—so far. I recognize that salespersons are both male and female. I want my female readers to know that the obvious overuse of "he" and "him" in referring to football scenarios is not reflective of any bias on my part, but of the state of football today. Sales, on the other hand, is generally a level playing field for both men and women (and I wouldn't bet against any female sales execs I have worked with).

Let's face it, the sales profession in any industry is highly competitive even when times are good. But if you think your sales work is competitive, you wouldn't believe the marketing and selling skills that are necessary to build a championship football team.

It's time to open your mind by learning how the famous coaches you see on television battle each other in the brutally competitive race to sign the nation's most prized, first-rate athletes. Are you ready? Down! Set! Hut!

Chapter 1

SALES BLITZ

How the Gridiron's Greatest Salesmen Build
Relationships, Close Deals and Beat the Competition

"We have a behind-the-scenes look at just what it took to land the latest football commit," a radio sportscaster teased his listeners one morning a few years ago as I drove to work. As a devoted football fan, my interest was piqued.

As it turned out, my favorite college football team had just received a verbal commitment from a highly coveted, blue-chip defensive back from California. He had all the key attributes that made college coaches drool and college fans daydream: the perfect height and weight, a blazing-fast 40-yard dash time, and a track record of success as a star high school player.

Like many faithful college football fans, I followed the recruiting process and already had studied this player. I knew what schools my alma mater had to beat out in order to get him, and before hearing this news on the radio, I knew we were in the lead among the suitors fighting to land his athletic services. So while I was thrilled, I wasn't surprised to hear the news.

I was surprised, however, to learn the back story.

Our new defensive back lived in the South Central Los Angeles neighborhood of Watts, famous for race riots in the 1960s and gang violence in current times. The player was one of many siblings growing up in a single-parent household struggling to scratch out a life in a tough urban environment. To make ends meet, his mother worked several jobs, meaning her schedule was void of time to meet any of the college coaches pursuing her talented son.

Now, there's something you must know about college recruiting. Mothers are incredibly important. Sometimes more important than the kids themselves. As many college football coaches will tell you, "You don't get the boy without getting the mom first."

As former Oklahoma Sooners coach Barry Switzer said, "Mommas pack the suitcases." The problem here was that the mother simply was not available. Alas, the recruiting efforts were seemingly stymied. That is, unless you are a tenacious, creative and highly competitive college football coach.

For one of her jobs, the mother drove a city bus. As the radio sportscaster told the story, our head coach and one of his assistants flew to L.A. Somehow they figured out her bus route and waited for her at one of the stops. As she pulled up to the curb, the coaches boarded the bus, introduced themselves and recruited her as she drove her rounds through the city. By the end of her shift, the critical relationship had been developed, and her coveted son was essentially on his way to Dear Old State U.

Several thoughts rushed through my head. How cool! What an incredible story! What a great example of real-life marketing! I was proud that the coaches of my alma mater were such dogged salesmen, so dedicated to the team's future success.

But after my initial amazement, I started to get a different feeling—guilt. I asked myself, Would I be willing to do such a thing for my job? Am I that committed to selling my wares? For just one prospective client, would I be willing to travel across the continent and spend a couple hours on a moving bus pitching my products and services to the driver?

I wasn't sure I was *that* committed.

I started to think of all the mind-boggling things college football coaches must do in order to convince great athletes to join their teams. I thought about the incredibly long hours and the sacrifices their families must make. I imagined what it must be like to work under the constant pressure of extreme, never-ending competitiveness in such a high-stakes environment.

Coaches must be great salespersons. They are constantly selling their programs against all the other fine programs out there. College coaches essentially sell Saturday afternoon glory to Friday night stars.

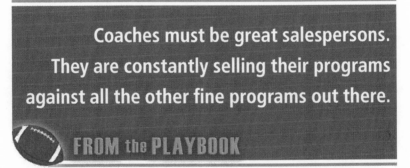

Coaches must be great salespersons. They are constantly selling their programs against all the other fine programs out there.

FROM the PLAYBOOK

Just how competitive is college football recruiting? It's downright brutal. For starters, there are 119 major college football teams, and each one of them can take up to twenty-five scholarship players per year. Do the math, and you will find a potential for 2,975 scholarships per year. The only problem is that elite football talent is an extraordinarily scarce resource. Only about 250 high school players each year can be classified as blue-chip players.

Of those, about a hundred are truly elite. Only about ten to fifteen are considered program-changing, sure-fire, can't-miss, All-American, future-first-round-draft-pick superstars.

Former Colorado and Northwestern head coach Gary Barnett said he would typically study a thousand high school players per year. Of those, there were typically twelve players who, barring injury, were certain to make the NFL someday. One can imagine how zealously all the college coaches would recruit those dozen superstars.

Coaches scour the nation looking for talented prospects. Some prospects are hidden like diamonds in the rough, just waiting to be discovered. Other prospects are known to everyone and courted aggressively and relentlessly. Through mailings, social media, phone calls, football camps and in-person visits, coaches build rapport with the young men. I call it "climbing the relationship depth chart."

First you build rapport, which eventually leads to relationships and ultimately to trust. In football, an incoming freshman player starts at the bottom of the depth chart and works hard hoping to earn a starting position someday. Over the course of his career, he climbs the depth chart. Similarly, salespersons start at the bottom with each prospective client and work their way up.

Once trust is established, and the prospect identifies his favorite school, coaches at the chosen team try to convince the young man to make a verbal commitment. These commitments are legally non-binding—and not always kept—but generally give a coach reasonable assurance that the prospect will be playing for him in the future. The coach can't truly relax until National Signing Day, the first Wednesday in February, when high school seniors sign binding letters of intent with their future schools.

With so many highly paid and highly motivated coaches chasing the same select pool of blue-chip athletes, the competition is overwhelming. For a professional working in some other industry, the responsibility to recruit elite personnel in such a competitive atmosphere would be enough to occupy the whole of every day of every year while providing a constant need for ibuprofen and antacids. For coaches, it's just one part of their work lives.

Successful coaches are downright obsessed with recruiting. There's a reason teams like Alabama, Texas, Oklahoma, Ohio State and Florida tend to be so good year after year. They have established programs that reel in a disproportionate share of the nation's best athletes. Make no doubt about it: recruiting is the lifeblood of the sport. Have one down year in recruiting, and a great team might overcome it. Have two consecutive down years, and the head coach will probably be looking for a new job.

It is impossible to overstate the importance of recruiting in college football. It's not uncommon for elite programs to have annual recruiting budgets of a million dollars. Former University of Minnesota head coach Tim Brewster said he thought about recruiting twenty-four hours a day, 365 days a year.

But recruiting is only one of the incredibly competitive tasks a college football coach must master. Additionally, he must prepare every week to beat a foe on the field that is feverishly trying to beat his team. A coach's stress is amazing. Ultimately, his success depends on how well he can manipulate the whims and passions of seventeen-year-old boys. The demands on his time are almost unreal.

How do coaches do it? For one thing, they devote an unbelievable amount of time. University of California head coach Jeff Tedford works sixteen to seventeen hours a day almost every day of the year. Among his colleagues, that grinding schedule is not unique.

Remember that feeling of guilt I had on my morning commute a few years ago? It was actually a familiar feeling. Many times over the years, when I thought about the lives of college football coaches, I have felt guilty. I worry that I'm not working as hard in my job. To fans, coaches are living the dream. They're doing what so many Americans, especially men, fantasize about—getting paid to coach football. But in reality, that dream might be more of a nightmare; coaches work so much harder than the typical person.

The more I thought about it, the more I realized that I needed to be like a college football coach—competitive, organized, motivated, committed, a great salesperson, a tireless marketer. I realized that if every professional worked like a coach, each individual would be more successful and the economy would soar. In particular, it occurred to me that there was so much that we all could learn from college football recruiting as a business process regardless of what we did for a living. In an "aha" moment, I realized college football recruiting is the ultimate marketing and sales process.

That was the genesis of this book. What better way is there to help people be more successful in sales and marketing than by using college football as the roadmap? After all, as a people, we love the game. It's full of tradition, pageantry and storied rivalries. Millions of us go to the stadium each fall Saturday or tune in on television. College football fans are unusually passionate, and because so many of them are zealots, a cottage industry has popped up around the pursuit of future players.

Thousands of fans at each of the premier football schools subscribe to Internet services that keep them up-to-date with the comings and goings of the most highly coveted teenage athletes. So important is recruiting in the eyes of hardcore fans that it has become known as the sport's "second season."

There's no doubt that college football is something that millions of men, women and children enjoy, so let's use it to be more successful. Let's use football as a way to make us better marketers, salespersons and networkers.

This book is intended to be entertaining and enjoyable for football fans, but its mission is much deeper than that. Frankly, I want this book to make you more successful. Each chapter recounts true stories from college football as told by coaches, players and the journalists who cover the sport. These stories are then used to illustrate important sales, marketing and other aspects of business and career success.

Please allow one disclaimer. While we are using college football "recruiting" stories to teach business and marketing lessons, this book is not written just for "recruiters." It is not a human resources book. The process of recruiting elite football players is all about marketing and sales. College football is a business, and in order to be successful in it, a coach must treat it like any other big business. Marketing and sales are essential components of any business.

To affirm and better understand the parallels between football and business, I went to the one man who might understand the similarities better than anyone else: Joe Moglia.

After working as a high school and college assistant coach for sixteen years, including a stint as defensive coordinator at Dartmouth, Moglia made a radical career change in 1983. He left coaching and went to work for Merrill Lynch in New York. In his orientation class that year, there were twenty-four MBAs and one football coach.

Although he missed coaching, Moglia worked hard and pushed his way up the Wall Street food chain. Eventually, he became chairman and CEO of TD Ameritrade, the Omaha-based online brokerage company. After building up TD Ameritrade, Moglia longed to go back to his roots.

At age sixty, he gave up his job as CEO of a *Fortune* 1000 company (but stayed on as chairman) and went back to coaching. To shake off the rust, he served a couple years as an unpaid intern for Nebraska coach Bo Pelini. He worked sixty to seventy hours a week for the Cornhuskers and was surely the wealthiest coaching intern in America! Soon after that experience, Moglia took a head coach job with a pro team in the United Football League. He now serves as head coach at Coastal Carolina University.

What does Moglia think?

"I was a much better business executive because of the sixteen years I spent in coaching," Moglia said. "Frankly, I've been a pretty senior guy in the business world for many years now. What I have had to go through, in very competitive environments, under significant stress is very similar to coaching."

Both CEOs and coaches must handle themselves under pressure, develop credibility and position people in the right roles. Just like an executive, a coach must have a competitive strategy and understand what's happening in his market, his league. When it comes to business leadership and coaching football, the parallels are plentiful.

So which one is tougher—coaching football or running an international company?

"There is nothing I've ever done in my career that's been more intense and more competitive than coaching football in season," Moglia said. "You don't get a day off for four or five months. You work eighty-five to ninety hours a week. Your entire career is dependent upon whether or not you win on Saturdays. It's incredibly stressful, but while a coach still has to work hard recruiting and planning during the off-season, there is somewhat of a break. In business, however, you never get a break. You just had your best quarter in history? You got to do better this year."

Leading a company to sustainable long-term growth in a competitive, global market never ends. So, during the season, football is tougher. Year round, being a CEO is tougher. That said, they both have their challenges, and they are a lot alike.

Moglia wasn't the only insightful expert I interviewed. I talked to current college coaches, players going through the recruiting process, high school coaches, national recruiting experts, and several legendary former coaches.

These former coaches were all successful. Some of them were extraordinarily successful. Several have won national championships. Several have been inducted into the College Football Hall of Fame. They are men who coached at the highest levels. To get there, they had to be great recruiters, great marketers, and great salesmen. These coaches are some of the greatest salesmen to ever walk the gridiron.

As you explore the fascinating world of college football recruiting, you are actually developing deeper insights into business success. Think how you might emulate these coaches and how you can transfer their strategies and techniques to your business.

Before you can learn sales and marketing lessons from college football recruiting, you must first understand the recruiting process and why fans go so crazy over it. That's what the next chapter will do. After that, the subsequent chapters will take you through the marketing and sales process by synergizing football with the business world.

It's time to roll up your sleeves and get to work, so you will be pleased with your personal "recruiting class" when your own "National Signing Day" arrives.

If you're frustrated or burned out by the heavy competitive pressure in your business, learn new ideas and find inspiration from college coaches who compete in one of the most competitive selling environments on Earth.

To make a sale, climb the relationship depth chart: rapport → relationship → trust → signed deal.

The most successful leaders are downright obsessed with sales and marketing.

If you want to succeed like a great football coach, be competitive, organized, motivated, and committed, as well as a great salesperson and a tireless marketer.

Chapter 2

BLUEBLOODS AND BLUE CHIPS
How It All Works

Almost a thousand red-clad fans filled the main ballroom of the Holiday Inn Central Convention Center for a banquet on the first Wednesday in February. There was great diversity of dress. Some were wearing suits and ties while others wore polos or sweatshirts, but the common color was red. Scarlet and cream, to be exact.

It was a celebratory environment, and people chatted each other up as the booze flowed steadily during the pre-dinner social hour. The attendees were zealots, big fans of the Nebraska Cornhuskers, gathering on National Signing Day to celebrate and learn all about the 2010 class that the Huskers had signed earlier that day.

The head coach and his entire staff were on hand to introduce the class. Each assistant coach stood up, showed film and analyzed his signees. The audience was mesmerized. It was a crowd sophisticated and well-schooled in the art of football as evidenced by breathless comments such as "look at that footwork" when film was shown of an unusually athletic 300-pound defensive lineman.

After the formal presentation, fans swarmed the coaches, requesting autographs, and asking specific questions about each new player. Because of Internet recruiting sites' extensive coverage throughout the recruiting process, most of those in attendance already knew the basic answers. This was an opportunity for in-depth probing. Questions focused on the behind-the-scenes sales maneuverings. In other words, "Coach, tell us exactly how you got Cooper to choose Nebraska over Notre Dame?"

When the event finally wrapped up at 9:30 p.m., most of the coaches looked tired. A few stayed for a beer or cocktail, but they didn't linger. It had been an exhausting day to wrap up a seemingly never-ending recruitment period. They needed sleep, because an identical dinner and program were planned the very next night fifty miles down the road in a different city.

If you think Husker fans are over-the-top crazy about their football team, then you apparently haven't heard about Florida State fans.

On the same day as Nebraska's recruiting dinner, Florida State held its football recruiting "War Party." That's when head coach Jimbo Fisher and his assistants announced the class and broke down video of each signee. It was a chance for the fans to hear first-hand about the newest crop of Seminoles.

More than a thousand fans bought tickets, selling-out the venue within hours of the event's announcement. Because of that interest, FSU boosters arranged to simulcast the event to two additional locations in Tallahassee and more than a dozen sites around the nation.

If you think Florida State fans are over-the-top crazy about their football team, then you apparently haven't heard about Louisiana State fans.

The Tiger Gridiron Club of Baton Rouge hosts the "Bayou Bash" every year on National Signing Day. It's an all-day party held to celebrate the announcement of LSU's brand-new recruiting class. The event includes a silent auction and corporate sponsors. Proceeds from the Bayou Bash go to a fund used at the discretion of head coach Les Miles to "enhance the LSU football program."

The Husker Recruiting Dinner, the Florida State War Party and LSU's Bayou Bash are impressive, but those are just once-a-year events. College football recruiting is actually a year-round passion.

But how does the process work? Before we can use college football recruiting to make us better marketers and salespersons, we have to step back and learn the system, the jargon and vocabulary. It's time to explore just how this complicated process works.

Rivals.com, an Internet-based recruiting information service, provides a website dedicated to every major college football team in the nation. On each team's site, Rivals provides regular news updates about young football players who are considering that team. The sites report on scholarship offers, campus visits and who might be influencing a player's decision. Rivals also provides highlight videos and stats for star athletes, a list of the colleges they're considering and even ranks the top players nationwide according to a star system.

A five-star recruit is truly special—one of the top twenty to twenty-five players in the nation. A four-star recruit is a highly coveted blue chipper as well. Even three-star recruits receive multiple scholarship offers from major conference teams. Rivals.com rates all the Division I recruiting classes based on combined rankings of each team's recruits.

In 2012 and 2011, Alabama assembled the nation's highest-rated recruiting classes. In 2010, it was the University of Southern California.

Perhaps the most popular part of the Rivals.com team websites are the discussion boards, the online forums where fans pay a monthly membership fee to chat twenty-four hours a day with fellow fans, sharing their hopes for the football team, commiserating when things don't go well and celebrating every time another high school stud verbally commits to their favorite college football team.

Just how popular are these discussion forums? Some fans are logged on to the forums seemingly round the clock. It's not uncommon to see users who have written several thousand posts (and sometimes tens of thousands). According to Sean Callahan of Rivals.com, the sites with largest membership lists include Alabama, Florida State, Texas, Nebraska, Michigan and Notre Dame. The Rivals discussion forums keep track of record use, when the highest number of users is online at any given time. The record at Michigan is 8,766. Alabama's is 7,581.

Suffice it to say, the public has a great deal of interest in college football. Professional football earns higher television ratings, but college football fills stadiums in a way the NFL does not. In fact, all of the ten largest football stadiums in America are college stadiums. The largest professional venue, FedEx Field in Landover, Maryland, is only the nation's twelfth largest football stadium.

College football engenders unusually strong passions among its fans. It could be the tradition and pageantry. Perhaps it's the marching bands, Greek organizations and cheerleaders that are still worth watching. It could be love for an alma mater. Whatever it is, college teams enjoy strong and large alumni bases, which tend to be spread across the nation. The great Vince Lombardi once said, "A school without football is in danger of deteriorating into a medieval study hall."

Not only is the game of college football a big deal in America, college football recruiting is a big deal too. Serious fans not only follow recruiting, they embrace it. They savor it. It's a hobby unto itself. To a lay person, such intense interest in recruiting must come across as odd. Why do so many fans care about seventeen- and eighteen-year-old boys who haven't even enrolled at the university let alone contributed on the field?

The answer is simple: Hope.

For diehard fans, recruiting is all about hoping for an idyllic, glorious future. No matter how bad the last season may have been, recruiting is a new start. Your favorite team could have played for the national championship in January and lost by one point on the game's final play, leaving you heartbroken. Yet, despite such a crushing disappointment, National Signing Day in February brings new life. Everyone feels like a national champion on National Signing Day.

The young recruits are full of life; they are potential personified. It's easy to get excited over them. They come out of high school or junior college seemingly dripping with unimaginable levels of God-given talent and boundless potential. What's more, they're fresh. Having not yet played a down in college, they have never fumbled, blown an assignment, missed a tackle, thrown an interception, given up a sack, skipped class, gotten in trouble with the law, or found a way to get the university on probation.

The recruiting process is drawn out over a lengthy period, so by the time National Signing Day arrives, fans have had months to build up their excitement and anticipation. Rivals. com's John Tallman likes to say, "National Signing Day is the dinner bell after you've made the meal."

College football fans enjoy recruiting for the same reason NFL fans enjoy the draft. As a fan, you transpose yourself into the coaches' positions. It's fun to pretend you're putting together the team. As Jeff Ketron, coach of Douglas County High School in Castle Rock, Colorado, put it, "Recruiting is like football on paper."

Former Texas A&M coach R.C. Slocum understands why fans obsess about recruiting. College football fans tend to be quite knowledgeable about their beloved sport. They know that as recruiting goes, so goes a program's on-the-field success. It's a natural way to keep up with the team and enjoy college football in the off-season. The Internet sites that have popped up over the past fifteen years add even more fuel to the fans' fire.

"Recruiting services keep the interest going, because they make a lot of money off the process," Slocum said. "It's just like the draft. The NFL draft wasn't always like that where they bring people to New York and have the two or three days of intense television coverage. The fans just have so much interest in football."

Following your favorite team's recruiting is really another form of arm-chair quarterbacking, said Jack Pierce, who served as Nebraska's off-campus recruiting coordinator for several years under Tom Osborne.

"You could be sitting on your couch watching the game, and say, 'That's the dumbest damned play I've ever seen run! They should have blocked the play this way,'" Pierce explained. "But your wife's sitting next to you, and she doesn't know a thing about football, so she's thinking you're so smart, 'cause you know all this stuff. Recruiting's the same way. I could be sitting with you at the bar, and say, 'Geez, you know, I was looking at Bama.com and this kid is going to Alabama.' You sound like you're part of it, in the know. Makes for a big ego."

So popular is football recruiting that it's become known by some as the "second season." Although former Colorado and Northwestern head coach Gary Barnett was quick to point out, "The second season is actually coaches' firings and hirings in December," so recruiting is essentially the "third season." After the real season ends, hardcore fans get excited for National Signing Day. Later in the spring, fans start following the recruitment of high school juniors.

But not all fans enjoy the recruiting process as much as those who follow the biggest names, the perennial powers of the game. You see, college football is an elite sport generally ruled by a small class of bluebloods, the "old money teams."

In his book *Football's Second Season*, renowned recruiting analyst Tom Lemming describes college football as a "caste system," in which the "super 16" have an inherent advantage when it comes to recruiting. Lemming identifies the sixteen premium teams as Alabama, Auburn, Florida, Florida State, Georgia, Louisiana State, Miami, Michigan, Nebraska, Notre Dame, Ohio State, Oklahoma, Penn State, Tennessee, Texas and Southern California.

These blueblood teams don't always win, but over the years, they tend to dominate the sport and usually boast highly rated recruiting classes. These teams enjoy storied traditions, huge stadiums and big-time Nielsen ratings when they play on television. Teams from the next tier appear often in the Associated Press Top 25 as well. Several of those teams come close to the elite level such as Virginia Tech, Texas A&M, Michigan State, Iowa, Wisconsin and Arkansas.

Recently, "new money" teams such as Oregon, Texas Christian, Stanford, South Carolina, Missouri, Rutgers, Boise State and Cincinnati have enjoyed success. A few years back, Colorado, Kansas State, Washington, Clemson, Georgia Tech and Brigham Young were in the limelight.

In the early years, the late 1800s and early 1900s, the best teams came from the Ivy League. Nowadays, because of differing views on athletic scholarships, an Ivy League school would be obliterated if it took on a traditional power from the Southeast Conference or the Big 10. Looking at the list of most national championships, one of history's most prolific teams is Minnesota, but the Golden Gophers haven't won a national championship since 1960 and have posted an overall losing record over the past forty years. Of course, Minnesota could develop into a great team again someday, but a prolonged and dramatic fall from greatness scares the hell out of athletic directors and coaches at the currently elite teams.

To retain their lofty status and membership among the nation's bluebloods, teams must keep winning. To do that, they must invest millions of dollars in state-of-the-art athletic facilities, hire a highly paid coaching staff, and, perhaps most importantly, sell the program to elite athletes.

Ultimately, it all comes down to recruiting, the lifeblood of the team's winning ways. If it is true that wars are won before the battles begin, then college football championships are won in living rooms and high school coaches' offices. Great teams need a never-ending supply of blue-chip athletes. Player turnover is a constant concern for coaches. A significant portion of the team exhausts its eligibility at the end of each season, but graduation isn't the only cause of player deficits. Some players suffer career-ending injuries. Exceptionally talented players may opt to leave school early and enter the NFL draft. Others might flunk out of school or find themselves kicked off the team for disciplinary reasons.

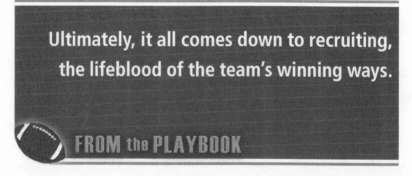

Ultimately, it all comes down to recruiting, the lifeblood of the team's winning ways.

FROM the PLAYBOOK

Recruiting is a never-ending process. In season and out of season, many coaching staffs devote time to recruiting every single business day—year round. They must constantly reload their squads with enough of the right players.

So what do coaches look for when recruiting? First and foremost is speed, speed and more speed. You can't coach speed, and you can only partly develop it. Speed is a natural talent that a few people have and most don't. As the old football adage goes, "Speed kills."

When building a football team, you simply cannot have enough fast guys. That even applies to linemen; the quicker your big guys are, the better your whole team will be. Speed is the most important physical asset a young player can possess. If you're a high school football player who can run the 40-yard dash in 4.4 seconds or faster, you are going have many multi-millionaire college coaches sitting in your living room, and they'll all want to be your new best friend.

After speed, coaches look for a variety of attributes. Contrary to the image of recruiting as perpetuated by the sports media, coaches want character. The higher quality a kid's behavior is, the easier it is to lead a coach's life.

Coaches want their players to play hard, love the game and show the appropriate amounts of aggressiveness. It's a brutal sport, so the right prospects demonstrate toughness on their high school highlight films.

Other attributes are strength, size and explosiveness. Flexibility and athletic ability make a big difference as well. Certain positions require specific sets of unique athletic ability. For instance, defensive backs must have very flexible hips in order change direction quickly and keep pace with the speedy receivers they must cover. Offensive linemen must possess unusual bending ability for guys of their size. Offensive tackles need to be light on their feet, able to move quickly in a small space and keep perfect balance while exerting great force against a blitzing defensive end.

Coaches work hard to assemble the right players. The recruiting process is ongoing, and at any given time a coaching staff is probably working on more than just one class. For instance, a staff could be just closing its final commitments for the 2013 class, but at the same time, they are communicating with kids who may enroll in 2014 or beyond.

While most teams require that all coaches on the staff sell, one coach is designated as the recruiting coordinator. As the title would indicate, it's his job to make sure the effort is well planned and coordinated. But it's not like he's alone. In addition to his fellow coaches, the major football teams have large staffs of non-coach employees who organize recruiting data, logistics, travel plans, communication strategies and special events.

At the blueblood schools, coaches have an army of administrative assistants and interns who serve at their beck and call. It's a good thing they do, because selling takes a lot of work, especially when you're also preparing the current players to win on the field.

Prospecting occurs all the time. Coaches comb through data and video clips provided by scouting services and other sources. High school coaches frequently send films to colleges, hoping their star players might receive scholarship offers. Coaches also work their assigned geographic territories, asking high school coaches what players impress them. High school players sometimes take the initiative and send their own videos to college coaches.

If a player expresses interest, he receives regular marketing mailings from the college team. These mailings, which increase in frequency as the kid moves closer to his senior year, are a mix of letters, handwritten notes, and glossy, full-color, expensive brochures showing pictures of everything from current players working out in a state-of-the-art weight room, to students sitting on leafy campus lawns under perfectly azure skies, to beautiful coeds walking along the picturesque quad.

Coaches go on the road each spring during "evaluation season." That's when they visit high schools, see players and talk to high school coaches. Summer is camp season. Major college teams hold several camps for different age groups of younger football players, starting as early as age twelve. The boys come to campus, stay in the residence halls and work out with the college's coaching staff. As the boys grow older, the camps become more in-depth and often are specialized— for example kicking camps or elite quarterback camps.

Hundreds of boys attend camps each year at each college. The vast majority of boys who attend the camps will never receive a scholarship offer from a college team. For them, it's a great life experience that helps them become better players on their high school teams. But for some kids, the camps are a place to be discovered.

For coaches, the camps allow them to evaluate prospects in person to see how they might fit in with the team. Just as important, the camps are sales tools. If a kid has a positive experience and is blown away by the coaches and the facilities, there's a good chance the team might earn his commitment and ultimately his signature on National Signing Day.

Meanwhile, coaches and prospects communicate regularly via telephone calls and Facebook messages. The athletes can call college coaches as often as they want, but National College Athletic Association (NCAA) rules restrict how often coaches can call the kids. Like any salesperson in any industry, college football coaches use the various communication methods to build rapport first, then establish a relationship and ultimately develop trust. Once trust exists, the coach knows he stands a good chance of landing the prospect.

Every sales process has a key step that normally makes a big difference in the salesperson's success. In football recruiting, it's the on-campus visit. Players can make unofficial visits at any time. In order to qualify as "unofficial," the player and his family must pay their own way. In the fall and winter, players can take "official" visits. The colleges pay for these visits. Each player is allowed to take up to five of these free trips, but many kids don't take their full allotment.

Almost as powerful as the on-campus visit is the in-home visit. It's essentially a sales presentation in the prospect's home court. This is when the assistant coaches or the head coach visit the player's home and get to know his family. The head coach is allowed to visit each prospect's home only once, so he must make the visit count. Most teams send assistant coaches to the home first. Typically, the head coach is the "closer," so he saves his one permitted visit until it's time to seal the deal.

At any point in the process, the player can make a verbal commitment. Such commitments are non-binding, and, frustratingly, some players each year renege on their pledges. Fortunately, most players do honor their verbal commitments.

Teams collect verbal commitments until they reach the number of scholarships they have available any given year. The NCAA allows a team to grant twenty-five scholarships per year, but because no more than eighty-five total players are allowed on scholarship at any given time, teams may take fewer than twenty-five freshmen if they had a small graduating class the prior season.

Like any athletic league, college football has its rules, but the sheer number of rules is astonishing. A look at the NCAA recruiting rule book is dizzying. It takes a great deal of time to get through it, but coaches and athletic administrators must understand it. In fact, before you can phone student athletes or go out on the road recruiting, you must pass your NCAA recruiting exam. In addition to the voluminous rules, each school has internal policies and procedures that coaches must honor.

Compared to the conditions under which most salespersons and marketers operate, college football recruiters have it rough. NCAA rules are onerous. But as football coach and corporate executive Joe Moglia points out, everyone operates under the same rules. In the business world, executives must cope with the burdens of Sarbanes-Oxley, the costly and time-consuming federal reporting-and-accountability law, but all publicly traded companies share that burden.

"I think the NCAA has the best interest of the student athlete at heart," Moglia said. "They're trying to create a level playing field."

Of course, where there are rules, there are cheaters. It's yet another way that college football mirrors the business world and life in general. While rule bending was far more prevalent in days gone by, it certainly happens today.

Recently, two of college football's bluebloods, Ohio State and Southern California, have embarrassed themselves because of NCAA violations. One anonymous national recruiting analyst knows a blue-chip athlete who was recently offered $10,000 to play for one of the big Florida schools. He took it. Apparently, someone got nervous, and the kid was told to "spend the money fast." He ended up taking his girlfriend on a cruise.

No matter what you might think about recruiting fraud today, it's merely child's play compared to the Wild West days of the 1970s and earlier. Things were especially lawless in the now-defunct Southwestern Conference.

From that conference came one of the lowest moments in football recruiting history when Southern Methodist University's "death-penalty" became the harshest penalty the NCAA can inflict on a member school. SMU was banned from participating in football competition in 1987 and 1988 because of multiple recruiting infractions that had occurred over several years prior to that. Things were so fraudulent for so long at SMU that people joked only half kiddingly that one of the school's star running backs in the early 1980s had to take a pay cut when he moved on to the NFL.

Former Nebraska assistant coach George Darlington said the Huskers made a conscious decision to stop recruiting in the Houston area for a period in the 1970s because too many high school coaches of that era made it known that "if you don't bring money, don't bother to come." Darlington claims that one high school coach told one of his colleagues, "Don't forget the green," when he was making arrangements to visit a prospect. Apparently, the coach saw himself as some sort of an under-the-table talent broker. In more recent years, a similar but smaller scale problem occurred in the Memphis area.

Back in the 1960s, the charismatic head coach of one Midwestern football program got in his car on a Tuesday evening and drove to a nearby city to visit one of his best prospects. The coach picked the kid up from his lower-middle-class home and took him out for drinks at a swanky hotel lounge downtown where they met an alumnus.

Over the course of the evening, the two adult men and the underaged high school senior downed so many drinks that all three were plastered. The coach and the young prospect stumbled to the car and drove back to the kid's house where, upon arrival, the coach immediately passed out on the couch.

The recruit's mother made breakfast and coffee for the coach in the morning and then sent him on his way. Unfortunately, the coach was still intoxicated, which explained why he collided with a telephone pole while driving back to campus. Somehow the severely damaged car limped its way back to the local car dealership that provided Coach with all the free transportation he wanted. Of course, the dealership owner was shocked to see the damage when Coach informed him he was swapping it for a new car.

"What the hell happened, Coach?" he asked.

"I hit a deer," Coach responded.

The dealer looked at the mangled automobile and responded that he had never seen such damage from a car-deer collision.

"You should have seen the size of that son of a bitch," Coach responded with sly grin.

It was a different world back then before NCAA rules tightened up and the media started monitoring celebrity football coaches 24/7. Another 1960s incident illustrates the point.

The "Big 33" is Pennsylvania's all-star high school football game in which the thirty-three best players in Pennsylvania take on the thirty-three best from a different state. Back in the 1960s, the Big 33 pitted Pennsylvania against Texas.

One year, the Texas all-star team had an unusually gifted player on its squad. College coaches from around country came to the game to see him compete. So coveted was this blue chipper that two collegiate coaches, one from California and another from Pennsylvania, literally got into a fist fight under the grandstand because both wanted the Texas kid so badly. Bystanders who rushed over to stop the contretemps quickly realized that separating the two coaches was like taking a grizzly bear away from the honey tree.

Some cheating stories are disturbing and discredit a great game, yet others are comical especially when viewed through the lens of time. College football recruiting gets a bad rap because of the widespread cheating that has taken place over the years. Most books written on recruiting focus on cheating as the authors wring their hands over the game's sordid underbelly. We must acknowledge that cheating does take place, but let's not get too carried away obsessing about it.

As long as highly competitive enterprises exist with high stakes and are populated by imperfect human beings, cheating will occur. That's sad, but it's a fact of life. There will always be cheaters as long as there are people, but for the most part, the majority of football programs follow the majority of the rules most of the time. The same thing can generally be said for most businesses—high-profile exceptions notwithstanding.

> **As long as highly competitive enterprises exist with high stakes and are populated by imperfect human beings, cheating will occur.**
>
> FROM the PLAYBOOK

With constant coverage of college football recruiting by the traditional media and especially the Internet-based recruiting services, it's frankly much harder to cheat than it was in the pre-Internet days. That has probably had more to do with cleaning up recruiting than the tougher rules.

The Internet has also made coaches more cautious in what they say publicly and in supposedly private conversations with their prospects. For instance, Rivals.com and its competitors frequently call and email the nation's top high school players and query them about who has offered them scholarships, which college coaches have visited them, and what those coaches have been saying.

In Rivals's early days, one of its reporters interviewed a handful of star receivers who were all being recruited by the University of Michigan among other teams. In separate interviews, each receiver said a Michigan coach had told him that he would be the "next Desmond Howard," the star receiver and kick returner who won the Heisman Trophy in 1991. There was really nothing wrong with what the Michigan coach said—all salespersons are prone to puff up their prospects—but it was embarrassing when their sales techniques were laid bare for the world to see, and prospects realized they weren't as special as they initially believed.

It appears as if many college coaches have a love-hate attitude toward the companies and people who cover recruiting and provide recruiting information online. Though they won't typically admit it, most coaching staffs at least take a peek at the online player data to make sure they're not missing any prospects. Coaches also want to know what their prospects are saying publicly. But it does irritate some coaches when they see fans and media put so much stock into player evaluations that are often conducted by people who have never coached major college football.

That leads to comments like, "Guys that run these websites… they don't know whether a football's blown-up or stuffed," as said by former Nebraska assistant coach Jack Pierce.

College coaches do have a point when they warn fans not to rely too heavily on the player assessments and rankings provided by the websites. As former Ohio State recruiting coordinator John Peterson said, the stats can be misleading.

"You have to get the kid into your camp and see him in person," Peterson said. "You look at the 40-yard-dash time, but how fast is the kid? Was the track really 40 yards or was it actually 39?"

What's more, some of the services only evaluate a small sampling of a player's high school film; whereas, a serious college coach will look at the young man's play for a whole game over multiple games to see how good he truly is.

Some coaches use the Internet services to their advantage perhaps even spreading misinformation through secret sources to sway the media, fan perception or a prospective player in a certain, desired way.

Former Colorado Coach Gary Barnett doesn't like all the Internet focus on and participation in recruiting, but he realizes it's here to stay. Coaches can complain about it all they want, but Barnett believes they must get used to it and somehow find a way to use it in their favor.

"Don't fight it," Barnett said, "Don't tell the kids and their parents that you hate it, because all that does is drive a wedge between you and them if they think it's cool … You're crazy to fight it."

The recruiting process is all about future success on the football field. It's critically important, but keep in mind that it's just one part of a football coach's job.

And what is football ultimately about? The answer depends on your perspective. For fans it's about pride, a good time and a sports version of psychological transference. For alumni, it's about good memories and affection for the alma mater. For college administrators, it's about revenue and publicity for the institution's many missions. For faculty, football is a mixed bag—some like it, others despise it and some don't care one way or another.

For players and coaches, the guys who live and breathe it, football means many things. One of those things is hard work. To earn playing time, a player must excel on the field. To keep his high-paying job, a coach must win and win frequently.

Because of the pressure to win, and because of the big dollars at stake, many observers assume college football is all about greed, egos and a lust for power. That's not a fair assumption. As it turns out, operating with integrity and a sense of purpose pays off in football over the long run just as it does in every business.

Coaches who believe in and focus on football's nobler missions are the ones who are ultimately the most successful on the field for extended lengths of time. Coaches like Bobby

Bowden and Tom Osborne come to mind. These men won five national championships between them, yet they always cared about their players as people, not just as football pawns.

Character matters a great deal in football. "The longer I'm in coaching, the more character means to me," Coach Tim Brewster said. "Every single night of your life, you're responsible for 115 kids doing the right thing and making the right decisions. I don't care how talented a kid is, if I've gotta worry about him at night, it's not worth it."

While you must win to keep your coaching job, Joe Moglia believes the college game is about converting eighteen-year-old kids into adult men. In Moglia's mind, a "man" is someone who stands on his own two feet, accepts responsibility for himself and understands the consequences of his actions. When you consider the number of young people who play college football each year and turn out to be contributing, tax-paying citizens, most coaches do a good job of this.

College football has its warts. It's far from perfect, but it's a good game played by mostly good people. It makes many contributions to our society. Football generates massive economic activity, creates jobs and provides a way for thousands of students, many of them ethnic minorities from disadvantaged backgrounds, to pay for a college education.

What's more, football provides healthy entertainment for millions of people while inspiring them and motivating them to do better and achieve greater heights in their lives. The game is a metaphor for life that provides us with so many analogies for our work. Football is a learning laboratory where we can test leadership and management theories, and, for purposes of this book, it teaches us valuable marketing and sales lessons.

Now that you know how the process works, you surely see that countless parallels exist between college football recruiting and the business of sales and marketing. The rest of the chapters will focus on one aspect of sales and marketing and illustrate what you can learn about it by studying the master salesmen of the gridiron.

We can learn much about success in our own profession by studying something different such as football.

Like players on a football team, clients are always turning over. That means you must constantly market even when you are "full-up."

Everyone on the team must sell even though one person is designated as the recruiting coordinator.

Prospecting is an ongoing, never-ending activity.

To maximize sales, exploit your strongest assets.

Because all competitors operate in the same market and under the same rules, external forces are no excuse for failing.

While some people cheat, those who resist the temptation tend to enjoy long-term success.

If there is a great deal of outside interest in your profession, don't fight it; embrace it and use it to your advantage.

Chapter 3

YOU CAN'T AFFORD
TO BE OUT-MARKETED
Passion and Commitment Required

Vince Dooley won 201 games while coaching the University of Georgia Bulldogs football team from 1964 to 1988. During that time, he won the 1980 national championship and captured six Southeast Conference championships. That's an impressive track record when you consider he was pitted against powerhouse teams like Alabama, Auburn, Florida and Tennessee every year. The College Football Hall of Fame inducted him in 1994.

One of the many reasons for Dooley's success was his passion for and commitment to recruiting. In his autobiography, *Dooley: My 40 Years at Georgia*, he discusses how demanding a coach's job is and how hard it is on his family.

When he started in the profession, recruiting restrictions were few and far between, meaning coaches could contact prospects whenever they felt like it. And they did. It was open season back in those days, and coaches marketed their teams year round and around the clock. Several times over the years, when Dooley was vacationing with his family, he would get restless.

"About five days into it, things would just start to bother me," Dooley wrote. "That was because I knew there was another coach out there talking to recruits while I was on vacation." To assuage that nagging feeling, he would tell his wife he had to take off for a day. During that time, he would visit a handful of prospects and then would return to his vacation feeling much more relaxed.

Such is the life of a coach. Such is the life of anyone trying to reach the highest levels of success in a highly competitive profession. The most successful salespersons and dealmakers don't let any grass grow under their feet, so to speak. They are passionate. They are committed, and they work extremely hard.

We hear many people talk about work-life balance today. That certainly is important. If you don't recharge your batteries, you'll eventually run out of juice, but you have to be careful. Success often requires more "work" than "balance." To reach the pinnacle of your profession, you will most likely have to work harder, smarter and longer than your top competitors. Doing that requires great passion and commitment. If you don't love what you do, you're not likely to put in the time and effort necessary to become a champion.

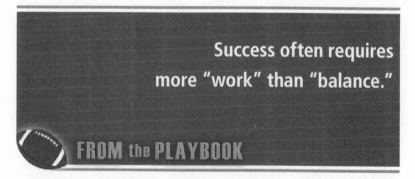

Success often requires more "work" than "balance."

FROM the PLAYBOOK

Like any competitive selling situation, college football recruiting is difficult. It's hard. It requires a tremendous work ethic. As University of California head coach Jeff Tedford said, "You use all the hours in the day, that's for sure."

Coaches sacrifice a great deal. They seldom eat meals at home. They miss most of their kids' sporting events, dance recitals and school plays. They must marry incredibly supportive and understanding spouses who are willing to serve as "single parents" most of the time.

A coach's wife leads a difficult life, with one big exception— head coaches bring home huge salaries, especially established winners like Bob Stoops, Nick Saban, Kirk Ferentz and Mack Brown. Saban, Brown and Stoops all earn at least $5 million or more per year.

The coaches who consistently sign highly rated recruiting classes are creative time managers, sneaking in phone calls or responding to Facebook messages whenever they get the chance, often shimmying their sales work into the tiniest bits of time.

"Recruiting is the lifeblood of our existence," said former Minnesota Gophers coach Tim Brewster, "so 24/7/365, we think about recruiting. It's part of every single staff meeting every single day because without it you're going nowhere."

No matter how good you are as a coach, Brewster believes a program's ability to win rests on recruitment. Unless a coaching staff is 100 percent committed to it, especially the head coach, the team won't succeed. If recruiting is the lifeblood of college football, then marketing and sales are the lifeblood of business. Those companies that become focused on operations and finance at the expense of marketing usually pay a steep price.

Serving as a college coach, and subsequently a football salesman, is not the appropriate lifestyle for everyone. Most people couldn't handle it. The same statement applies to all forms of sales work as some people just don't have the temperament or the burning desire necessary to succeed. If you want proof of this, just look how many people try and fail as independent salespersons. Just look at how many people would love to be a football coach, but can't hack it because of the profession's oppressing demands.

There's no denying it: football recruiting is hard work. Hall of Famer John Cooper, who coached at Arizona State and Ohio State, is glad to be out of the college recruiting business. "I don't miss making those phone calls, and getting turned down and lied to," he said.

Cooper now serves as a consultant for the NFL's Cincinnati Bengals. "I help them a little bit with their draft," he said. "I can tell you right now, sitting in that draft room is a heck of a lot easier. Picking who you want is a heck of a lot easier than recruiting who you need."

But difficulty is no excuse for not doing it well. Extraordinarily rare is the coach who is a mediocre salesperson and still wins consistently. Just as selling is the lifeblood of a business, recruiting is the lifeblood of a football program. Its importance cannot be exaggerated.

Most coaches agree that no matter how good you are with the X's and O's, winning comes down to talent. "You're kidding yourself if you think you're going to out-coach many people," Cooper said. "You out-recruit them. You win with talent."

Another Hall of Fame coach agrees completely. "Talent is number one," said Jim Donnan, former coach of the Georgia Bulldogs and the Marshall Thundering Herd.

Even though you can develop players, Donnan says it's hard to beat a team that has superior talent. "Bad coaching will get you beat, but good coaching isn't always enough," he said. "Good coaching can keep a team in the game, but when it comes down to it, the best teams are usually the ones with the best players."

One of the greatest football salesmen of all time was Barry Switzer, head coach of the Oklahoma Sooners from 1973 to 1988. He won three national championships during that tenure and came darned close to winning a couple more. While he was a solid coach and a great motivator, Switzer's ability to attract the right talent to Norman, Oklahoma, was what ultimately made him great.

"Any coach can line 'em up on both sides of the ball," he said. "It's very difficult to out-coach anybody, out X-and-O anybody."

Switzer had a knack for beating heavyweight rivals late in closely contested games. Usually the difference was a highlight-reel play from one of his extraordinarily gifted blue-chip players.

During post-game interviews, he would sometimes sum up the thrilling finish by saying, "We out-athleted 'em." Switzer's ability to recruit the most elite athletes to OU allowed him to build impressive records against some of the best teams in the land. He was 12-5 against Nebraska, 9-5-2 versus Texas and 3-0 against Bobby Bowden's Florida State Seminoles.

His series against Nebraska particularly illustrated Switzer's ability to recruit. Throughout the 1970s and 1980s, Switzer's Sooners played in many ferocious nail-biters against Tom Osborne's Cornhuskers.

Despite the fact that Osborne was one of the game's true geniuses, Switzer's players were almost always quicker and more athletic. That athleticism, along with Switzer's easygoing, loose demeanor, allowed OU to pull a lot of rabbits out of hats with some athletically amazing, last-second victories against the hard-nosed Huskers. To this day, many OU fans refer to those victories as "the Nebraska miracles."

Sometimes coaches receive too much credit for "developing" a player, when the player really had a great deal of talent and potential to work with. Antonio Gates played basketball at Kent State University, but tried out for the NFL's San Diego Chargers in 2003. Because of this extreme athleticism and limitless potential, the Chargers signed him as an undrafted free agent. He went on to become a Pro Bowl player.

Gates's position coach when he started with the Chargers was Tim Brewster who received much praise and credit for developing Gates so quickly. "Everyone thought I was an amazing coach," Brewster said. "While I do take pride in my coaching ability, it had a lot to do with his talent."

Because talent is such a key part of football success, it logically follows that selling to blue-chip athletes is impressively competitive. In order to succeed in such a demanding environment, you need to do whatever it takes to build relationships with prospects. You must also adapt to unfamiliar surroundings, keep up with the changing nuances of the game, think like your client and always, always, always be passionate.

Doing Whatever It Takes

Early in his coaching career, when John Cooper was an assistant at the University of Kansas, he was chasing a highly coveted, blue-chip player from Kansas City, Missouri. The prospect liked KU, but this wasn't an easy sales job. Even though Lawrence, Kansas, is only forty miles away from Kansas City, Cooper and the Jayhawks were fighting an uphill battle. The boy's parents were University of Missouri alumni and his older sister was already enrolled there. Cooper knew it would take a Herculean effort to pull this guy away from Mizzou, but that didn't stop him.

Cooper wanted this player badly and made him his top recruiting priority. Back then, there was no limit to the number of times a coach could visit a player, so Cooper would see the kid at his high school almost every single day.

When the kid got out of class, Cooper was there. At lunch, he would stop by the kid's house and chat with the mother.

"She might be ironing or doing her housework, but I'd be there," Cooper said. "Each day, I'd say, 'Hey, I'll be here again tomorrow.'"

On Friday nights, Cooper not only attended the prospect's high school football games, he would pick up the parents, take them to the game, sit with them the whole time and drive them back home when it was all over.

"I pretty much told that family, 'Hey, I'm going to lose other prospects, because I'm going to be with you every Friday night, but you're the most important person I'm recruiting, and whatever it takes, that's what I'm going to do,'" he said. Not only did this cement Cooper's relationship with the family, it kept competing coaches away from them.

When you're selling something as competitive as football scholarships, you must do whatever it takes to build the right relationships and make the deal come to fruition. This means you are willing to go the extra mile, and then some, because the competition is so intense. Highly competitive situations should bring out your creativity, your boldness and your resolve. Sometimes that means you find yourself doing something quite out of the ordinary to make an impression.

Former Tennessee coach Phillip Fulmer did it all during his recruiting career including visiting parents of prospects in prison. One parent worked at the prison as a guard; a couple others were actually inmates. He once visited a parent who worked at a military ammunition depot. Before he could get in, however, he had to pass a federal background check.

When Indiana Hoosiers co-defensive coordinator Mike Ekeler was working at Nebraska, he found himself in a heated battle to sign Bonne Terre, Missouri, linebacker prospect Will Compton. Ekeler made quite an impression when he arrived at the family home, rolled up his sleeves and showed he had tattooed (temporarily) Compton's name on his arm. It worked; Compton signed with the Huskers.

Years earlier, a couple other Nebraska coaches traveled to Liberal, Kansas, to win over a star running back's mother. They ended up recruiting her while she played bingo in a church basement. When the legendary Woody Hayes was trying to sell a devotedly Christian kid on Ohio State, he would often go to church with the young man and his family.

In his book *Top Dawg*, author Rob Suggs highlights the work ethic and commitment of Georgia assistant coach Rodney Garner. A few years ago, on the last day coaches were allowed to visit players' homes, Garner showed up at a blue-chip prospect's house at one minute after midnight Saturday and slept on the living room sofa.

On Sunday morning, he woke up, attended church with the family and stayed at the prospect's home until 11:59 p.m., the last possible minute a coach was allowed to visit. Not only did this 23-hour-and-58-minute visit make an impression, it kept opposing coaches away from the prospect at a critical time in the recruiting process. It worked, because the kid signed with the Bulldogs.

As a salesperson, you occasionally encounter an awkward conundrum when two important prospects need or demand your attention at the same time. That requires some quick thinking, a creative solution and a bit of sweet talking. Legendary Oklahoma Sooners coach Barry Switzer experienced that in 1975.

Switzer was one of the greatest recruiters in the history of college football, but his 1975 signing class was impressive even by his standards. It has to be one of the greatest classes of all time. It produced a Heisman Trophy winner, an Outland winner, ten All-Americans and numerous NFL draftees.

As he neared National Signing Day in February 1975, Switzer was faced with a problem: who should he sign first? Unlike current times, head coaches could personally sign players on National Signing Day. In fact, the best players expected that the head coach would show up and personally attend their signing ceremonies.

Two of the nation's best running backs that year, Billy Sims and Kenny King, had verbally committed to OU. Both lived in Texas, but they lived on opposite ends of the Lone Star State. Sims was the more highly recruited of the two, yet Switzer was more confident about Sims's commitment than King's.

Texas A&M was still hot on King's tail, and Switzer was afraid they would make a last-minute play. So what was Switzer to do?

He had to be with Kenny King to make sure he signed first thing in the morning, but he couldn't disrespect Billy Sims, who was considered by many to be the nation's finest high school running back that year.

Switzer convinced Sims to go into hiding and delay his signing ceremony. Switzer told Sims, "Look at it this way, Billy. You know you're comin' to Oklahoma. Let me sign everybody else and hide you out, and when all the smoke clears, people are gonna say, 'Where's Billy Sims?' Then, all of a sudden, two days later, you sign with Oklahoma, and you get all the attention, all the press." Sims thought this was a great idea, so Switzer secreted him 300 miles away from home to Houston, where nobody would think to look for him.

Once Sims was tucked safely away in Houston, Switzer traveled to the Texas panhandle town of Clarendon, where he could stand watch over King all night long until he was legally able to sign at eight the next morning.

He then flew all over the state of Texas personally signing many of the blue chippers who had committed to OU—guys who would go on to become legendary players including Greg Roberts and Thomas Lott among others.

Sure enough, two days later, Switzer and Sims came back to the star running back's hometown. The high school stadium was full, because interest in the signing ceremony grew with the mystery surrounding the whereabouts of the nation's most coveted player.

Adapting to Unfamiliar Surroundings

Regardless of your industry, avoid being a "situational salesperson" or "situational marketer." Some professionals excel in certain situations but fail in others. Tim Brewster believes too many football coaches are merely "situational recruiters."

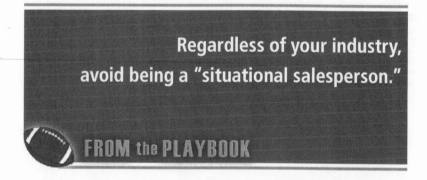

Regardless of your industry, avoid being a "situational salesperson."

FROM the PLAYBOOK

In other words, they don't recruit very well when they are forced out of their comfort zones. They may have a hard time recruiting in a dysfunctional home or in a dangerous neighborhood. Perhaps they don't relate as well to people of certain racial, cultural or religious backgrounds. A situational recruiter might be flustered when the process doesn't go exactly as scripted. Whatever the reason, a situational recruiter will never be a great recruiter. A situational seller will never be a great seller.

Great salespersons adapt to their surroundings. They adjust and think quickly on the fly. When selling their team to a prospect, they have no trouble handling objections and refocusing the sales process, pushing it back on the road to closing. The best salespersons are team players and tow the company line, but they function independently and flourish while under duress in multiple environments even when they are away from the safety net and supply line.

Because they are essentially traveling salespersons, college football coaches do much of their quick thinking while on the road.

When Jack Pierce was working as off-campus recruiting coordinator for Nebraska in the 1980s, he literally spent most of his time on the road. Like any traveling professional, he was seemingly always running to the next flight or trying to find the location of his next meeting in an unfamiliar city.

One time he was in a D.C. taxicab and running late for an important flight to Atlanta. Not only did the cabbie have no idea where he was going, he was indecisive and had no sense of urgency. Eventually, Pierce couldn't take it anymore.

"Stop the car, man," he shouted. "Move over. I'm taking it from here." The flustered cabbie pulled over. Pierce jumped into the driver's seat and sped toward Dulles International Airport. The suddenly demoted cabbie sat in the passenger seat with a bewildered look on his face.

One of the biggest problems coaches face while visiting prospects' homes might come as a surprise—dogs. Of course, a barking dog typically calms down by the time a coach sits down in the living room and starts chatting with the family.

That was not the case on one of former Nebraska assistant George Darlington's visits to a junior college player's home in California. He was scheduled to meet the player's mother at her apartment in a rough neighborhood. As an apparent form of protection, the mother owned a Doberman Pinscher. From the moment Darlington entered the apartment until he left, the Doberman stared piercingly at him, showed its teeth and literally shook with intensity. Darlington feared that any false move could trigger the coiled dog, so how did he adapt to that tense situation? It was the shortest sales pitch of his career.

Howard Schnellenberger is famous for coaching the Miami Hurricanes in the early 1980s, but long before that, he was an assistant coach for the legendary Paul "Bear" Bryant at the University of Alabama. During the 1960–1961 recruiting cycle, Alabama received a late opportunity to go after a western Pennsylvania blue chipper by the name of Joe Namath.

In his book *Coach: The Life of Paul "Bear" Bryant*, Keith Dunnavant describes the spartan conditions Schnellenberger faced while spending a whole week recruiting Namath in his hometown of Beaver Falls, Pennsylvania. Schnellenberger had expected to be on the road for only a couple days, not the entire week it took to convince Namath to take an official visit to Tuscaloosa, Alabama. So he was low on clean clothes and even lower on money.

When it came time for the two of them to fly to Alabama, Schnellenberger wrote a bad check to pay for Namath's airline ticket. He wrote a second bum check at a hotel when weather problems caused an unexpected stay-over in Atlanta.

As Dunnavant writes, "Like the Marines, Bryant's [assistant coaches] were taught to improvise, adapt and overcome!" The decision paid off as Namath ended up leading the Crimson Tide to a 29-4 record and the 1964 national championship.

Not only do coaches have to improvise while out on the road selling, most of them have had to learn the craft mostly on their own. Because of time demands on head coaches, most young assistants receive little or no formal training on how to recruit. Sadly, many for-profit businesses are similarly ill-focused when it comes to sales training. If that's the case in your company, you have to figure out how to do it on your own.

As a new coach, you learn recruiting from talking to your veteran colleagues and asking questions but mostly from old-fashioned trial-and-error. In other words, you just have to jump into it. The more you do it, the better you get.

That's exactly how the great Barry Switzer got his start. In 1961, Switzer landed his first assistant coaching job at his alma mater, the University of Arkansas. He worked for Hall of Fame head coach Frank Broyles, who would later become athletic director and an ABC television broadcaster.

The rookie Switzer earned Broyles's confidence by successfully selling in remote parts of Texas—west of Wichita Falls and Amarillo and up into the panhandle—places where Arkansas never previously recruited. Switzer signed three players from the area his first year, and all of them eventually started for the Razorbacks. One earned all-Southwest Conference honors by the time he finished his college career.

Keeping Up with the Changing Game

To stay relevant in your profession, you must keep up with the changing landscape of business. Norms and expectations change. Your competition is always on the move. Technology changes so fast that even technologists have a hard time keeping up with it. Nevertheless, you must try to embrace new gizmos and gadgets just to keep up with the competition let alone beat it. Football is no different.

Because the stakes are so high, major college football coaches are always looking for new angles, new tricks to one-up the competition in the sales race. The NCAA's rules for recruiting are probably stricter than the rules legislated for any other aspect of football. Even though the rules are both broad and detailed, coaches often find little loopholes they can exploit in order to gain an advantage. Technology tends to create or at least expose these previously unanticipated white spaces in the NCAA rule book.

Text messaging was a perfect example. Before the NCAA handed down strict rules about text messages, coaches across the nation were using them as a way to contact student athletes much more frequently than the NCAA ever intended. Technically, there were no rules against texting, so it was open season.

Well, as is the case with most NCAA loopholes, the texting era of recruiting came to an abrupt end when the rules changed. Frankly, some coaches see strict rules as a relief. It's not easy remembering to text your prospects multiple times a day, and it's hard to keep your messages "fresh." Coaches were only doing it because they knew their competition was. You never want to be out-marketed in a competitive business.

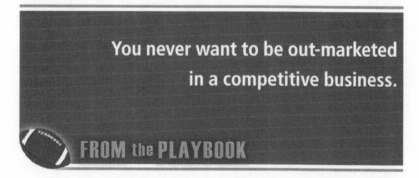

You never want to be out-marketed in a competitive business.

FROM the PLAYBOOK

Once texting was banned, coaches discovered social media. The NCAA didn't have the same rules in place for Facebook that they had for more traditional forms of communication. It doesn't matter what communications technology is currently in vogue, football salesmen will find a way to use it to their advantage. It doesn't matter what new marketing strategies consultants will dream up, they will be leveraged until the NCAA has had enough. It's a never-ending battle to stay ahead of the competition when your job depends on winning.

Changing technology affects football recruiting in ways beyond prospect communication. It wasn't too many years ago when coaches evaluated prospects next to a clicking projector while feeding flickering celluloid from reel to reel.

Eventually, video came into being, which made it easier for coaches to move the footage forward and backward allowing them to closely study a player's footwork and technique. Now coaches watch their prospects on digital video, which gives them the ability to study game footage like never before. Digital film also provides instantaneous access to footage. In the old days, a coach could hear about a prospect but might have to wait several days for the kid's game film to arrive in the mail. Now the coach has immediate Internet access to thousands of player videos.

Technology has changed the way coaches view prospect videos and how they break down game footage to help current players play better. Hudl.com is a great example. The Internet company works with thousands of high schools and several major college football teams.

Hudl, with offices in Lincoln, Nebraska, and Austin, Texas, digitizes all of the team's and each player's plays for entire games and entire seasons. The technology allows plays to be dissected, categorized and catalogued. It's effective for improving a player's own performance and for studying the opposition's tendencies.

Hudl is playing a key role in recruiting as well. High school players hoping for scholarships have an easy way to send any appropriate plays to recruiters. The college coaches, on the other hand, find the technology to be helpful as they prospect and qualify athletes.

Because college football is so incredibly competitive, it's hard for a coach to achieve a nice routine, allowing him to coast for a couple years. There's no such thing as "being comfortable" as a football coach, because as soon as you relax, several competitors speed past you.

Understanding Your Client

Another way to keep up is by thinking like your clients. In football sales, the client is a seventeen- or eighteen-year-old boy, who just so happens to possess an extraordinarily rare combination of speed, power, strength, balance, intelligence, temperament, discipline and commitment. Though these young men are blessed beyond imagination, they are still teenagers. The success of a nationally famous, $2-million-salary coach ultimately comes down to the whims and passions of a group of kids who aren't old enough to vote, legally drink a beer or rent a car at the Avis counter.

> The success of a nationally famous, $2-million-salary coach ultimately comes down to the whims and passions of a group of kids who aren't old enough to vote, legally drink a beer or rent a car at the Avis counter.

FROM the PLAYBOOK

And if you know anything at all about teenagers, you know how fickle they can be. You know how hard it is to relate to them, how hard it is to keep up with fads, fashions, styles and slang words.

To succeed in college football, "You have to think like a seventeen-year-old," said former Colorado Coach Gary Barnett. "That means you have to sort of retool your focus every year, because seventeen-year-olds are always thinking differently."

Multi-millionaire, fifty-five-year-old college football coaches, therefore, better know the names of popular video games, movies and the music kids are listening to this year if they want to relate. Just like salespersons of any industry, coaches need to relate. They must study their clients constantly and be prepared to sell their teams using the client's language.

All-American Passion

Given the difficulty and cut-throat competition in recruiting, coaches must be passionate in order to succeed. Not only does passion imply discipline and commitment, it means a coach actually enjoys the process. Selling your team may be taxing, but it can be fun for those with a positive outlook.

"I loved recruiting," said former Tennessee coach Phillip Fulmer whose Volunteers won the 1998 national championship. "I enjoyed the young people, the families, the sales process. Having been a Tennessean and a Tennessee player, I knew an awful lot about the place. I liked East Tennessee. [The university] was a great place to go get a great education and play in a fabulous facility and with a great history."

Barnett enjoyed recruiting because it was another form of competition. "I liked the competing part of it," he said. "I also wanted to see first-hand how a kid interacted at school, with coaches and other students. Those things were really important, because you're hand-picking a family."

NCAA rules restrict how often the head coach can go out on the road; only assistants are allowed out on the sales trail for much of the year. "I miss getting out on the road in springtime," said Cal's Jeff Tedford, who consistently signs highly rated classes.

"They've taken the head coaches off the road, and I really miss that. I used to love spring recruiting, getting out and meeting [high school] coaches, seeing guys at spring practice and evaluating them. We used to be able to go to all the combines, I really enjoyed that and miss it." Despite the tight rules, Tedford still thoroughly enjoyed the times in the fall and winter when he could go out and recruit.

Even though he lived in one of the most talent-rich football states in the country, former Texas A&M coach R.C. Slocum deserves credit for being an outstanding salesperson. Slocum acknowledges that recruiting has its downside in that it's tiring and takes you away from your family. That said, he doesn't believe a person can be a successful coach if he doesn't enjoy selling the team to the next generation of players.

"You're going into a home. You're meeting a nice family. You're talking about their most prized possession—their son. That shouldn't be a chore," said Slocum, who led the Aggies from 1998 to 2002. "Over the years, I've made so many great friendships. I didn't get all the players, but to this day, remain friends with those young men and their families, because of the relationships during recruiting."

When it comes down to it, you can't fake it. You have to enjoy your work in order to have the passion necessary to reach the pinnacle of your profession.

Long-term success demands a commitment to marketing and selling.

Being successful requires constant effort. Things fall apart quickly when you avert your focus.

Successful organizations think about marketing and selling 365 days a year.

Serious professionals are willing to do whatever it takes to seal the deal. If necessary, they take extraordinary measures to win a prospect's favor.

Avoid being a situational marketer. Be ready and willing to adapt to a shifting playing field.

To stay relevant in your business, keep up with the times. Don't resist the change-forces that are bigger than you.

Think the way your clients think. Your client determines what is valuable, not you.

Passion is required to succeed at the highest levels, so make sure you work in a field you truly enjoy.

Chapter 4

GOOD VS. GREAT
Second Don't Mean Nothin'

If you're going into business, you might as well go all the way and shoot to reach the pinnacle of your profession. It's a competitive world, so set your sights high. If you're going to take the risk and invest the time, strive for greatness.

Ever since Jim Collins wrote his best-selling book *Good to Great* in 2001, business people worldwide have been fixated on what separates goodness from greatness. Why do some companies do so well when a fairly similar competitor languishes? Why do some companies transition from being merely successful to being truly great? What traits and behaviors separate the good from the great?

Of course, good-versus-great questions apply not only to companies; they can be asked of people too.

Whether you're selling medical equipment, brokering international business transactions or recruiting star athletes to a major college football team, it's easy to fail. Salespersons, marketers and dealmakers in every profession commonly fail. Some succeed, but only a tiny percentage achieve greatness.

If we can understand why some football coaches become great salespersons, we can apply those coaches' behaviors and traits to sales and marketing in general.

A++ Leadership

A different definition of greatness applies to head coaches than it does for assistant coaches. Determination of the head coach's recruiting effectiveness depends greatly on his ability to lead. He must depend on the orchestrated efforts of his nine assistant coaches and the athletic department's vast administrative support staff. That means he must cast a compelling vision and manage the efforts of many. Head coaches are essentially CEOs, and football programs are in essence big businesses.

Whether it's a head football coach or a CEO, certain leadership traits separate the good from the great. Joe Moglia, who has served as both a *Fortune* 1000 CEO and football coach, identifies three big ones: an ability to relate to people, stress management, and a focus on core competencies.

Not everybody relates well to people. Some new head coaches may have been great coordinators, but they might not possess the strategic thinking and big-picture perspective necessary to lead a team to a conference or national championship. A CEO may work his or her way up over time thanks to great technical or operational ability, but that does not always translate into leadership effectiveness.

It's a fact: the higher you go, the greater your stress level. "There are many guys who can paint an incredibly cogent picture of why we should be investing in China or why we should be running a spread offense," said Moglia, who serves as both chairman of TD Ameritrade and a collegiate coach.

"The reality is, when things are not going well, when you're losing money in China, your guys are fumbling the ball, when you have injuries, how do you handle yourself?" In Moglia's mind, responses to pressure and stress are huge determinants of success.

Both football teams and businesses must focus on their core competencies and thereby leverage their competitive advantages. Once this is determined, only a handful of things matter. "You've got to get an A-plus-plus on this," Moglia said. "Too often we lose sight of what those select few things are, and we waste energy in other areas. All your energy needs to be focused on the things that really make the difference, really matter in your program or your organization."

You Can't Afford Not to Be Honest

Those coaches who reach the pinnacle of the profession place a great value on character—both their own and that of each player. Hall of Fame coach Tom Osborne led Nebraska to three national championships, 255 wins and twenty-five bowl games in twenty-five years. In his worst season, he still won nine games.

Osborne excelled for so long because he placed a premium on character. He was honest with his players, and he expected them to respond in kind. Being honest as a head coach means you never promise someone playing time or offer anything you can't deliver.

The legendary Joe Paterno commanded Penn State from 1966 until his sad and shocking demise in 2011. He served as an assistant there starting in 1950. His coaching career spanned twelve U.S. Presidents and quite a few Penn State University presidents. You don't win more than 400 games unless your career rests on a foundation of honesty. While his career—and ultimately his life—ended sadly when a shocking and disgusting series of accusations were unveiled about the Penn State Athletic Department, he did have a respected reputation for decades. He was known for telling the truth.

"My parents were more impressed with him than any other coach," said former quarterback and current television broadcaster Todd Blackledge as quoted in *No Ordinary Joe* by Michael O'Brien. "He asked if he could take his shoes off. He made himself at home. That really made an impression."

Paterno was always frank with his prospective players, O'Brien writes. The octogenarian coach talked a great deal about academics. He told prospects they will work hard, be tested for drugs and have the opportunity to prove they are worthy of playing time. Paterno essentially believed it would be wrong to promise playing time to an incoming freshman because it would be disrespectful to his veteran players.

Phillip Fulmer's recruiting prowess and coaching abilities helped him win a national championship at Tennessee in 1998. Year in and year out, he would assemble one of the nation's highest-rated recruiting classes. He identifies honesty as one of the most critical traits especially as a recruiter.

"We were honest with families, and they felt that," Fulmer said. "I wanted my coaches to tell the families what we were all about as an organization. We had our share of guys who played in the NFL; a lot of guys drafted, but it was not necessarily a path to the NFL."

Fulmer told parents of recruits that the top priorities were academic, spiritual and social development. If pro football was a possibility for a player, that would be great—and Fulmer would certainly support his players in such a career pursuit—but he wanted the University of Tennessee to be the immediate focus. Even the most extremely talented members of a recruiting class often have a difficult time making it to the NFL. The odds are against them.

"We took it seriously that they would go to class," Fulmer said. "We took it seriously that they would come away with a degree. Not everybody finished, but those who stayed with the program were better off academically, socially and spiritually. A lot of them did get their degrees and went on to things other than football."

High school coaches too play a major role in the recruiting process, and while the stakes aren't quite as high for them as they are for their college counterparts, a sense of honesty is just as important. College coaches need high school coaches to tell the truth and the whole truth. High school coaches can be tempted to puff up a kid and portray him as a better prospect than he really might be.

There are a number of motivations for this. For one thing, the high school coach probably has developed fondness for the kid and wants to see him get a college scholarship. Another reason is much more selfish: the more college prospects a high school coach produces, the more praise and attention the coach receives. That means he gets to hobnob with the famous college coaches who are on television every Saturday. Even better, a brown-nosing high school coach could be positioning himself for a future job on a collegiate coaching staff.

"I tell our kids, 'Look, I'm not going to lie for you,'" said Cedar Hill (Texas) High School coach Joey McGuire, who has sent countless blue chippers to Texas, Oklahoma and other football powerhouses. "I'm going to tell them the good, the bad and the ugly ... because at a program like ours, I can't afford to not be honest."

McGuire realizes that his reputation as an honest high school coach is good for his players. If he developed a bad reputation, colleges might start skipping over his school thus harming future students.

Hard Work and Fierce Competition

Anything worthwhile is worth hard work. Success in football, or any other profession, typically comes only with a great deal of effort, especially smart, efficient effort.

Throughout his thirty-six-year head coaching career, Hayden Fry was known as a hard worker. At each of his three head coaching assignments, he took over programs that had been struggling and turned them into winners. He is best known as the long-time coach of the Iowa Hawkeyes.

In 1962, when the thirty-one-year-old Fry took over Southern Methodist's football program, he had an annual recruiting budget of $8,000, a paltry sum compared to nearby competitors like Oklahoma, Texas and Texas A&M. He badly wanted to attend the American Football Coaches Association convention in Los Angeles that year, but he couldn't justify taking precious funds out of his budget. To pinch pennies, he bought a bus ticket from Dallas to Abilene, Texas, and then hitchhiked to Phoenix.

Once in Phoenix, he splurged and bought a bus ticket to L.A., because he didn't want the embarrassment of fellow football coaches seeing him hitchhiking. On another occasion, Fry wanted to attend a lecture by legendary coach Paul Brown so badly that he hitchhiked from Dallas to Cleveland and back. Fry was so dedicated to succeeding that he was willing to go to great lengths and make tremendous personal sacrifice.

When asked to identify what ultimately separates a good recruiter from a great one, a former Ohio State Buckeye coach wasted no time in answering.

"Let's just say, hard work would be a factor," said John Cooper, who recruited countless future first-round draftees. "Everyone knows who the great athletes are, so everyone is fighting for them." Coaches must exercise perseverance and discipline, constantly battling for players against fierce competition.

Hard work paid off for Cooper as his teams were consistently loaded with blue chippers. During his time in Columbus, Ohio, he recruited Heisman, Outland, Biletnikoff and Thorpe award winners. In fact, Jim Tressel's national championship Buckeye team in 2002 consisted mostly of star players recruited during the Cooper era.

What does "hard work" mean for a coach? It means they constantly prospect and qualify potential players year round. They are forced to place phone calls to high school players whenever they can. They carve out time during the typical day to discuss recruits, analyze prospects' game films, strategize with fellow coaches, and compose handwritten letters to blue-chip prospects who are being hounded by the competition. All of this takes place while coaches are trying to develop their existing players and preparing game plans for the next opponent.

Now, let's acknowledge that coaches aren't the only people who have a lot to do. The world is a busy place. We all have so many things we must do. Employers expect employees to accomplish more with less. Ask almost anyone and he or she will argue that his or her life is crazy busy, but football coaches' lives are like almost no others. They are unbelievably busy; they bring a new meaning to the word busy. They work under constant competitive pressure. Their demanding schedules rival those of top corporate CEOs and prominent politicians.

Those who choose a demanding profession should know it will take hard work. If they're not willing to make the sacrifice, they might want to pursue a different line of work.

Nothing Falls Through the Cracks

Prospecting is a critically important part of the sales process, and good prospectors think like detectives. They are constantly searching, questioning and trying to find any shred of advantageous information possible. A detective-like prospector turns over every stone and scratches the dirt, looking for hidden gems, unexpectedly great clients. Just like a detective, a savvy prospector pays attention to detail. Nothing falls through the cracks.

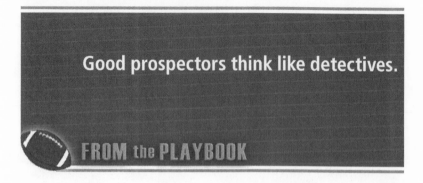

Good prospectors think like detectives.

FROM the PLAYBOOK

Attention to detail not only helps you find prospects, it is necessary to find out all you can about the prospect. You must do your homework by learning all you can about the person you're trying to sell. When you're selling a college football team, some pieces of intel are more important than others. You must discover who influences the kid. Are there academic or behavior problems? What evidence can you find in his past play that makes you comfortable he can project to the next level? Be careful and pay attention to detail, because you can't afford too many "busts."

Tom Osborne says one of the most difficult yet important things a prospecting coach faces is to ascertain what people play key roles in the player's life. You might assume it's the mother or the father, but might later discover it's the grandmother. Learn everything about the kid. What does he like to eat? Who is his girlfriend and what's her story? Are there people at the school who influence the kid? Can you develop any advocates in the kid's community?

Additionally, you need attention to detail to manage large amounts of information. Each assistant coach is responsible for developing a personal relationship with a certain number of recruits each year. This is complicated by the fact that he is recruiting a couple years' worth of recruits simultaneously (that is, he's recruiting both high school juniors and seniors while tracking younger kids for future classes). He must remember when to contact each player and keep track of where he is in the recruiting process. Is the prospect warm or cold? Is he a verbal commit who needs to be maintained or a good prospect who needs to be moved along the decision-making process?

You need to have a good client-contact management system, most likely electronic, which allows you to track what you said to each kid/client and when. Then you must have the discipline to use it properly and fully.

Communication

Nobody can be effective as a detective-like prospector if he or she isn't a good listener.

"Recruiting teaches you the importance of listening," Tom Osborne said. "You don't always want to be talking. Spend some time figuring out where the other person is coming from."

Former Northwestern and Colorado Coach Gary Barnett believes the greatest football salesmen are the ones who not only listen but truly *hear.*

"Most people, a lot of young recruiters especially, are just waiting to talk," Barnett said. "They don't really listen to what the recruit is saying, or what the recruit's parents are saying." When a coach makes this error, he doesn't really know where he stands in the process. He doesn't know what buttons to push, because he doesn't know what the prospect thinks.

> ## The greatest football salesmen are the ones who not only listen but truly *hear.*
>
> ### FROM the PLAYBOOK

If you ask the journalists who cover college football recruiting to name the most gifted recruiters over the past decade, there's a good chance Tim Brewster's name will come up. Brewster served as an assistant coach at North Carolina and Texas before working a couple years as Minnesota's head coach. What does Coach Brew identify as a recruiter's number-one skill? It's a quick and easy answer: listening.

"Coaches talk too much," Brewster said. "They spend too much time talking and not listening. The art of listening is a hidden secret in recruiting. Many recruiters want to just talk to kids ... and I'll talk to kids after they talk to a guy at a different school, and they'll say, 'Coach, I can take the phone off my ear for fifteen minutes.'"

Coaches who listen well create a level of excitement in their prospects' minds.

"Some coaches call, and the kids don't want to pick up the phone," Brewster said. "Other coaches call, and the kids says, 'Well, I'll pick up the phone, but I'm not really interested.' And then some coaches call and it's like, 'Dang, I can't wait to talk to Coach Brewster. Goll, it's Coach Brew.' Then you develop that type of relationship with a kid where he's really looking forward to your phone call. And it's not always, 'Hey, how many touchdowns did you score?' You better get to know a kid on a personal level."

The most effective recruiters listen, because they know the process is not about them. It's about the player, the prospective client.

Of course, good listening skills are not the only component of communication.

Not every great salesperson is an extrovert, but it sure helps. Those coaches who are comfortable interacting with new people take to recruiting more naturally than the introverted guys who would rather be back in the office watching film and playing with X's and O's.

"You have to be a great communicator, someone who has the ability to feel comfortable and be genuine, honest and sincere in your approach to people," said Hall of Fame coach Barry Switzer.

Recruiters are essentially salespersons, and great salespersons relate to people. They explain the product by painting a picture with words while simultaneously building relationships and establishing trust.

Switzer was one of the best salespersons in the history of the game, and one of his most valuable assets was his ability to communicate with families. He was comfortable in his own skin, and he made the people around him feel comfortable too. That made it possible for him to win over even the most skeptical mothers—the women who often made the final decisions where their sons would play.

Communication is facilitated when the communicator has a charismatic personality. Like gregariousness, charisma is not required per se, but it makes the sales process a hell of a lot easier.

Before he became a head coach, Jim Donnan worked as Barry Switzer's offensive coordinator. That gave him a front-row seat and first-hand insight into how a master salesman plied his trade. He learned up-close how Switzer sold Saturday afternoons to Friday night stars.

"He had a knack for seizing the moment," Donnan said of Switzer's uncommon recruiting ability. Switzer had the ability to see what made a prospect tick and then use his dynamic personality to win him over, while still coming across as sincere.

On one of their many recruiting trips together, Donnan and Switzer arrived late for a meeting with a blue-chip prospect. By the time the two OU coaches pulled into the parking lot, school was out and the hotshot prospect was not only already on the school bus, he was actually driving it. The young man saw Switzer and waved at him from the driver's seat.

Switzer jumped out of the rental car, held up his hands while running toward the bus, boarded the vehicle and then rode the whole bus tour until the last student had been dropped off. You can imagine that a bunch of small-town school kids were thrilled to be entertained by a famous college football coach on their way home. More importantly, the stunt made the high school senior Switzer was pursuing look like quite a hero in the other kids' eyes.

"It was one of the most impulsive things I've ever seen, just a great impulse, and it was a big deal for that kid that Switzer would take all that time," Donnan said. "He would go into a school and you'd think the President was coming in there. Everyone in the school wanted to get their picture with him and talk to him."

Donnan said it was clear that Switzer enjoyed being with people in crowds and that his genuine sincerity was palpable and only further bolstered his charisma.

Lou Holtz is famous for his national championship tenure under the golden dome at Notre Dame University and more recently for his game-day commentary on ESPN. Holtz's charismatic personality has allowed him to overcome his speech impediment and become a successful coach, a popular broadcaster and a highly sought-after public speaker.

That charisma helped Holtz early in his career, long before his glory years at Notre Dame. In 1984, he left his head coaching job at the University of Arkansas and ventured up north for a new challenge in Minneapolis as head coach of the struggling Minnesota Gophers.

One of Holtz's first orders of business was to build a metaphorical fence around the Land of 10,000 Lakes. For several years, blue-chip talent from Minnesota high schools was heading off to Iowa, Nebraska and Wisconsin, according to Holtz's autobiography *Wins, Losses, and Lessons*. So, right away, Holtz went on statewide television and implored all high school football stars to attend the University of Minnesota.

"The heart and soul of our team must come from the state of Minnesota," he said during his television monologue before looking squarely into the camera. "But you do realize the arms and legs must come from elsewhere. It's hard to run in snowshoes."

The good people of Minnesota loved it. They ate it up faster than a pan of hotdish at a Lutheran potluck supper. The mass-media appeal was just what the doctor ordered. Holtz claims that for the next two years he signed every major prospect in the state except one.

Focusing on Others

When a salesperson truly masters the art of communication, he or she tends to be highly empathetic, the type of person who tries to understand what it's like to walk in someone else's shoes. An effective salesperson knows that greater success will eventually come if he or she puts the client's interest before his or her own.

Real estate agents, accountants and trustees are said to have "fiduciary" responsibilities to their clients. In other words, they are legally required to put the client's interests before their own. No matter what you do, pretend you have a fiduciary duty to the clients you serve. If you do this, you will build rapport, which leads to a relationship, which leads to the holy grail of sales and marketing: trust. Once trust is established, deal-making is easy.

Although football salesmen are not technically fiduciaries to the young men they recruit, the successful ones are committed to the players' best interests. As Joe Moglia likes to say, "It's not about you; it's about the kid."

One of the most important parts of a recruiter's job is to determine if the young man is a fit for the institution and if the institution is a fit for him. As much as the coach wants to sign great athletes, he will be doing nobody a favor, including himself, if his school is not the best choice for the prospective player.

Early in his career, when he was coaching at Dartmouth College, Moglia remembers parents saying, "I'd love my son to play for you," and while such nice words naturally stroke any coach's ego, Moglia never felt comfortable when he heard them. So he would ask the parents and their son not to put too much stock in him and his personality.

"I could get another job tomorrow," Moglia would say. "I want your son to come to here because this is the right place for him. That's the decision you gotta make. A lot of coaches say, 'I'll take care of your kid.' That sounds great, but you have to be careful you can live up to your promises."

Coaches who think like fiduciaries and put the players' interests first, end up having more solid programs, Moglia believes. Keep in mind that current players have a big influence on recruiting. They are the ones who host the high school hotshots on official campus visits. If the players aren't happy, if they don't feel the coaches fully have their backs, those negative feelings and beliefs will probably be conveyed to the prospects.

Similarly, things don't work well in business when a salesperson walks prospects through an office where they can overhear employees griping about the company. Even worse, sometimes a prospective client can "feel" negative energy in the air, which could cause him or her to take the business to a competitor.

> Sometimes a prospective client can "feel" negative energy in the air, which could cause him or her to take the business to a competitor.
>
> FROM the PLAYBOOK

Over the course of time, fiduciary-like selling builds a strong base of happy clients—not just players but parents and the high school coaches who refer players. In recruiting and other forms of sales, you need a huge network of people who will sing your praises and constantly funnel prospects your way. Make them feel special, treat them like gold and put their interests before your own. If you do that, you will have more influencers and champions in your back pocket than you ever imagined possible.

Relentless Competitiveness

In the mid-1970s, Oklahoma's Barry Switzer pulled out all the stops trying to recruit a gifted running back out of Tyler, Texas. The young man had an unusual combination of size, speed and strength. On top of all of that he was smart and emotionally mature for his age. His name was Earl Campbell.

When Switzer looks back on all the blue-chip players he recruited, only two had the physical ability to go straight from high school to NFL stardom—Earl Campbell and Marcus Dupree. Only one of those guys had both the physical *and* mental abilities to skip college ball and go straight to the big show, and that was Earl Campbell.

Oklahoma didn't win the battle for Campbell's services. The superstar signed with OU's arch-rival, the University of Texas, where he amassed 4,444 career rushing yards and won the 1977 Heisman Trophy. He went on to have a memorable career with the Houston Oilers.

To this day, Switzer identifies Campbell as his "biggest fish that got away." OU and Texas fought a ferocious recruiting battle for Campbell, but in the end, his mother worked for the owner of the local bank. That guy was a Texas alumnus and a big Longhorn fan. It was a tough battle for the out-of-state Switzer to win. Under the circumstances, some guys might take some solace in coming in as runner up especially since so many football powerhouses wanted the kid.

"Second don't mean nothin', but I was second," Switzer said. "Second don't mean a thing."

Those simple words, "second don't mean nothin'," speak volumes about Switzer's success. In order to succeed in any competitive enterprise, you have to think and act competitively. You have to do everything you can to win. You have to fight every fight to the end and tell yourself, even when victory isn't looking likely, to keep battling. When you're in a winner-take-all game, never be pleased when you beat out all the competitors except for one, because second don't mean nothin'.

Think Strategically

Blue-chip football talent can be found almost anywhere in the United States, but it tends to be concentrated in a few specific areas: Texas, Florida and California make up the top tier. Behind those three fertile states are the southeastern states plus New Jersey, Pennsylvania and Ohio. If you're looking for one metropolitan area that produces the most talent, the candidates would include Houston, Los Angeles, Miami and the Dallas–Fort Worth Metroplex.

Cedar Hill High School in the Dallas suburb of Cedar Hill, Texas, is located in a middle-class area on the southern side of the Metroplex. It's a powerhouse high school football program that competes in class 5-A, the largest high school competitive classification in the biggest high school football state in America.

Cedar Hill's nearby rivals include DeSoto and Duncanville, among other big high schools in the same general area. These three prep schools produce amazing numbers of Division 1 football players each year. That's impressive, but there are hundreds of high schools in the Metroplex. Altogether, they crank out some of the nation's best football players and quite a large number of them.

Cedar Hill coach Joey McGuire claims a college coach could win a national championship simply by recruiting the Metroplex (assuming he landed most of the area's best players each year). Such a statement is probably not much of an exaggeration. The place is talent rich.

That means the great college football teams from around the nation come to the Metroplex to recruit players. It's logical, right? You go where the talent is.

Blueblood programs like Notre Dame, Nebraska and Tennessee are not located in the most populated, talent-rich states. That means those schools must go to places like Dallas in order to get their talent. Oklahoma sits in a sparsely populated state, but it's next door to Texas. Alabama and Auburn are located in a small-population state, but the number of players per capita in the Yellowhammer state is near the top, plus it's located in the talent-rich Southeast. Even schools like Michigan and Penn State, which sit in highly populated states, have to recruit significant portions of their rosters from southern states, because there is simply more and better talent south of the Mason-Dixon Line.

That's part of the strategic thinking that goes into selling a college football team to a small group of elite prospects. You have to go where the prospects are. Meet your prospects where they live.

The great coaches do what it takes to develop winning recruiting strategies. They hire the right coaches—at least a certain percentage of the coaching staff needs to be exceptionally blessed with strong recruiting skills. Great coaches train and organize their staff and lay out a sales philosophy that everyone at the university follows. They assess their needs and are willing to change targeted client profiles when necessary.

Former Nebraska coach Tom Osborne did this several times over the years. Long before he won his three national championships, Osborne struggled to make the leap from good coach to great coach. Part of the problem was recruiting.

In 1981, Osborne had a solid team. The Huskers struggled early in the season, losing two of the first three games, but started to excel in the fourth game after it discovered a sensational sophomore quarterback by the name of Turner Gill. Under Gill's leadership, Nebraska went on an impressive winning streak, ended the regular season ranked fourth and earned a trip to the Orange Bowl to play number-one-ranked Clemson for the national championship.

Gill suffered an injury before the bowl game and wasn't able to play. Clemson captured the national championship with a 22-15 victory. Although the Huskers were still a good team without Gill, they were not as fast as Clemson, which was loaded with speedy players from the Southeast.

After the game, a disappointed Osborne huddled with his assistant coaches on the plane ride home.

"Recruit speed," Osborne demanded. "Every position—I want, speed, speed, speed."

The game was changing. Increasingly sophisticated offenses required defenses to be more athletic and much quicker. Osborne changed with the times by changing his recruiting strategy and the type of prospect he would sell. That eventually helped him lay the foundation for much greater success years down the road.

Prospecting and Qualifying

As a coach chases top-notch players for his team, he has to be careful not to be overly dazzled, not to get blinded by brightly shining talent. In the same way a salesperson can become too enamored with a big prospect, a coach can fall under an unusually gifted player's spell, daydreaming about him scoring touchdowns or making a goal-line-stand tackle. God-given talent notwithstanding, a player who doesn't fit the program is never worth taking.

In his twenty-one years as head coach of the Michigan Wolverines, Bo Schembechler won or shared thirteen Big 10 Conference championships. He took his teams to the Rose Bowl so often, he should have kept an apartment in Pasadena. When it came to prospecting, Schembechler preferred those players who would become "Michigan Men," guys who dedicated themselves to the Wolverines' team-first culture.

"I can't tell you how many times we passed up hotshots for guys we thought were better people, and watched our guys do a lot better than the big names, not just in the classroom, but on the field—and naturally, after they graduated, too," said Schembechler in his book *Bo's Lasting Lessons* co-written with John Bacon.

"Again and again, the blue chips faded out, and our little up-and-comers clawed their way to all-conference and All-America teams. And even when some bad-acting blue chipper did the job on the field for some other school, I never felt any remorse over not taking him," he said. "When you recruit for character, you sleep a lot better too."

While Schembechler was determined to find players who fit his team's culture, don't be fooled by his humility. He had more than his share of highly coveted blue chippers over the years. He was just a stickler for character.

In order to move from good to great, a coach must find inspiration in other places. Perhaps you have seen the movie *The Blind Side*. It's an acclaimed movie based on a true story first described in a best-selling book by Michael Lewis.

The Blind Side introduces us to Michael Oher, one of thirteen children born to a mother addicted to crack cocaine living in a Memphis housing project. When the story begins, the teenage Oher doesn't know his father, his birthday or even his true last name. His reading and writing skills are almost non-existent. A victim of utter neglect, he spends his days and nights unsupervised, wandering the crime-ridden, inner-city streets.

Through a twist of fate—or perhaps divine intervention—Oher finds himself enrolled in an upscale, suburban prep school where he meets an affluent family that eventually adopts him. With this new love and support, he overcomes culture shock, catches up academically and discovers the game of football.

He not only discovers football, he turns out to be darned good at it and receives a full-ride athletic scholarship to the University of Mississippi. Today, Oher is a star offensive lineman for the National Football League's Baltimore Ravens and consequently a very wealthy man.

While the compelling story behind *The Blind Side* is the amazing metamorphosis of a young man, there's a second story line: the evolution of the game of football. You see, there's a reason why Oher is such a wealthy player today. He plays a position that is critically important and perhaps the most difficult one for a coach to staff: left tackle. There is a scarcity of truly great left-tackle talent. That makes Oher unbelievably valuable to coaches and team owners.

Why is the left tackle so important? Because he protects the quarterback's blind side. Most quarterbacks are right handed, so when they drop back to pass, they can't see pass rushers coming from their left sides. Given that, defensive coordinators usually line up their most ferocious athletes on the quarterback's left side.

As the highest paid and typically most valuable player on the team, the quarterback must be protected at all costs. But it's not enough for a left tackle to be big and strong. He must possess the rare combination of size, strength, speed, balance and agility. In other words, a left tackle must be a huge guy with the agility of a little guy. Very few human beings possess this priceless combination of abilities. Michael Oher is one of them.

As a quarterback, you need a world-class left tackle covering your blind side, your greatest vulnerability. If you get blindsided too much, you not only lose the game, you might lose your career.

Since there are few developed left tackles coming out of high school, great college coaches know they must develop these players—"create" them over time through strength and conditioning and great coaching. Knowing this, they look for transferable skills.

This might come as a surprise, but basketball is one of the greatest indicators of future success as a college or professional left tackle. Coaches look for big, strong guys who not only play basketball but are quick, exhibit good balance and look "light on their feet" for a big guy. With good coaching, that combination of abilities could evolve into a future All-American lineman.

Asking for the Order

When it all comes down to it, you simply cannot be a great recruiter or salesperson unless you seal the deal. Great salespersons are closers. As Joe Moglia says, success in any business ultimately comes down to getting somebody to say "yes."

It's interesting that for many salespeople, regardless of industry, including football coaches, the close is the hardest part of the process. It shouldn't be. If you have done a good job with earlier parts of the process—prospecting, qualifying, relationship building—the close ought to be a formality. But for some reason, the pressure and importance of the close cause some salespersons to become tongue-tied, wobbly-kneed and short of breath. The great ones overcome this fear, find ways to handle the pressure and get the job done.

You simply must be able to close the deal. Ask for the order. Call the question. You must get the sale. You must get the contract signed. As the old saying, goes: "ABC" or "Always Be Closing."

"A lot of guys are good recruiters, and they do a good job of making contacts and relationships," said R.C. Slocum, the winningest football coach in Texas A&M history, "but in the end, a lot of times, those guys never get the sale. To me, that's the most important thing separating a good recruiter from a great one. You can spend a whole lot of time and money on recruiting, but the object of the game is to get the guy signed."

Don't settle once you reach "good." Keep growing.

To be a great leader, you must relate to people, manage stress and focus on core competencies.

Honest professionals tend to enjoy more career longevity.

Success typically comes only with great effort, especially smart, efficient effort.

Just like a detective, a savvy salesperson pays attention to detail. Nothing falls through the cracks.

The greatest salespersons don't just listen; they truly hear.

Once you decide to put your clients' interests ahead of your own, you're on your way to the top.

Never be pleased when you beat out all your competitors except one. Second don't mean nothin'.

Effective salespersons spend most of their time and effort where they have the highest likelihood of finding the largest number of qualified prospects.

Don't be blinded by shining, dazzling prospects who just might be too good to be true.

Ultimately, all marketing efforts should be geared to accomplish one thing: a signed deal.

Chapter 5

WINNING TRADITION
Building a Brand People Want to Buy

"Some time, Rock, when the team is up against it, when things are going wrong, and the breaks are beating the boys, tell them to go in there with all they've got and win just one for the Gipper. I don't know where I'll be then, Rock. But I'll know about it, and I'll be happy."

These words were made famous in the 1940 Warner Brothers film *Knute Rockne, All American*, starring Ronald Reagan, among others. The movie tells the story of the legendary Knute Rockne, who coached Notre Dame from 1918 to 1930 during which time he became the most successful coach in history in terms of winning percentage.

Reagan played George "the Gipper" Gipp, a player on one of Rockne's teams who ended up dying from an infection while he was an otherwise healthy young man in 1920. Gipp struggled to utter those words to Rockne while he was lying on his death bed.

In 1928, Rockne's Fighting Irish team was not playing up to his usual standards. After posting a 4-2 record in the first six games, Notre Dame prepared to take on undefeated Army. Finding his team trailing at halftime, Rockne delivered his "Win One for the Gipper" speech in the locker room. Those eminently motivational words inspired the team to go back out on the field and play their hearts out, upsetting Army 12-6.

Not only did the film give the future U.S. President his lifelong nickname, it immortalized Rockne and further cemented Notre Dame's widely respected and nationally recognized "brand." Sure, Notre Dame enjoyed tremendous success and a big following before the 1940 film, but after millions of moviegoers saw the Notre Dame mystique on the silver screen, the brand was bolstered. Just think of the iconic images and words that are now universally known to be associated with Notre Dame—"Four Horsemen," "Golden Dome," "Wake up the echoes."

For years after that film, Notre Dame enjoyed top-of-mind brand status. That made it easier for the Irish to sign blue-chip players. In fact, during Coach Frank Leahy's tenure, 1941 to 1953, Notre Dame won four Associated Press national championships and registered six undefeated seasons. Since Leahy, Notre Dame has won national championships under Ara Parseghian (1966, 1973), Dan Devine (1977) and Lou Holtz (1988).

Notre Dame has experienced its ups and downs in recent years, but the team remains wildly popular. Even when the Irish suffer through a lackluster season, games are still broadcast nationally on NBC. Notre Dame Stadium is still full on Saturdays, and the team generally puts together highly rated recruiting classes each year on National Signing Day.

The reason Notre Dame continues selling itself successfully to blue chippers each year is simple: it has a phenomenal brand. When you have a great brand that many people covet and desire, you sell more of whatever you're trying to sell. An organization that has achieved great brand status has convinced a significant portion of its target audience that it is the only brand worthy of attention. Loyal customers believe in the brand so strongly that no other provider measures up. So it is with fans of the nation's most elite football programs.

While Notre Dame's brand is more established and recognized than other college football programs, all the major teams have brands. Many of those teams, especially the bluebloods, have brands that are highly coveted and widely recognized.

The University of Oregon is famous for its cutting-edge approach to the game and its eye-catching uniforms that come from the university's unique relationship with Nike, Inc. The Ducks have countless variations of their basic uniform, which means they never look quite the same from one game to another.

Penn State is "Linebacker U" not only because it has produced so many great linebackers but because it has a history of fielding hard-nosed defenses. The Virginia Tech Hokies are famous for their outstanding special teams play and their tendency to force turnovers at key moments.

Stanford is an academic school. It demands higher grade point averages and SAT scores from its incoming players, so naturally the Cardinal is thought of as one of the nation's most "intelligent" football teams. Stanford alumni revel in that brand.

Boise State is known as an up-and-comer that tends to slay college football's giants (and for the blue turf in Bronco Stadium, where Boise State plays its home games). The Miami Hurricanes are known as the outlaws of college football. That "bad-boy" brand worked for several years until it became so unsustainable and out of control that it blew up in the university's face, so to speak.

All organizations have brands, and they use their brands to position themselves in the marketplace. Football teams use their brands to recruit blue-chip players, sell game tickets, promote licensed merchandise, attract sponsors and secure donations from prominent boosters.

> ## All organizations have brands, and they use their brands to position themselves in the marketplace.
>
> FROM the PLAYBOOK

In short, a well-established brand is essential for any team that wants to succeed. Like selling, branding is a part of the overall marketing process, but it comes before selling. Branding is a prerequisite that must be established before sales tactics are of any use.

More Than a Logo

So what is a brand? We know it's necessary to have one in order to sell, but what exactly is it? According to the American Marketing Association, a brand is "a name, term, design, symbol, or any other feature that identifies one seller's goods or services as distinct from those of other sellers." Similarly, Entrepreneur.com defines a brand as "the marketing practice of creating a name, symbol or design that identifies and differentiates a product from other products."

Marketing guru Seth Godin defines a brand as "the set of expectations, memories, stories and relationships that, taken together, account for a consumer's decision to choose one product or service over another. If the consumer (whether it's a business, a buyer, a voter or a donor) doesn't pay a premium, make a selection or spread the word, then no brand value exists for that consumer."

Godin's definition comes closer to the modern and true definition of a brand, and it certainly applies to big-time college football teams. We should no longer think of a brand as a name, symbol or trademark. Coca-Cola's brand is far more than its famous red-and-white logo. The University of Michigan Wolverines' brand is far more than those unique, maize-and-blue football helmets or the big "M" logo. Those things are part of Michigan's image and help make the brand recognizable, but Michigan's actual brand comes from its winning tradition, great players, iconic games and "The Big House," the university's 110,000-capacity stadium.

If you view Godin's definition through the lens of a major football team, it's suddenly crystal clear why the winningest and most glamorous football teams continue to out-sell their competition when fighting to sign the best prospective players.

Brand Power

Have you ever heard someone say, "The rich get richer, and the poor get poorer?" If there's any truth to this old saying—and there probably is—then branding is a big part of the reason. The more success a person or an entity enjoys, the more desirable the brand becomes. The more people want to buy or be a part of that brand, the richer the entity becomes.

People have a deep desire to associate with organizations and people who have highly respected and widely recognized brands. If you doubt this, think of how famous actors and actresses capture their fans' attention. If famous football coaches such as Bob Stoops, Nick Saban and Urban Meyer go out to dinner, other restaurant patrons will probably swarm them, seeking autographs or to just be in their presence.

> ## People have a deep desire to associate with organizations and people who have highly respected and widely recognized brands.
>
> **FROM the PLAYBOOK**

Desirable brands make customers loyally love companies like Apple, Nordstrom and Southwest Airlines. Branding makes Coca-Cola much more desirable than Shasta or R.C. It's because of branding that a young athlete's ears perk up when his mother says the University of Texas is on the phone. Letters that have the USC Trojans logo on the envelope will be opened and read promptly.

A highly respected and widely developed brand gives a successful organization "perception power" in which organizations are perceived to be even greater than they actually are.

For instance, let's say one of college football's bluebloods, Florida State, happens upon a high school football player who is rated as only a two-star prospect. Despite his low ranking, FSU coaches see something on the prospect's game film that catches their eyes. They determine the kid is a late bloomer, a diamond in the rough.

As soon as the Seminoles offer the young man a scholarship, other football programs take notice. Suddenly, the football recruiting services may be apt to up his rating to a three- or four-star level. As the old saying goes, perception is reality. Because FSU is perceived so positively by people inside and outside college football, the prospects they are targeting become the prospective players everybody else wants too.

Simply put, a great brand makes it easier for a salesperson to achieve greatness. Barry Switzer was one of football's greatest salesmen, but he always had a great product to sell. Oklahoma was the only school where he served as a collegiate head coach. He never had to recruit kids to some middle-of-the-road school in the Western Athletic Conference. He was at Oklahoma, home of multiple national championships, Heisman Trophy winners and rabid fans who filled the huge stadium each Saturday.

Brand Components

John Cooper was wildly successful in selling blue-chip athletes on Ohio State University. He was a good salesman with a well-developed sales plan, but let's face it: he was selling the Ohio State Buckeyes, one of the bluest of the bluebloods.

"You've got to have a great product to sell, which we did," said Cooper, who coached Ohio State from 1988 to 2000. "You gotta have facilities. You've gotta have resources. Tradition certainly helps. Schools like Ohio State, Florida, USC, Texas, Notre Dame, they have an awful lot to sell a kid. I mean, they've got it all. They have the things you're looking for."

So the moral of the story for any business or organization is this: If you're going to sell more and sell more efficiently, you better have a great product. If your product isn't truly great, then "job one" is to improve it. Of course, you have to continue selling while you are improving your product, because you need revenue now, but make the commitment to improve the product as soon as possible.

It is similarly important to identify your company's biggest strengths and attributes, as well as those of your products/ services, and exploit them in your branding. In other words, truly understand your brand and know what you really sell in order to be effective.

While at Ohio State, Cooper emphasized four primary things when selling the Buckeye brand to prospective players: education, winning, recognition and professional football.

"Everybody sells education," Cooper said. "You automatically know if you come to a Big 10 school like Ohio State, you're going to receive a high-quality education, but because everybody emphasizes it, we made sure we did too."

After education, Cooper reminded prospects they would be winners if they came to Columbus, Ohio. He had the facts to back up that assertion as Ohio State is one of history's most successful programs.

Then there was recognition. "I'm going to do all I can as head coach to get you the recognition you deserve," Cooper said. "If you look back—and I say this with a lot of pride—my teams were probably the most recognized teams in college football. You name it; my players won it. Heisman, Outland, Lombardi, all of them. They won just about every award that you could win, because we pushed for them. We campaigned for them."

Cooper's fourth selling point is somewhat controversial in college football circles: He sold "pro football." Some coaches don't like to do that because they want their current and prospective players to focus on the here and now and have total loyalty to the college program. Nevertheless, the tactic appeared to work for Cooper, who did send an incredible number of players on to the next level.

"You're going to play on Sundays," Cooper would tell the most talented prospects as he was wooing them. "All the great high school football players dream of playing in the National Football League. If you start fighting it, if you say, 'We don't care about getting you into pro football,' that hurts you. We sold pro football. My last recruiting class had the most players drafted than any team in college football history. We had fourteen players drafted."

Since Cooper left Ohio State, the Buckeyes have focused less on selling professional football, but there is still a major emphasis on the team's glorious tradition, stout academics and the likelihood that players will win games.

"The story line at Ohio State kind of speaks for itself," said 2011 recruiting coordinator John Peterson, who now coaches at University of Alabama–Birmingham. "You bring a kid on campus, and you look at all the championship trophies and the academic success the kids have, it's impressive. It's a big commitment to play for Ohio State, but also, it's full of great opportunities, plus a lot of opportunities after football."

At the University of California–Berkeley, head coach Jeff Tedford incorporates the school's academic reputation and the Bay Area's beautiful weather in branding the Golden Bears.

"Cal is the number-one public institution, really, in the world, so you get a great education. The strength of a Cal degree is important for the next fifty years of your life," Tedford said. "And the perfect weather! It's a great place to live. The quality of life here in the Bay Area is pretty nice."

When former Minnesota coach Tim Brewster was selling Golden Gophers to high school players, he focused on the fact that the university was committed to becoming one of the top three leading public research institutions in the world. While many seventeen-year-old athletes probably couldn't care less about a university's research mission, it does sound good to parents. Perhaps more effectively, Brewster focused on facilities and the diversions available in the Twin Cities.

"We've got the finest, brand-new football stadium in America," he said. "There are some stadiums that are a little bigger than ours, but they're not as nice. We've got a beautiful city. You've got the Twins. You've got the Timberwolves.

You've got the Vikings. Shoot, I could recruit the heck out of anybody."

When Jack Pierce was working as Nebraska's off-campus recruiting coordinator in the 1980s, he believed there were a couple key assets that reinforced the Huskers' brand. According to Pierce, prospects liked the stability, the long tenure and low turnover of Nebraska's coaching staff. Additionally, the commitment to honesty as demanded by head coach Tom Osborne eventually became so interwoven into the program that it was almost palpable.

Former Husker assistant coach Turner Gill had a more succinct message when selling players on the Huskers: "You'll win a lot of games."

In modern college football marketing, great facilities and the commitment to constantly improve facilities are critical components of a team's brand. By facilities, we are talking about weight rooms, locker rooms, food-service areas, medical facilities, player lounges, academic-support centers, indoor practice fields and massive stadiums.

"If you're not building, you're behind," said Cedar Hill (Texas) High School coach Joey McGuire, who has sent an unusually large number of blue chippers to big-time football colleges. "Put a dad-gum bulldozer on your campus and a sign that says, 'future something,' even if you're not building, because it's one of those deals where so many people are competing to have the state-of-the-art facilities. Everybody's building."

McGuire's blanket statement is not too far from the truth. You would be hard pressed to find a big-time college football program that isn't improving its facilities now or just coming off a major construction project.

As head coaches brand their teams, it's common for them to take advantage of attributes near the campus. The University of Colorado talks about the majestic Rocky

Mountains that soar above the city of Boulder. Southern California and Miami can tout their proximity to beaches. Teams located in the nation's largest metropolitan areas can promote their easy access to big-city entertainment and other amenities.

Notre Dame is located in a smallish city, but it just happens to be in the same town as one of college football's shrines, a place that beckons countless football pilgrims each year. Dr. Bernie Kish, former executive director of the College Football Hall of Fame in South Bend, Indiana, said that Notre Dame would typically bring recruits over to the Hall during on-campus visit weekends. Of course, Notre Dame is the reason the Hall is located in South Bend, so it would be foolish for Notre Dame's coaches not to sell that to each prospect who visits town.

Brand Management

Regardless of what goes into forming any organization's brand, the primary decision maker—no matter whether that's a head coach, a CEO or a company owner—needs to set the overall framework or paradigm in which the brand will exist. In other words, a company or a football team may have a sophisticated marketing department, but overarching brand themes need to come from the top. Just as important, an organization's leader needs to make sure the operations side of the entity is truly delivering what the brand promises.

As business CEO and football coach Joe Moglia believes, the boss needs to make sure marketing and the rest of an organization work in harmony.

"What's our brand promising? Are we actually delivering on that?" Moglia would ask his leadership team when he was CEO of TD Ameritrade. "If our marketing people were saying we deliver great value and give you great service, then it was my job to make sure our operations people really were giving good value and providing clients with good products and services."

Moglia also believes that the CEO or the head coach needs to look at marketing messages with an outsider's perspective, a third party's eye.

"Let's say I'm previewing one of [TD Ameritrade's] ads before we go national with it," Moglia said. "If the vice president of marketing needs to explain that ad to me, it's not a good ad. I am intimately aware of what we're trying to do, so if I have to say, 'I'm not quite sure what you're saying here,' then I know our typical prospects aren't getting it."

Moglia acknowledges that it was rare that he would ever nix a major advertisement, because ideally a leader and his or her staff would be on the same page as the project is under development. Ideally, the leader would have done a great job in communicating the most important aspects of the organization's brand. But, when all else fails, the boss sometimes is forced to exercise brand veto power.

Like major corporations, the big-time football teams have in-house marketing staffs. As CEO, the head coach must exercise some influence on and have authority over the messages that come out of the university's marketing department.

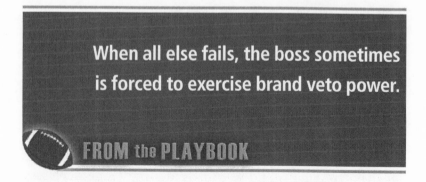

When all else fails, the boss sometimes is forced to exercise brand veto power.

FROM the PLAYBOOK

Brand Lifecycle

Once a brand achieves a high level of respect and recognition, the challenge is to keep it there. Brands have lifecycles. They're born. They grow. At some point, they may have a dramatic, rapid ascent to the top of an industry. Once there, they go into the maturity phase. You want the maturity phase to last a long time, because after that comes decline and eventually death.

Nothing lasts forever—Harvard and Yale were once the titans of college football—but leaders can take measures to keep brands at the top. Commitment is critically important. If a brand's leaders lose their enthusiasm, become lazy or no longer value the brand, decline sets in. For instance, Harvard, Yale and other Ivy League schools at some point decided that elite college football teams were no longer consistent with their missions. In those cases, decline was deliberate.

Assuming you want to keep your brand at the top, remember that excellence is fundamental. If the product or service remains outstanding, you have won a big part of the branding battle. Great college football teams such as Oklahoma, Alabama and Michigan may experience some peaks and valleys, but administrators and coaches at those schools do what it takes to excel over the course of time.

Next, organizations must keep up with consumers' changing tastes and consequently tweak the brand from time to time. If a football team runs a boring, old-fashioned offense, they are not appealing to one of their most important consumer audiences: prospective players. Those young athletes are likely to choose a different school, one whose team is more exciting and runs a dynamic offense. The great athletes want a team with a game philosophy that increases their chances of making the NFL after graduation.

A team's other constituency, ticket buyers, may have a similar reaction. If the on-the-field product is exciting, fans will fill the stadium. If not, empty seats may be visible on Saturday afternoons.

When a brand makes it big, the brand manager, whether that's a football coach or a business executive, needs to balance two things: a commitment to the fundamentals that built the brand in the first place and the need to keep the brand responsive to the changing desires of the target audience. The longer you can keep these two things in balance, the longer you stay viable.

When you have a great brand that many people covet and desire, you sell more of whatever you're trying to sell.

Branding is a prerequisite that must be established before sales tactics are of any use.

People have a deep desire to associate with organizations and people who have highly respected and widely recognized brands.

Take advantage of your unique selling points, both internal and external, when building your organization's brand.

No matter the size of an organization, overarching brand themes should be set at the top with expert advice from the marketing team.

If leadership loses interest or lessens its commitment to a brand, the brand will decline.

Chapter 6

BIGGER THAN LIFE
How Personal Branding Makes Marketing Easier

At six feet, four inches and 245 pounds, Noah Spence casts an imposing shadow, but it's not only his size that catches your attention.

He also happens to be blessed with a competitive nature and a mixture of natural athletic talents. That's why big-time football teams from coast to coast zealously sold themselves to Spence during the 2011–2012 college football recruiting cycle. Rivals.com tagged Spence with the coveted five-star rating and ranked him as the ninth best high school football prospect in the entire nation.

As Spence was wrapping up his final football season at Bishop McDevitt High School in Harrisburg, Pennsylvania, it looked more and more like he would sign with the University of Maryland Terrapins. Maryland was putting together a solid class under the leadership of first-year coach Randy Edsall, plus the university was less than ninety miles from Spence's hometown.

But oh how quickly things can change in the college football sales game!

Plans began transforming shortly after Ohio State hired former Florida coach Urban Meyer, a charismatic leader who owned two national championships and an 82 percent career winning percentage. Meyer is unequivocally a great salesman, one of the best recruiters in the business.

"Noah Spence was essentially going to Maryland," said national recruiting expert Mike Farrell as reported by BuckeyeGrove.com. "Had Urban Meyer not been hired, [Spence] still would be going to Maryland. [Meyer's] ability to change minds of prospects is really unmatched as a head coach ... He's the best at doing that ... He's relentless."

One of the reasons Noah Spence is now a scarlet-and-gray-wearing Buckeye is the Buckeyes' new head coach. Urban Meyer is a powerful force in college football. He is the type of person players and fans flock to. He is fascinating. He has an aura about him. He wins on the football field, and he has a winning personality.

This has allowed Meyer to build a personal brand, and like any smart salesperson, he exploits that brand.

Whether you're selling a football team, selling professional services or trying to reach the pinnacle of any other industry, everything is easier when you have a great personal brand. People are excited to associate and be seen with people who have widely recognized and highly respected reputations. When your name is regularly dropped in conversation, you have power.

A Powerful Presence

Just imagine the power a famous football head coach wields when he calls a prospective player on the phone or visits his home. Guys like Nick Saban, Bob Stoops and Mack Brown are larger than life. They appear on television and are interviewed in newspapers and radio. People buzz about them year round in the social media.

In today's sales world, it's growing more and more difficult to catch your would-be clients' attention. Regardless of your industry, prospects return fewer than 25 percent of the voicemails left by salespersons. Do you think Bill Snyder's messages are returned when he calls a prospect from the state of Kansas? You bet they are! When Steve Sarkisian leaves a voicemail for a young man from the state of Washington, the call is returned promptly.

Once you establish a widely recognized and highly respected personal brand, your sales calls are more likely to be returned.

> **Once you establish a widely recognized and highly respected personal brand, your sales calls are more likely to be returned.**
>
> FROM the PLAYBOOK

Coaches' personal brands are bolstered and filled with even more mystique when a coach has a memorable personality. LSU's Les Miles is known as the "Mad Hatter" because of the risks he has been known to take at key moments in big games. Washington State head coach Mike Leach came across like some sort of mad scientist while he coached at Texas Tech because his offenses were so unique yet highly prolific. Leach also drew national attention for his varied interests outside of football including a fascination with pirates. What's more, he is known to say outrageous things in the media at any given moment. Florida's Will Muschamp is known as a defensive football genius.

Several former coaches maintain powerful brands years after they have left the game. Ohio State's Woody Hayes and Michigan's Bo Schembechler battled each other ferociously on the field and on the recruiting trail throughout the 1970s. Both were famous for being tough as nails. When Jimmy Johnson coached Miami in the 1980s, he was seen as the permissive leader of a bunch of bad boys because of the way so many Hurricane players behaved on and off the field.

Perhaps no coach in history owned a more powerful personal brand than the legendary Paul "Bear" Bryant who led Alabama from 1958 to 1982. Bryant was recognized by his trademark houndstooth hats, was revered because of the championships he won, and was famous for his larger-than-life presence, his unique personality.

Many compared Bryant to John Wayne, the bigger-than-life American movie-star hero of the time, according to Keith Dunnavant, author of *Coach: The Life of Paul "Bear" Bryant*. Years after they exhausted their playing eligibility, many former players would admit to still feeling in awe of their old coach.

Before Pat Dye became a successful head coach in his own right, he worked as one of Bryant's assistants. In his book, *In the Arena*, Dye described Bryant's recruiting style as "intimidating." His personal brand was so massive that Bryant frankly scared the hell out of some people, especially seventeen-year-old prospects. Because of that, Dye said Bryant was better at closing deals as opposed to building the rapport necessary to start the selling process.

Bryant was most effective sitting behind his desk. "High school boys would come into his office like they were in God's presence," Dye said. When Bryant would make a personal visit to a prospect's home, it was usually only to sign him.

No doubt a personal brand is important. It was so much easier for Bear Bryant to sell the University of Alabama than it was for some first-year coach at, say, Northern Alabama University to sell his team to prospective players.

Personal brands give salespersons a huge head start. A big personal brand makes the competitive process seem downright unfair. It's a fact: People are more excited to do business with someone who carries a big name. People want to associate with those who are perceived as well-known.

But what exactly is a personal brand and how can you build one when you're not a major football coach who is on television every week?

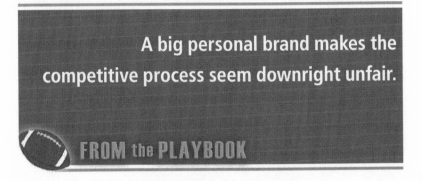

A big personal brand makes the competitive process seem downright unfair.

FROM the PLAYBOOK

Slightly Famous

To start, all professionals should seek to become famous in their own spheres of interest by tapping into the group of people who in any way can help you reach your goals— clients, prospective clients, anybody who could refer clients to you. Each professional has potentially thousands of people in his or her sphere of interest. Some have millions, but whoever you are and whatever your goals may be, you want to become a celebrity among those people who can have an impact on your success.

When someone needs the talents you have or the products you sell, you want your name and face to pop into that person's head. That's what personal branding is all about—

being recognized as the go-to source, the safe option, the obvious choice.

How do you become a celebrity in your own sphere of interest?

First, be excellent in your work. Successful football coaches live and breathe the game. They relentlessly prepare for their team's on-field performance while constantly selling the program to future players. You must work just as hard at your business as a big-time football coach works at his if you hope to become great.

Unfortunately, however, excellence is far from enough. In this competitive world, your talent and hard work are simply expected. Performance is merely foundational. Assume your competition is working just as hard as you and is even more talented than you. In such an environment, your personal brand is one of the few things that sets you apart.

Step one in becoming a celebrity in your own sphere of interest is to see yourself as an entity, not just as a human being. You are a man or a woman, but you are also a brand, a business, a business of one, a business unto yourself. Every business worth its salt jealously guards the integrity of its brand while zealously promoting it. So must you. You need to approach your personal brand promotion with the same intensity as your company promotes its brand.

Next, think like a politician. That's not to say you should adopt the nefarious and tawdry behavior of too many politicians, rather it means you understand you are in a lifelong series of "campaigns" seeking to be "elected" to whatever it is that matters to you. A politician works hard to build a core group of people who would "run through a brick wall" for him or her. That core is built and strengthened by networking—going out and deliberately meeting and building relationships with as many people as possible.

Unfortunately, politicians never meet most of the voters in their spheres of interest. For everyone outside the core, politicians at least want people to recognize their names and have a positive feeling associated with them. To reach these people, politicians use mass media, social media and word of mouth.

All sorts of analogies exist between political campaigning and the personal branding game. Like a politician, you need to build your core relentlessly and never stop building it no matter how big and strong it becomes. You can then use mass media, social media, and word of mouth to project your personal brand to your "voters," the people in your sphere of interest.

Football coaches and all other "celebrities in their spheres of interest" deliberately lead active lives and focus externally. They are involved, energetic and engaged in their communities. At the same time, they are focused on meeting new people and building relationships. Great salespersons are never satisfied with their current number of personal contacts. They're never satisfied with the current status of relationships. They realize that if those things don't continually grow, they might actually be declining.

Being Everywhere

Successful football coaches regularly work sixteen-hour days, and a significant chunk of those hours is typically dedicated to marketing and sales work such as prospecting, marketing planning, making phone calls, responding to emails, hosting guests, visiting high school coaches and traveling to prospects' homes.

Thankfully, most of us don't have to put in the hours coaches do, but we must work vigorously and smartly if we are going to become celebrities in our own spheres of interest and reach the peak of our professions.

Like football coaches, we need to spend time on the phone making meaningful conversations with prospects and the people who can refer clients. We need to get out of the office and show up at networking events. We need to reach out and engage the world around us. Unfortunately, in order to become a celebrity in your sphere of interest, you need to have at least one encounter in your sphere of interest per day—including weekends.

The good news is that these encounters don't necessarily have to be at formal functions held in formal venues. Your sphere of interest is always around you. Strike up conversations with people around you. Reach out to people and get to know those who might refer a blue-chip prospect to you some day.

The majority of prestigious, big-time clients in the typical industry can only be reached through relationships. They do not commonly walk into your office asking to be your customer. They aren't amenable to cold calls, and they won't respond to your direct mail piece no matter how pretty it is.

"Big elephant" clients know they are important, and they expect to be wined and dined, so to speak. They are big deals and expect to be treated like a big deal. Such clients are quite analogous to the blue-chip prospects all the college coaches so desperately want. These young men are well aware of how coveted they are.

To get a chance to sign one of these hotshots, you have to go out of your way to build relationships with them, their family members, girlfriends, high school coaches, community influencers and others. That requires a coach to get out into the world and actively communicate.

Getting access to the highly desirable blue chippers requires a coach to be out among his sphere of interest on a regular basis. Same applies to you. Get out there and meet everyone you can. Ask questions. Be like a detective turning over every stone, looking for any shred of evidence that can help you make the sale.

Great salespersons are seemingly "everywhere." They live their lives so actively that other people feel as if they see them everywhere. If someone ever says to you, "I see you everywhere," you know you're doing something right.

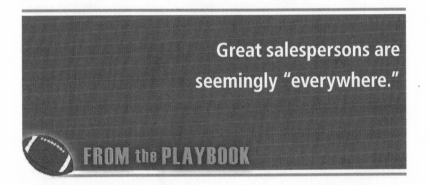

Great salespersons are seemingly "everywhere."

FROM the PLAYBOOK

Once you have the "everywhere" thing down pat, start working on your personal branding message. This is known as your "area of self-marketing expertise." In order to determine your area of self-marketing expertise, think about what you do for a living, then determine what about it is most fascinating to people who do not do what you do. What is the most interesting part of your business, profession or career to the lay person? Once you determine that, you officially have an area of self-marketing expertise.

After establishing your own area of self-marketing expertise, it's time to exploit it. When you're out networking, chatting with people on the phone, blogging or making posts in the social media, focus on the area of self-marketing expertise. Don't focus on the boring stuff. Don't talk about inane, meaningless and monotonous drivel. Find the fascinating. Find the intriguing. Find what makes people raise their eyebrows and perk up their ears.

Although your life very possibly is not as glamorous as a head football coach's, there certainly is something about it that can be portrayed in a fascinating way. Your area of self-marketing expertise is your ticket to media coverage, social media followers, access to prestigious events, association with impressive people and ultimately celebrity status in your sphere of interest.

Practice how you will convey your area of self-marketing expertise. How will you describe it? What's your twenty-second elevator speech? Avoid using a bunch of industry jargon or "salesperson speak" when describing what you do. For best results, explain your area of self-marketing expertise using descriptive, real-world English.

If someone asks a football coach what he does for a living, he's probably not going to start describing defensive alignments. Instead, he should say what he does for a living and focus on the most fascinating aspects of it to the non-football person.

Now it's time to take your personal brand to the market. If you truly have an area of self-marketing expertise, expose it to your sphere of interest (also known as your personal target audience). The most foundational way to do this is through good, old-fashioned networking.

National Championship Networking

Believe it or not, in this day and age of social media, face-to-face networking is not only effective, it's still essential. In fact, many professionals use social media as a way to set up, enhance or facilitate face-to-face meetings. In many cases, especially when dealing with professionals older than thirty-five, a face-to-face encounter is ultimately needed to sign a deal.

> ## In this day and age of social media, face-to-face networking is not only effective, it's still essential.
>
> FROM the PLAYBOOK

Also, remember that the relationship depth chart ultimately starts with rapport. Once rapport is established, you then focus on relationship building and ultimately trust, which makes deal-making possible. Networking is an effective way to build rapport with a lot of people. The more people who enjoy rapport with you, the more famous you are among your sphere of interest. The individual parts of the personal branding process feed on each other in a perpetuating way.

If you become a skilled networker, you can employ the art of networking to gain access to those who can put you in the media, to those who influence others, to those who have large Internet platforms and to those who are good connectors. Network with everyone but devote particular effort to those influential people who can drop your name in front of decision makers.

When you network, make sure you are focused on results. In other words, don't network just for the sake of networking. That's a waste of time. A busy football coach who has to put in hundred-hour weeks isn't going to network without a purpose. Neither should you.

Unfortunately, many people think they are networking when they are actually just socializing. In order to turn your socializing into highly effective networking, you need to have a goal. It's called "goal-based networking," and it's quite simple.

Don't network just for the sake of networking.

FROM the PLAYBOOK

As you are about to step into a room where networking will take place, plant a three-tiered set of goals in your head:

Goal number one: "I will get a direct opportunity from this event." Sadly, goal number one doesn't happen at most networking events. Sometimes it does, which is great, but usually it's a pleasant surprise. Even though it's not a common outcome of a typical networking encounter, it is nonetheless the ideal for which you should strive.

Goal number two: "I will get a very good lead on a direct opportunity from this event." Goal number two should happen at almost every networking event you attend. If it does not, it means you are not talking to enough people or not asking the types of questions that will lead you to opportunities or good leads on opportunities.

Goal number three: "I will meet people I did not know, and I will learn valuable information that will advance my goals." Goal number three should happen every single time you network. If you have trouble achieving goal number three, you're probably a ways off from being an effective salesperson. Rather, you need to practice your interpersonal skills and push yourself to develop more assertiveness and self-confidence.

Some football coaches are the serious, introverted, technician-like guys. These coaches are more comfortable breaking down opposing offenses and defenses and sitting in front of computer terminals designing plays and analyzing opponent tendencies.

But when these behind-the-scenes guys land a full-time coach's job at a major university, they have to sell. Every coach on the staff has to sell, because recruiting is the lifeblood of the program. This isn't easy for introverts. Nevertheless, they must find a way. Similarly, if you are the introverted type, it's important to force yourself to get out among your sphere of interest and network your tail off. It will build your personal brand and facilitate your professional work.

Some people mistakenly assume that personal branding is superficial—like having a cheesy catch phrase to describe yourself or wearing the same outfit. Having a certain "look" is a personal branding tactic, but it's just a tactic. In other words, you don't need a gimmick in order to become a celebrity in your own sphere of interest.

> You don't need a gimmick in order to become a celebrity in your own sphere of interest.
>
> FROM the PLAYBOOK

That said, many football "characters" have used this tactic. Coach Bryant had his houndstooth hats. South Carolina coach Steve Spurrier and Oklahoma coach Bob Stoops wear their trademark sun visors. Oklahoma State's Mike Gundy is recognized by his spiked hair.

Showmanship

Personal branding is even more effective when you throw a little "theater" into it. In other words, put on a bit of a show when you're among your sphere of interest. When you go see a stage performance in a live theater, you don't see behind the stage, and you don't see the actors fall out of character.

Similarly, in your life, put on a bit of a show. That's not to say you are pretending to be someone or something you are not, but it does mean you put forth the best image possible.

Think of it this way: Most people are afflicted with the grass-is-always-greener-on-the-other-side-of-the-fence syndrome. Take advantage of that. Exploit that common human weakness. Paint a picture of yourself that is so desirable that everyone will want to reach their heads through the fence and eat your grass. People don't need to see your dirty laundry. They should see you as someone who leads the kind of life they envy.

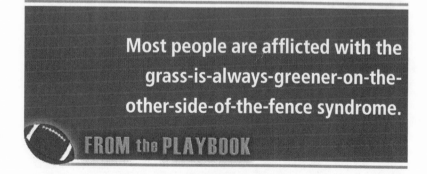

Most people are afflicted with the grass-is-always-greener-on-the-other-side-of-the-fence syndrome.

FROM the PLAYBOOK

One of the reasons former Texas A&M coach R.C. Slocum pursued a career in college football and worked so hard to become a head coach was because of the image college coaches portrayed when Slocum was working in relative obscurity as a young high school coach.

"The college coaches would come by, and they were always dressed sharply and had the great personalities," Slocum recalled. "I really admired those guys, and said to myself, 'Man, I gotta get me one of those jobs!'"

Former Nebraska recruiting coordinator Jack Pierce always made sure to project the image of a big-time coach to impress young prospects. That's important when your target audience consists primarily of teenage males. A competing college coach once asked him why he always rented Cadillacs while selling out on the road.

"When you pull into a school yard, you've got every kid in the school coming up to the car," Pierce answered. "They either think you're selling dope or you're a big-time football coach. In both cases, you've got their attention."

In fact, Pierce's fancy-car philosophy once got him out of a potential jam. As a brand-new coach in the late 1970s, his very first road trip was to a rough high school in a terrible neighborhood of Oakland, California. Even back in those days, this was a dangerous area. Security was tight, and Pierce was escorted through the school building and grounds by a police officer.

After the visit, Pierce walked to his rented Cadillac outside the school grounds and noticed a group of guys sitting nearby drinking beer out of paper bags at ten in the morning. At the same time, he realized his keys were missing. He went through his pockets and briefcase but couldn't find them.

Meanwhile, one of the hoodlum-looking beer drinkers shouts, "You a coach?" Pierce responded that indeed he was.

"Where ya from?" The guy asked.

"Nebraska," Pierce said.

The young man turned to the other guys. "I told you, man, he's one of them big-time coaches. He's from Nebraska."

"Yeah, I gotta problem, though," Pierce said before being cut off mid-sentence.

"You can't find your car keys, can't you?" the guy asked. "They're in the car."

Pierce was amazed.

"I told them, man, we don't want to steal a car from a big-time coach like that," the guy said. "It would have been gone if you was anybody else."

You should always try to maintain your professional image and perpetuate your personal brand, but sometimes things go wrong. Sometimes even the biggest celebrities in their spheres of interest have to perform under conditions that are not the most flattering.

Tim Brewster recalled a time in the 1990s when he was an assistant at North Carolina and Mack Brown was the head coach. The two were courting a star prospect from central Pennsylvania. In the heat of the annual recruiting battle, the coaches arrived at the Harrisburg airport late at night. Much to their dismay, every rental car company was out of cars. This generated quite a bit of anxiety for the two coaches. They needed to get to the prospect's house that night or risk losing him to a competitor.

Overhearing the conversation, and sensing their desperation, a random stranger volunteered to drive the coaches in his personal vehicle to the player's house.

Unfortunately, the car was a nasty-looking, 1950s-era rattletrap that should have made its way to the scrap heap decades earlier. The floorboard was so rusty and disintegrated that the passengers could actually see the pavement as they drove down the street.

But like any great salespersons with important jobs to do, the coaches jumped in the car and directed the Good Samaritan driver to the kid's house. You can just imagine the look on the kid's face. Expecting to see a Cadillac or Mercedes, the young man watched two coaches pull up in a jalopy. Perhaps he and his family were suddenly concerned about financial conditions inside the UNC Athletic Department.

Authenticity

Adopting a theatrical approach to your personal branding efforts in no way whatsoever should cause you to be someone you are not. Be animated, play the part and highlight your strengths but never ever lie or deliberately mislead.

Cedar Hill High School (Texas) head coach Joey McGuire knows when coaches are keeping it real and showing their true personalities. As a coach of a powerhouse high school football program, he would know, as he sees many college coaches come through his office each year.

McGuire likes Mack Brown's charisma, Ron Zook's sense of humor, Bob Stoops's professionalism and Gary Patterson's ability to relate to young men. More important than keeping it real with high school coaches, the college recruiters must exhibit authenticity around their prospects.

"You got to be genuine," McGuire said, "because kids can sense a load of B.S. faster than most adults."

Regardless of what you sell, everything is easier when you have a great personal brand.

If you have a widely recognized and highly respected personal brand, your voicemails and emails are more likely to be returned.

All professionals should seek to become celebrities in their own spheres of interest.

Excellence is not enough. In a competitive marketplace, talent and hard work are simply expected.

You are not just a human being. You are an entity, a business of one, a business unto yourself.

You are in a lifelong series of "campaigns" trying to be "elected" to whatever matters to you. That's why you should think like a politician.

Live actively and focus externally. In order to become a celebrity in your sphere of interest, you need to be seemingly "everywhere."

Develop an area of self-marketing expertise, something related to what you do but is fascinating to people who do not do what you do. This is what you talk about when you network.

Don't network just for the sake of networking. Focus on results.

Put on a show. Don't be someone you are not, but play up your strengths and put forth your best image possible.

While you are portraying yourself in a positive light, do keep it real. Your prospects can sense authenticity as well as a lack of it.

Never go back on any promise made to any prospective client.

Honor your strategic plan, but always stand ready to tweak it and adjust on the fly.

Chapter 7

GO WHERE THE PLAYERS ARE

Developing Your Sales Strategy

Miami's Carol City High School sits in an economically disadvantaged part of town, but it has quite a reputation for producing great football players.

Back in 2003, Rivals.com's Sean Callahan and a few of his colleagues put on a football camp at Carol City High. The Rivals guys worked out the entire team, putting the players through various tests and conditioning drills. Conditions were spartan to say the least. The 40-yard dashes were timed on the driver's education parking lot because the practice fields were in such poor shape. But the lack of quality facilities didn't keep the Carol City Chiefs from making a positive impression.

"I have never seen a more impressive collection of talent and speed on one team in my entire life," Callahan recalled. Carol City produced eleven Division 1 players that year.

If the sheer number of phenomenal athletes on that high school team wasn't impressive enough, what would happen next is something Callahan will never forget.

After the camp ended, and the players started heading home, a group of middle-school students showed up—a bunch of skinny kids wearing jeans and plain old tennis shoes. Having watched the older kids go through the drills, the youngsters wanted a shot. The Rivals guys had some extra time, so just for fun they put the kids through the same drills. Though they had probably never worked out, lifted weights or run timed 40-yard dashes in their entire lives, several of the middle schoolers ran electronically timed 40s in 4.7 seconds or faster.

That's beyond impressive.

For perspective, Callahan was involved in a high school summer camp at Penn State University known as the Central Pennsylvania Coaches Combine. Four hundred high school players from the area participated, hoping to impress college coaches. In some cases, entire teams showed up. These kids had all the right gear, and many had parents who paid for off-season training.

Despite all those advantages, only ten of these four hundred players ran the 40-yard dash in under 5.0. Think about that. The Miami middle-school kids, wearing jeans, bad shoes and using terrible technique, outran the experienced and well-trained high school players in Pennsylvania.

What does this story teach us? That's easy. There's a hell of a lot of raw talent in South Florida! But it's not just Florida. There is simply more talent down South than there is up North. That's not to say the North is without talent. Ohio, Pennsylvania and New Jersey high schools produce huge numbers of outstanding college players each year, but that amount of talent is nothing compared to what college coaches find in the southeastern states plus Texas and California.

Because such a disproportionately large number of great prospects live in the South, northern coaches are forced to have southern selling strategies if they hope to win national championships. You may be able to build the core of a northern team with in-state or regional players, but you will have to supplement them with at least a few southern blue chippers. If you look at the northern teams that have won national championships over the past twenty to thirty years—Nebraska, Michigan, Ohio State, Penn State, Notre Dame—most of them had quite a few southern players on their national championship rosters.

On the other hand, it typically does not make sense for southern coaches to look up North for talent unless there's an unusually great prospect who fits a need on the team right away. With all the talent down South, it would frankly be a waste of resources for Sunbelt coaches to travel north to the Rustbelt.

In 2006–2007, CBSSports.com columnist Bruce Feldman was granted insider access and spent parts of a whole year observing the recruitment practices at the University of Mississippi under the leadership of then-head coach Ed Orgeron. The result of that experience was Feldman's acclaimed book *Meat Market: Inside the Smash-Mouth World of College Football Recruiting*. Recognizing the hotbed of talent in which Ole Miss was located, the bombastic Orgeron reportedly told his assistant coaches, "Planes don't fly north!"

A big part of the strategy is to find a way to sell the right prospects on your team. You have to go where they are, develop rapport, build relationships with them, establish trust and close deals.

Like any sales endeavor, college football recruiting can only be successful if the coaches and the university's marketing support staff have a coordinated, well-developed strategy that rests on a solid philosophical foundation.

Strategy vs. Tactics

The concepts of "strategy" and "tactics" came originally from military philosophy. Thousands of years ago, the Sun Tzu writings in China set the foundation for much of modern military thought.

In contemporary times, marketers have borrowed the concepts of strategy and tactics in designing master plans for the movement of products from their producer to their eventual buyer. Ironically, football, which provides the metaphor for this sales and marketing book, is historically and philosophically inspired by military conflict: irresistible force vs. immovable object, offense vs. defense, the element of surprise, positioning. At its heart, football is an analogy for traditional battlefield clashes.

Just as some military scholars argue over the fine line separating strategy from tactics, so do marketers. In fact, many of the so-called strategies identified in sales and marketing books are actually tactics. Furthermore, most sales books are heavy on tactics but light on strategy. That's okay. Most marketers probably spend more day-to-day time on tactical issues, but they have to make sure their tactics grow out of a well-defined, carefully planned strategic framework.

Generally, strategy relates to the broad, big-picture view. Strategy seeks to solve the overarching problem. It's the 30,000-foot view. Strategy is based on your philosophy, comes from your goals and determines where you put your focus and your money. Tactics, on the other hand, are the details, the actual things you do to carry out the strategy. For example, part of your strategy might be to become a faster team. To make that happen, tactics would include new prospecting methods, different prospect qualification standards, a new sales pitch, or even adding facilities and equipment that the fastest skill-position players would find appealing.

Creating a Culture

Leaders must take many steps in order to develop an effective strategy. One of the first steps is to determine "who you are" as an organization. This also means "who you are not" and "who you never want to become." Strategies simply are not as effective if an organization hasn't created a culture. Determining what you are and why you want to be that is hard work. It can be tedious and sometimes argumentative if there are conflicting opinions among the leadership.

In order to determine who you are and create a culture, leaders must set their philosophies and beliefs. Ultimately all marketing should rest on a philosophical foundation. When a new football coach is hired to take over a team—and it's usually a struggling or underperforming team—one of his biggest challenges is to establish a healthy, winning philosophy. If he skips this step and goes straight to sales and coaching tactics, his long-term success is not likely.

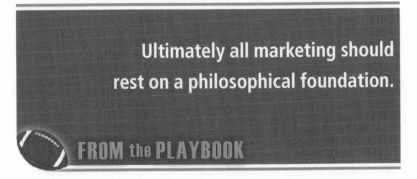

Ultimately all marketing should rest on a philosophical foundation.

FROM the PLAYBOOK

Philosophy and beliefs are your unshakable, solid foundations. They are crystalized by focusing on values, mission and vision. First, leaders should record their core values. These are the qualities that mean the most to them, the lines they will not cross, the expectations they will not compromise.

Once these values are agreed upon and recorded, it's time to develop a mission statement. A relatively short written passage, the mission statement summarizes the organization's purpose, its reason for existence. Almost as important is the vision statement, which is a description of where the organization will be or what it looks like at some snapshot point in the future.

Core values are a big determinant of any organization's culture. These are the commitments that drive you each day. Core values indicate what is truly important to you. On a broad level, these values are related to your beliefs and philosophies. More narrowly, they relate to your behavior. Core values are important to success because they keep your inner self and your outward actions synergized.

If you know where your team stands philosophically, you are more likely to make decisions in harmony with your organization's true character. Acting this way will enhance your team's long-term career success. Before taking your products and services to the market, understand what actions you will not tolerate, what corners you are not willing to cut and what ethical boundaries you are not willing to blur.

Who Are You?

The next part of developing a sales strategy requires a frank assessment of who you are or what your organization is really all about. For instance, are you developing strategy for a "client-recruitment" or a "client-retention" shop? Some companies operate in industries or markets that are rich in prospective clients. Other companies exist in an environment of client scarcity.

Of course, you should always have a healthy respect for client retention. As the old saying goes, "It's cheaper to keep a customer than to find a new one." That said, some businesses have more opportunity to find and attract a steady stream of new clients.

In his career, Gary Barnett had the chance to coach teams that operated in both an environment of scarcity and moderate abundance. Northwestern, a school that has never been considered a football powerhouse, is known as a rigorous academic institution and is overshadowed by several big-time football teams nearby, so Barnett had no choice but to be solidly focused on retention and development.

When Barnett moved to the University of Colorado, he decided he could be more of a "recruitment" program. Colorado had a bigger budget, wasn't overshadowed by teams in its own region and had already established long-standing ties to talent-rich California.

In other words, Barnett would have been beating his head against the wall trying to go after highly coveted blue chippers at Northwestern. He would lose out almost every time. Those players simply aren't interested in going to an "academic" institution with a small stadium and a historical paucity of conference championships. Instead, Barnett knew he had to find "diamonds in the rough" or late bloomers or that hard-working, over-achieving, smart kid who could develop into a solid player by his senior year.

At Colorado, there was an established history of bringing in highly recruited blue chippers, so it was worth his while to go for the big prize. At the same time, he still placed emphasis on client (player) retention, because his team was still located a thousand miles or more from all those talented prospects in Texas and Southern California.

As you prepare your sales strategy, figure out how much of an emphasis you can place on client recruitment versus client retention. Look at your business honestly. Assess your industry, your marketplace and your standing within that marketplace.

Several additional external factors have an impact on "who you are" and on the approach. How competitive is your environment? In college football, teams in the powerful Southeast Conference have it rough—every team they play is loaded with talent. Other conferences, or divisions within conferences, aren't so competitive. The level of competitive pressure directly influences marketing strategy.

> **As you prepare your sales strategy, figure out how much of an emphasis you can place on client recruitment versus client retention.**
>
> FROM the PLAYBOOK

Financial resources play a huge role in marketing strategy development. Barnett had a much larger marketing budget at Colorado than he did at Northwestern, but that must be kept in perspective. Colorado's marketing budget still paled in comparison to Michigan's or Oklahoma's.

Additionally, honestly assess where you stand vis-à-vis your competition in the arena of public opinion. Auburn University, located in the quintessential college town of Auburn, Alabama, is one of college football's undisputed bluebloods. The Tigers boast a rich history and won the national championship as recently as 2010.

But despite its glorious standing in the football pecking order, Auburn is overshadowed in its own damned state! The University of Alabama, which won the 2009 and 2011 national championships, is an even bigger brand name. As good as it is, Auburn tends to be an underdog when recruiting against its hated in-state rival.

When Auburn's coaches formulate their marketing strategy and set their goals each year, they must be constantly aware of the 800-pound gorilla located up north in Tuscaloosa, Alabama. Auburn coaches can never take their eye off the competition.

Goal Setting

College football coaching staffs probably have an easier time setting quantitative goals than most companies do. All Football Bowl Subdivision teams (formerly known as Division IA) have the same maximum number of new scholarship players they can take in a given year and the same total number they can have on scholarship at any given time. They can set goals about what types of players they need to get in terms of athletic ability, character, personality type and the positions they could play on the football field.

Whether you are setting marketing and sales goals for a for-profit company, a charitable organization or a major college football team, it's best to start first with dreams. Before writing a single goal, take some time to dream.

Dreaming dreams is the highest, most important position on the planning-process hierarchy. Dreams can range from the reasonable to the outrageous and from practical to whimsical.

Organizational leaders should sit down at least once every few years and just dream. Imagine your organization's "ideal." What does your company look like if all your marketing is done perfectly, your operations are flawless and money is no object? Think about every single thing you would like to accomplish or experience. A dream could be as far-fetched as winning three national championships in a row or as practical as winning a conference title within the next three years. All dreams are good dreams if they are your dreams.

Record your company's dreams. Write down every single dream that enters your mind. Your list should be a stream of consciousness. Record what every leadership team member says. Don't evaluate the practicality of the dreams and don't edit the wording. Just get them on paper. Don't judge anything at this point. Don't worry if your list grows long. That's a good thing.

After you have thought of every dream you can (don't be surprised if your dreams number in the hundreds), you may want to reorganize your dreams into categories. At this point it's okay to clean up your writing and edit the dream list as long as your editing doesn't change the meaning of your organization's true desires.

After all of this, it's finally time to start on your goals. Set goals that help you move closer to your company's dreams. Set goals that honor your core values and are in harmony with your mission and vision. There are a number of reasons to set goals. They help you match actual with desired progress and give you a regular mile marker to chart your progress. Goals clarify and quantify your needs and wants.

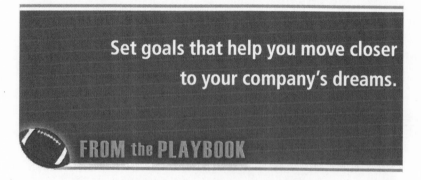

Set goals that help you move closer to your company's dreams.

FROM the PLAYBOOK

It is wise to have short-, medium- and long-term goals. Long-term goals would be in the ten- to twenty-year range. Medium-term goals are in the five-year range. Short-term goals are in the one-year range. Goals are the bread and butter of your success plan. While the earlier steps can be conducted every few years, goals must be set yearly and evaluated at least monthly.

Goals drive the rest of your strategic marketing and sales plan.

Target Audience

In 1979, Howard Schnellenberger left his job as offensive coordinator of the NFL's Miami Dolphins and accepted the job as head coach of the struggling University of Miami. In those days, the Miami Hurricanes were downright awful.

Like any good leader, Schnellenberger had a plan to bring glory to the moribund Hurricane football program, and a big part of that plan involved sales and marketing. Coach Schnellenberger realized he was sitting atop a football goldmine as the state of Florida was typically (and still is) one of the top football-talent-producing states in America.

Even better, the greater Miami area was particularly rich in talented prospects. Schnellenberger announced that he would mine the "state of Miami" and build a metaphorical fence around South Florida, making sure "the U" signed all the great local talent while keeping the northern competitors out of his own backyard. South Florida had so much talent that Schnellenberger could focus 90 percent of his sales effort at home, choosing to venture farther out only when there was an especially phenomenal prospect who may have had a particularly keen interest in Miami.

The strategy worked. Within five years, Miami won a national championship, the first of five within the next eighteen years. Before Schnellenberger's recruiting strategy, football fans ignored the University of Miami. Now, the very mention of the team's name conjures up images of ultra-talented teams, displaying bravado and swagger while winning big games on national television.

Schnellenberger's marketing strategy worked in large part because he had a thoroughly researched and clearly defined target audience, a group of prospects upon whom he would depend for his "business's" success.

Every business has a target audience. The key is to decide exactly what types of people you need to target, determine where you can find them and establish the best ways to expose your brand to them.

In determining who is in your target audience, focus on exactly what kinds of clients you need. At the University of Tennessee, former national championship coach Phillip Fulmer valued one attribute among his prospective "clients" more than anything else: fit.

Just like all coaches, Fulmer and his staff wanted special individuals, those rare athletes who possessed great athletic talent and the competitive heart of a lion.

"It's easy to get too infatuated with media hype, if you're not careful," Fulmer said. "We always felt like character was a very important part of it." In other words, during the Fulmer era, Tennessee wanted "character" not "characters."

"Often times those four- and five-star guys turned out for some reason not to fit our program either talent-wise, academically or character-wise," Fulmer said. "We had our share of the great athletes—Peyton Manning, Jamal Lewis, John Henderson, Albert Haynesworth, Shaun Ellis, Deon Grant and on and on, but we were looking for guys that had the special talent and ability and size and speed and all the tangible dynamics, but we also were looking for guys who had the intangible things: character, work ethic, leadership. Sometimes they were five-star guys; sometimes they weren't."

Targeting the right group of prospects is therefore deceptively difficult. Many prospects who on the face of things looked highly desirable for the Tennessee Volunteers could actually turn out to be liabilities down the road. So it is with every organization.

A too-good-to-be-true client could end up costing you more money than they make for you. Sometimes, the best deals for you are the ones you choose to decline. Sometimes it's best to walk away from someone who at first glance *looks* like a great customer.

Selling Points

Once you know who you want, then you need to determine what you say and how you say it. What will be your main message? What about sub messages? This goes back to the qualities you established earlier in the strategy development process—mission, vision, core values, long- and short-term goals.

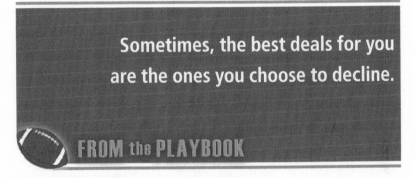

Sometimes, the best deals for you are the ones you choose to decline.

FROM the PLAYBOOK

Next, focus on what benefits of your organization would be most appealing to your target audience. Do your prospective clients care more about academic support programs, state-of-the-art weight-training facilities and player-coach relationships, or do they care more about winning tradition, big stadiums and national championships? Whatever it is, craft your communication tactics in such a way that drives these messages home in the prospects' minds.

Regardless of your message, prospects will not be receptive unless you "climb the relationship depth chart" by first establishing rapport, then developing a relationship that leads to trust. The message should facilitate the attainment of trust and should be spread out over the entire trust-building process.

Prospecting

Before you can climb the relationship depth chart with your prospects, you have to find them first. College football coaches use a variety of means to generate early prospect leads—recruiting services, rating services, relationships with high school coaches, their own personal scouting efforts and information sent to them by prospective players themselves.

One of the first prospecting decisions you should make is a geographic one. If you work in a large geographic market with a seemingly endless supply of prospective clients, there's probably very little sense in venturing afar unless you are chasing a particularly extraordinary lead that could have a profound impact on your business.

Some college football teams have almost all the players they need right at home; others must venture across the country.

"In a given year, we might have five or six high-quality prospects in the entire state of Oklahoma," said former Sooners coach Barry Switzer. "The coach of USC drives by that many players on his way to work."

Frankly, the sales business is geographically unfair. Go where the clients are. Go where the players are. In Oklahoma, that means you have to take quite a few business trips to Texas, California and elsewhere.

Switzer's solution to his geographic handicap could generally be summed up in one word: Texas.

"I had to spend more time in Texas than I did in Oklahoma, because Oklahoma was a given," he said. "We were going to get those kids in Oklahoma. They were going to be Sooners.

Texas has the numbers. They have 1,600 high schools that play football. Oklahoma has 200."

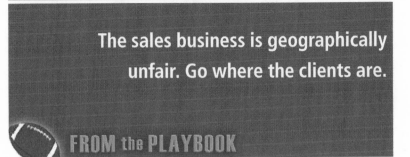

The sales business is geographically unfair. Go where the clients are.

FROM the PLAYBOOK

Switzer made up for the geographic disadvantage by "owning" the next-door state of Texas. During his tenure, he cherry-picked the Lone Star State and drove coaches at Texas and Texas A&M absolutely nuts. Switzer's 1974 recruiting class epitomized his Texas successes. The now-extinct *Dallas Times-Herald* had a confidential blue-chip list each year of the greatest players in Texas. Of the nineteen high school football stars who made the list that year, thirteen signed with Oklahoma.

The legendary Iowa coach Hayden Fry enjoyed a healthy Big 10 Conference rivalry with Joe Paterno of Penn State. One year, after Iowa had a particularly good season, Paterno called Fry and said, "Coach, congrats on the great season, but I also wanted you to know I vote for you for coach of the year every year."

Fry was surprised and confused by the comment, but Paterno chuckled and explained.

"Just out of curiosity, I looked at the Iowa almanac and noticed you have two-and-a-half million people in your state," Paterno told Fry. "I've got seventy-five million within a hundred-mile radius of my campus to recruit from."

Those words stuck with Fry for many years.

"I appreciated him saying that," Fry said, "because out of necessity, I did have to recruit nationwide. We'd have four or five players in Iowa each year who could develop into major Big 10 guys, so I would hire assistant coaches from different geographic areas where the high school coaches knew and respected them."

Hall of Fame former coach John Cooper earned a well-deserved reputation as a salesman. Fourteen players from his final recruiting class were eventually drafted into the National Football League.

"Great recruiters go find players," Cooper said. "You go nationwide. We got the three best players out of New York one year. We got great players from the West Coast. You gotta go out of state unless maybe you're Texas or USC. They have thirty-five million people in California, so USC gets the cream of the crop out there, yet they still recruit nationwide. You gotta go where the players are."

In your business, always start with the low-hanging fruit, those prospective clients who already know your brand and like you. But if there isn't enough of that quick-and-easy business, be prepared to go to whatever lengths are necessary to find the right kind of clients who fit your business model.

Dividing the Labor

Great selling organizations select staff and assign duties in an efficient and rational way that makes most sense to that organization. Depending on your industry, you may also have to decide carefully who is focused on operations and who must focus on the selling.

The NCAA limits the number of full-time assistant coaches each school can hire. That means the head coach must skillfully balance those who are great coaches with those who are great recruiters. When Switzer was roaming the sidelines at Oklahoma, he expected all of his assistants to be competent at both selling and coaching, but he made sure about half the staff was particularly strong in at least one area and the other half had a great aptitude in the other.

"You gotta have particularly strong coaches in certain areas—offensive coordinator, defensive coordinator. You gotta have a great secondary coach," Switzer said. "But then you take a few coaches who are great recruiters, a guy that can get players, over his coaching ability. I've done that before."

During Switzer's time, he didn't have the same limitations on the size of his coaching staff, but nevertheless, he still maintains that it is so important to have a great salesman on your coaching staff that you may overlook a lesser ability that he may have as a pure field coach when compared to his colleagues.

Football coaching staffs divide the labor in a number of ways. One of the most common divisions is a geographic one. Each assistant coach receives a geographic territory that he prospects.

When John Peterson was recruiting coordinator at Ohio State, he made sure that each of the Buckeye's nine coaches first had an in-state territory. Peterson's, for example, was southwest Ohio.

"We worked hard maintaining our state boundary," Peterson said. "Then we broke down the surrounding states, followed by different pockets in states that may have large alumni bases or areas that have been good to us in the past. Florida is one of those states that has a large population of not only athletes, but Ohio State alums living there."

While Ohio is one of the top producers of blue-chip football talent, Tennessee is not.

"We just weren't blessed with a population base that allowed us to just recruit our state," said Fulmer, the former Volunteers' coach. Therefore, Fulmer and his staff declared north Georgia, western North Carolina, Kentucky, eastern Arkansas and northern Alabama to be "in-state" territory. They used the same tactics in those areas as they would in Nashville, Chattanooga, or Memphis.

Outside the two concentric rings of in-state and "almost in-state" territories, Fulmer and his staff would then venture a little farther out in the Southeast Conference states, but wouldn't sell as hard and as intently as they would in the in-state areas. The fourth concentric territorial ring would include special athletes from far-flung places as long as those athletes had a particularly strong interest in the Volunteers.

Barnett's philosophy at Colorado was very similar. Like Tennessee, Colorado does not boast a huge population, but there are five million people in the Centennial State. That population is big enough to produce a handful of blue chippers each year.

"First of all, Colorado is your home," Barnett said, "so you've got to recruit that first. I assigned every one of our coaches a Colorado [territory] to recruit. I wanted to make sure we had constant contact; we always knew who was coming up through the ranks. I wanted the high school coaches to always have a college coach at the University of Colorado they could talk to and they would see every year. They would know our coach, so that if they had a kid, they would feel comfortable sending him to us. Always look at home first."

While the heart and soul of Barnett's Buffalo teams came from Colorado, the majority still were imported. When it came to the out-of-state selling strategy, Barnett focused almost all his resources on California and Texas. Those two states had long-established pipelines through which many players had signed with Colorado for many years. Colorado's California strategy was so strong for so long that a look at the roster always showed a large number of hometowns followed by "Calif."

After Texas and California, however, Barnett was highly cautious about recruiting other parts of the country. Colorado simply never has had the budget that the bigger football schools enjoy.

"For us, finances always came into play. I was always trying to get the biggest bang for my buck," he said. "What I didn't want to do was to go to North Carolina and spend $10,000 and come in second or third. I didn't think that was a good, wise use of my resources."

Now, if Barnett had reason to believe there was a remotely located player who had legitimate interest, and it looked like Colorado was one of the prospect's top two choices, it was a different story. Barnett would find the money to send coaches to visit him.

When working a territory, football coaches use a practice that is sometimes referred to as "sales farming." You find "sales farmers" in many industries. For example, some residential real estate agents choose a particular geographic area for special emphasis. A real estate "farm" is typically comprised of one subdivision or neighborhood consisting of a few hundred houses.

There's nothing to stop such a real estate agent from doing deals in a variety of neighborhoods throughout the city, but an agent places particular prospecting focus on just one neighborhood. The agent memorizes all the houses in that subdivision and tries to get to know all the current owners, sends calendars and newsletters to everyone in that neighborhood and tries to meet people who live there. He or she becomes the specialist or expert in that neighborhood.

The hope is that anyone thinking of selling a house in the neighborhood would think of the agent and list the house with that expert agent.

If you farm the neighborhood correctly and thoroughly enough, you know when residents are even just thinking about putting a house on the market. Such advance knowledge is critical in securing clients before your competitors do. Those real estate agents who are part of prospective clients' lives are the ones who get the listings. Their competitors just shake their heads and wonder, "How does she get so many listings? It's not fair!"

To be effective in territory-based selling, make the territory a big part of your life. Know your "farm" like the back of your own hand. Own it. Live it and breathe it.

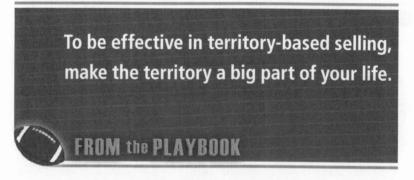

To be effective in territory-based selling, make the territory a big part of your life.

FROM the PLAYBOOK

Football coaches use similar techniques when they farm their assigned territories. They study everything they can about the high schools in their territories especially those that perennially produce blue-chip talent. They deliberately build friendships with high school coaches, principals and guidance counselors. It also doesn't hurt to build relationships with the sports journalists who cover high school football in the territory. They must study the culture, economy and politics of the territory and learn it so well that it feels as if they live there.

Territorial management would include public relations, networking and keeping tabs on happenings.

"You want to build relationships and trust over time, so a high school coach can feel confident in picking up a phone and saying, 'Hey, I got this kid, and I think he's Ohio State material. Come take a look at him,'" Peterson said.

The assigned coach serves as the primary talent scout within his territory. He is always digging, investigating and turning over rocks looking for the best prospects in his territory. Then he uses his established relationships to learn about the prospect's character, work habits and personality. He also uses those relationships to find out what it would take to sign the prospect. He searches out what buttons he must push in order to attract the prospect's attention and climb the relationship depth chart—rapport, relationship, trust, done deal—with him.

Just as salespersons must climb the relationship depth chart with prospective clients, they must make the same climb with the influencers and referral sources in the assigned territory. For college football coaches that means they deliberately build trust with scores of people who influence where blue chippers ultimately sign.

The War Room

The room itself is a tactic, but the activity that takes place in it is strategic. Some call it the "war room." Others have different names for it, but almost every college football coaching staff has a designated place inside its office complex where coaches can talk freely and openly about prospects, sales strategies and future needs. It's a place where confidential trade information can be spread out and displayed without the worry of an outsider seeing it.

If you work in a particularly competitive industry, you might want to borrow the war room idea from college football.

Whatever it's called, coaching staffs protect the secrecy and integrity of their war rooms with great zeal. According to Rivals.com's Sean Callahan, a fan managed to breach Nebraska's war room a few years ago and posted what it looked like inside on Rivals's Nebraska discussion forum. Husker coaches found out about it and requested that Rivals erase the discussion thread. Callahan understood the sensitivity and deleted it.

Recruiting, as the essential sales process for a football team, is the life-and-death of the program. Given that, the war room is sacred and hallowed ground.

Inside the typical football war room, you will find the "recruiting board," a listing of all the top prospects the team is pursuing divided by position—quarterbacks, linebackers, defensive backs, and all the others. The board itself can be constructed in a number of ways. In some war rooms, it's simply a marker board or chalkboard. Other teams take the high-tech approach and have an electronic recruiting board projected onto the wall.

One of the most common techniques is to have each prospect's name printed onto a large magnet and then stuck to a metallic wall. This allows the staff to easily arrange names in priority order in an easily changeable and highly visible manner. If a prospect commits to a different team, you can stick his magnet on the dead-prospect wall. If he commits to your team, you can easily move the magnet to your commit list. If you decide that your second priority at running back is now your first, it doesn't take much to flip the magnet order.

At Purdue, the recruiting board is actually a paper printout, according to Boilermakers assistant coach Donn Landholm. Purdue's recruiting coordinator keeps the recruiting board in a secured database. The coordinator simply gives each coach an updated printout at the beginning of each recruiting meeting. Purdue's war room also serves as the recruiting coordinator's office.

To make things even crazier, some football war rooms have a wall for each year's class. You might be working hard on the 2013 class, but you simultaneously have an eye on the 2014 and 2015 classes. The board must also factor in your current players. If you are going to lose all your best receivers next year to graduation, you will want to factor in particular sales emphasis on that position now to replenish your ranks. You have to think "positionally"—what do you need at each position this year, next year and beyond?

When Peterson served as Ohio State's recruiting coordinator, the Buckeye staff used its war room as a way to guide discussion and to make strategizing more visual and even tangible.

"You sit in the room and determine the odds that you'll get your top two kids or top three to four kids at each position," Peterson said. "Then you determine how many people you have to offer to get those players. You have to play devil's advocate sometimes and ask things like what are the odds that this kid from Texas is coming to Ohio State? He may be a great player and you really want him, but maybe he's not going to go so far from home."

Sometimes Ohio State would identify an incredibly gifted athlete who didn't readily appear to fit into a specific position. If the guy was talented enough, the coaches would put him in the "wild" category, which meant they wanted him and would find a place for him on the field if they ended up being fortunate enough to sign him. Peterson's recruiting board changed daily during the heat of the battle. Unforeseen events, such as the sudden transfer of an existing player to a different school, can upset the board very quickly.

Balancing Act

Like any industry, football selling is essentially a numbers game. Nobody, not even Texas, Florida or USC, signs all the prospects they pursue. Every business must have a plan for how many prospects are needed to equal one completed deal. Some lucky organizations, like Ohio State, enjoy a low prospect-to-client ratio. Others aren't nearly so fortunate.

To protect their downsides, even the blueblood programs over-offer. If a team is hoping to sign twenty-five players in a given year, it might offer more than two hundred scholarships. That makes total sense, but what happens when two prospects accept your offer at the same time for a position that only has room for one player? What happens when your number-three prospect at a position says "yes" but you really want to hold out hope that you'll get your top choice? It's a balancing act, and the smart sales strategist determines contingencies for these things before they actually happen.

In college football, the balancing act is particularly tricky when it comes to attracting quarterbacks as most schools typically want to sign only one QB per year. Quarterback recruiting is tricky, because these players tend to be your leaders and have a higher likelihood of being prima donnas. Coaches hold differing opinions as to how to manage the balancing act.

When Tim Brewster was coaching at Minnesota, he had a "first-come, first-served" policy when it came to recruiting quarterbacks. "I made sure my coaches, as they did their evaluations [of players] understood that if any of your five quarterback prospects calls at any particular time and wants to commit, you had better be really excited about them."

Not all coaches have such a black-and-white approach. It is common for a team to single out one high school quarterback and tell him, "You're our guy. You're the man. You commit to us, and we will not recruit another QB." This works if the prospect verbally commits early in the process and does not renege on his promise late in the process. That can be a big problem with elite quarterbacks who verbally commit early. The team stops communicating with other prospects at that position, but because the young man is so good, other teams don't stop trying to catch his attention. Many teams are left without a good quarterback in a recruiting class because the one guy they were counting on flew the coop late in the process.

At the University of California, head coach Jeff Tedford and his staff stratify quarterback prospects when they offer five in hopes of signing one. If the fifth-rated guy wants to verbally commit, and there's a big discrepancy in his abilities versus the top guy, Tedford waits.

"Just be honest with him, and tell him that this guy is ahead of you, and we have to wait out the process," Tedford said.

But if the fifth guy's ability is very close to the number-one ranked prospect, Tedford lets all the prospects know that the first guy who accepts the offer is the one who gets the spot.

When playing the balancing game, maintain your integrity and always be honest. If you mislead prospects, especially if it's a regularly occurring practice, word will get out. You will be labeled as untrustworthy, making future sales efforts all the more difficult. It is possible be honest with a prospect without giving away too much or divulging your competitive secrets.

"Remember your promises," Barnett said. "If you've told each quarterback that you're only going to take one, then by gosh, you better just take one. You don't want to go against what you said to a kid ... Be careful what you say."

Adaptation

Successful selling organizations are good planners. They plan meticulously. They brainstorm about the possible problems that could rear their ugly heads and snag the process. They develop contingency plans for a wide variety of potential complications.

No matter how diligently you plan, you will never plan for everything. Unforeseen external forces can play the devil with your strategy and tactics. That's why you must also plan for adaptation.

Be prepared to tweak your plan. Realize that no matter how hard you work, something will go wrong and something unexpected will always happen. Honor your strategic selling plan and keep its integrity, but always stand ready to think quickly and adjust on the fly. That combination of planning and flexibility can be just what it takes to push you over the top in a highly competitive selling situation.

Go where the prospects are. Develop rapport, build relationships with them, establish trust and close deals.

Spend time developing both your strategies and tactics and allocate adequate resources toward both.

Strategic planning must wait until the organization has clearly established its culture and understands what it is and what it never wants to be.

Honestly assess where you stand vis-à-vis your competition in the arena of public opinion.

Goals should be a product of your dreams and be in harmony with your core values.

In determining your target audience, focus on exactly what kinds of clients you need to succeed.

Start with the low-hanging fruit when prospecting but be prepared to go to whatever lengths are necessary to find the right kinds of clients.

Live and breathe your sales territory. Know it like the back of your hand. Own it.

Build a "war room," which is a place where you can spread out confidential trade information and display it without the worry of an outsider seeing it.

Never go back on any promise made to any prospective client.

Honor your strategic plan, but always stand ready to tweak it and adjust on the fly.

Chapter 8

PUTTING PEOPLE IN STRETCH ASSIGNMENTS
Sales Management

At one point during his long tenure as head coach of the Tennessee Volunteers, Phillip Fulmer unexpectedly lost one of his assistant coaches to a job in the National Football League. The sudden defection happened right in the middle of recruiting season, which created a hardship for the rest of the coaches left behind. Trying to hire a top-notch assistant coach at that time of year is next to impossible.

As it turned out, the Volunteers had a woman on staff who worked in the academic center. Possessed of a charismatic personality, she had an uncanny ability to relate to people and establish rapport with prospects and their families when they would come to campus for official visits. Not wanting to be short-handed during college football's prime selling season, Fulmer turned to the academic center employee and asked her to serve as an interim assistant football coach for seven weeks until he could find a permanent replacement.

"She was a full-fledged coach. She was my ninth coach," Fulmer said. "You should have seen the looks we got crossing paths with some of the competing coaches as they were coming out of players' homes and we were going in or vice versa. We must have been turned in five times, but it was perfectly legal. We checked the NCAA rules. She was our coach."

As head coach, Fulmer assumed the role of Tennessee football's sales manager, the person responsible for making sure the sales staff was in place, equipped to succeed and motivated to compete. Like all good sales managers, Fulmer had to think quickly on his feet and take immediate, decisive actions to mitigate any threat to the organization's ability to sell. Sales managers facilitate the sales process and protect the organization's ability to do deals.

While the term "sales manager" is the typical, generally accepted title of the person in charge of sales, the term "sales leader" is more appropriate. A manager supervises details. He or she makes sure tactical work is accomplished in an efficient manner. A leader makes sure those tactical tasks are completed but sees the business from a broader, more global perspective.

A head football coach is a sales "leader." The recruiting coordinator is more akin to a sales "manager." Even if your company is a small one, with only one person in charge of the sales staff, sales leadership is more important than sales management. The sales leader empowers the sales staff to carry out their work and rewards them for deals completed. Anyone who serves as a company's sales manager would be wise to see himself or herself as a leader and behave accordingly.

As the sales leader, you need to carefully analyze employees' personalities and push the right buttons to help them succeed at the highest levels. Urge them to accomplish more while still setting them up for success.

"It's putting people in stretch assignments," said Joe Moglia, former CEO of TD Ameritrade and now head coach of a college football team. Moglia believes two primary things are critically important when choosing people for a job and when assigning new goals to an existing employee:

alignment and listening. You can't succeed with one and not the other.

The leader must thoroughly understand the assignment and the people being considered for it. The most talented people in the world will fail if their personalities and abilities are not in alignment with the job. When it comes to listening, the leader must ask the right questions and then focus on what employees say and what body language they exhibit. Listen to find out whether the staff member is really excited about the assignment.

"I don't want to force somebody to take on a job they're uncomfortable with," Moglia said, "because I want them to hold themselves responsible for what they do. But if I'm putting them in a job that they don't have the skill sets for, shame on me."

Effective sales managers accept responsibility. They realize that they are in charge and accountable for what happens, but they don't see themselves as bosses. A leader is not a foreman. As a leader, you must depend on the abilities and hard work of your staff members. A successful sales leader is one who establishes interdependence. He or she trusts and depends on the staff while the staff trusts the sales leader to guide, provide resources and create a safe, pro-selling atmosphere.

Football coaches do very well in some aspects of sales leadership but tend to lag behind other professions when it comes to training and development. In the football business, there appears to be a "sink-or-swim" mentality or a belief that "you either have the ability to close deals or you don't." Many head coaches are so busy, they feel as if they can't take the time to train an assistant coach how to sell. If they do, it's probably only once a year. This is a mistake. Those head coaches who take the time to build sales skills usually are more successful than those who do not.

Resource Acquisition

Although training may be lacking, head coaches are very good when it comes to selecting and hiring good recruiters. Most schools also have fairly well-developed mentoring programs in which more experienced assistant coaches help teach the less-experienced ones how to sell.

There's one area of sales leadership where coaches tend to excel—securing resources for their salespersons. Head coaches are known to do whatever it takes to make sure staffing and marketing budgets are maximized, especially at the blueblood schools.

Attracting new clients is so important that every organization should devote considerable resources. That said, not all do. Leaders of various organizational departments jockey and position for resources. Some are better at it than others. If the sales leader isn't good at playing corporate politics, the sales staff might be at a resource disadvantage against the competition.

> ## If the sales leader isn't good at playing corporate politics, the sales staff might be at a resource disadvantage against the competition.
>
> FROM the PLAYBOOK

If you're a sales leader, do not let this happen. One of your single most important duties is to provide your sales force with everything they need to succeed. You don't ever want to give your salespersons an excuse for not performing. Lack of resources is a convenient excuse for a sales *person* but should never be an excuse for a sales *leader*.

The big-time football schools have large staffs that support recruiting operations year round. Staff members organize prospect databases, design brochures, maintain websites and handle mailings. Everything is set up so the coaches can evaluate film, make their calls and go on visits. The actual coaches don't do anything that a support staff member could do.

One of the best ways to ensure abundant sales resources is to establish clout inside your organization. At blueblood schools, football coaches enjoy tremendous clout, and they're not afraid to use it. Keep in mind that head coaches make far more money than their bosses—the president and athletic director. They are also far more famous, and if their teams have been successful, far more beloved by influential alumni and deep-pocketed donors.

Coaches know this. Big-time head coaches are not afraid to demand bigger weight rooms, fancier locker rooms and more attractive training tables with restaurant-quality food. If the recruiting budget isn't big enough, head coaches clamor for more funds. Of course, the smart head coach makes these requests at the right time. A coach has more clout at the end of a successful season or right after beating a hated rival.

The same timing applies to sales leaders of any industry. Make a pitch for greater sales resources right after you score a high-profile victory. Make the pitch when the higher-ups most value you and believe they could least afford to lose you.

Avoiding Blindness

One of the first values a good sales leader must establish is the belief that team is more important than the individual. This is tricky because salespersons tend to be very independent personalities. They tend to be self-confident and like making decisions for themselves without a lot of management oversight. Managing sales workers can be tougher than maintaining order the first day of freshman orientation!

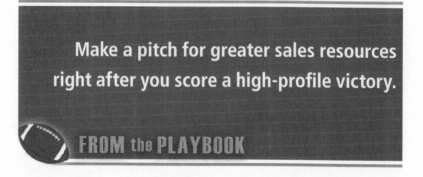

Make a pitch for greater sales resources right after you score a high-profile victory.

FROM the PLAYBOOK

In such an environment, the sales leader needs to respect and celebrate each salesperson's individualism and extend a level of trust and autonomy to each of them. At the same time, the leader can't allow a salesperson to go rogue. The good of the organization ultimately must be placed above the selfish desires of any individual no matter how talented he or she may be.

In college football, there have been outstanding assistant coaches who are extremely motivated recruiters and exceptionally talented salesmen. Those are exactly the types of guys a head coach wants to hire, but he must be careful not to be blinded by talent. If you're not careful, you could be so enamored with a prospective assistant coach's recruiting abilities that you might fail to notice his flaws.

Many of the assistant coaches who have landed their schools on NCAA probation for recruiting violations over the years were actually very skilled salesmen. They just went too far or were lacking in ethics. In the long run, no team, no business and no organization will come out on top if it hires ethically questionable salespersons even if those salespersons look great on the outside.

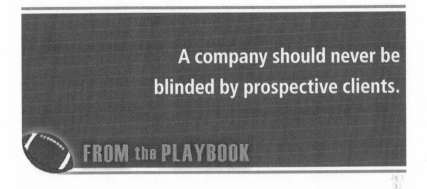

A company should never be blinded by prospective clients.

FROM the PLAYBOOK

Similarly, a company should never be blinded by prospective clients. Some football coaches have essentially sold their souls in order to attract a single great player. That once-in-a-lifetime athlete, who at 245 pounds can still run a 4.4 forty, is not worth it if he gets you in trouble and causes dissention in your locker room. Look for great prospects who will actually boost your business, not those that will end up costing it more in the long run. Those clients that look too good to be true most likely are.

Frequent Past Behavior

Hiring an assistant football coach is more complicated than choosing a salesperson in most other professions. Selling is only part of an assistant coach's job. He must also break down opposing teams' performances, help develop game plans, teach football basics and motivate a group of players to transcend their preconceived limitations and perform at levels they never before dreamed possible.

Despite all the varied tasks an assistant coach must perform, wise head coaches still place great emphasis on an assistant coach candidate's ability to recruit, his ability to establish rapport, build a relationship and develop trust, which can lead to signed deals with great players.

"If they can't recruit, they can't be good college coaches in my opinion," said Hall of Fame former coach John Cooper, who believes that you can only teach so much when it comes to a salesperson's personality and interest in working with people. Cooper wasn't interested in hiring a great X's-and-O's coach who couldn't close deals with talented prospects.

Tennessee's Fulmer held a similar opinion when he interviewed prospective coaches for his staff. "Everybody has their strengths and weaknesses," he said, "but at Tennessee, you had to be a good communicator."

R.C. Slocum looked for exceptional communication skills when hiring assistant coaches at Texas A&M back in the 1990s. What's more, he sought outgoing, gregarious guys for his staff.

"Someone who just likes people is a starting point," Slocum said. "Someone who enjoys being around people— if he's sitting in an airport, he's going to say 'hello' to the person next to him. Strike up a conversation. A guy who has a bent toward being introverted and doesn't really like to be around people and has an aloof nature isn't going to be a very good recruiter."

Because of the high stakes and high pay (assistant coaches at blueblood schools regularly make north of $200,000 per year), the big-time football programs tend to hire assistants who cut their teeth coaching and recruiting at smaller schools first. This gives the head coach something upon which to base his hiring decisions.

"Frequent past behavior is always the best predictor of future behavior," said former Colorado and Northwestern head coach Gary Barnett. "The other places he's worked—has he shown the ability to recruit? Is he someone you've competed against and you know how tough he is to beat? It comes down to what you've been able to accomplish in the past."

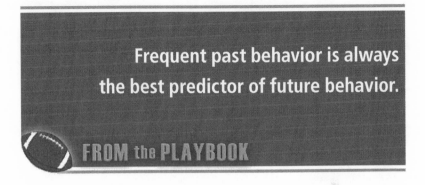

Frequent past behavior is always the best predictor of future behavior.

FROM the PLAYBOOK

University of California head coach Jeff Tedford also looks for recruiting experience when hiring assistants, but if he ever did hire a first-time coach, he would want someone who worked in the athletic department or a former player who hosted recruits when they would visit campus.

Tedford's beliefs imply that it is possible to develop an assistant coach with good selling skills from the ground up. In fact, former Georgia Bulldogs coach Jim Donnan would encourage his graduate assistants to take the NCAA recruiting exam, be involved in recruiting support roles and assist with on-campus recruiting programs.

"Through the years, I'd try to move graduate assistants up as much as I could," Donnan said, "because they already know our system on the field, academically and recruiting. But if it's a coordinator job, normally you wouldn't do that. I do think it's good to build from within when you can."

Former Iowa Hawkeyes coach Hayden Fry was successful on the field, but his greatest legacy is as the mentor and developer of head coaches. Twenty-one of his former assistants have gone on to be head coaches at either the collegiate or professional levels. Some of these names are huge in the football business: Bill Snyder, Bum Phillips, Barry Alvarez, Bob Stoops, Mike Stoops, Bo Pelini, Bret Bielema and Kirk Ferentz. Fry credits his father for providing him the philosophical foundation that made him such a prolific developer of great coaches.

"My dad told me, 'Son, if you're going to be a winner, you have to surround yourself with winners,'" Fry said, "so I never hired an assistant coach unless I knew he was completely motivated to become a head coach someday. Then I knew he would be ethical and see that his players graduated. I knew he would do the things a head coach ought to do."

Sales Training

Some industries are famous for their outstanding sales training programs. Others are notorious for essentially throwing new reps to the wolves. The insurance industry is known for thorough training programs that can go on for months and months.

Generally, the more you train, the better you sell. But let's be realistic. Most companies and most industries do very little training. Some do none at all. Though they sell in an über-competitive environment in a high-stakes business, new football coaches don't get a great deal of formal training. Those teams that do take at least some time to prepare their coaches as salesmen, however, tend to enjoy better results.

At Cal, Tedford takes a macro view to sales training, because he tends to hire only experienced coaches. Priority one is the rule book. Tedford and his assistants spend time in staff meetings making sure they are compliant with NCAA rules—the dos and don'ts of college football sales. After ensuring that the staff understand compliance, he focuses on his sales philosophy and values. For instance, he tells his staff not to negatively recruit by cutting down the competition as opposed to building up the Cal program.

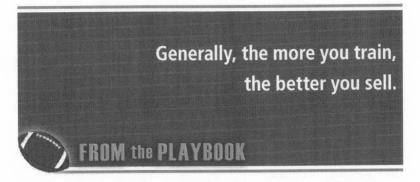

Generally, the more you train, the better you sell.

FROM the PLAYBOOK

Some head coaches bring in outside sales consultants on an annual or periodic basis to teach sales techniques to the staff. Often those trainers are from the insurance or financial planning industries. Instead of high-powered and high-dollar sales consultants, some staffs just go straight to the practicing insurance professionals to get their input. When going that route, the head coach will use a local company where most of the agents are probably big fans.

Cooper did that when he was at Ohio State. The whole staff visited the Columbus offices of a successful insurance agency to learn how to answer the phone, present the contract, find prospects' hot buttons and, most importantly, close the sale. The coaches learned from sophisticated sales professionals, who in turn got to rub elbows with the coaches from their beloved Buckeyes.

"They loved it," Cooper said, "but we loved it too, and we got a heck of a lot more out of it than they did."

When Fulmer was a young assistant for the Wichita State Shockers, he was impressed with a corporate trainer who came in from a prominent insurance company. He took that experience with him and would bring in outside sales seminars when he was head coach at Tennessee.

Along with sales training, Fulmer was very concerned about keeping his assistants up to speed on the latest happenings at the university. In addition to selling football, his staff had to sell the entire university. That meant all the coaches had to know something about each of the colleges and all of the majors. They also were expected to know about student-support programs.

To keep up-to-date, Fulmer expected each assistant coach to serve as a liaison with one of the university's colleges. As liaisons, the coaches monitored their assigned college and alerted the rest of the coaching staff about curriculum changes or when a new faculty member was hired or promoted.

At Georgia, Donnan built a recruiting book that was almost as detailed as the team's playbook. But instead of X's and O's, the recruiting book spelled out the standard operating procedure for sales work. The book was impressive in its comprehensiveness, listing such step-by-step detail as how to make a high school visit or a home visit and how to evaluate talent. Donnan also borrowed the psychological testing that some professional teams used to determine which players they would target in the draft.

Beyond providing detailed information, Donnan brought in trainers who would focus on presentation skills, overcoming objections and closings. Assistant coaches would role-play. One would pretend to be a coach selling the team while another one would be a demanding, skeptical parent or a high school guidance counselor who graduated from one of Georgia's bitter rivals like Tennessee or Florida.

Mentorship

If your company or industry lacks the time and resources for or commitment to sales training, you should at least consider a strong mentoring program in which new salespersons are matched with successful veterans. In some industries, the mentor-mentee relationship actually works more effectively than traditional training. Mentorship also appeals more to the action-oriented person who can't stand sitting in a conference room listening to the blathering of scripted sales trainers.

When Jack Pierce was a brand-new assistant at Nebraska in the late 1970s, he was paired with a terrific mentor, the veteran assistant coach Clete Fisher. The two coaches set off on a three-day recruiting trip through rural Nebraska. Fisher had strong in-state ties and was particularly effective relating to the local boys.

After a couple hours of driving, the two coaches arrived at a high school in Humphrey, Nebraska. Fisher talked to the high school coach while they watched kids in P.E. class. The athlete who was the object of Fisher's interest was in that class. The coach and kid made eye contact, but just nodded at each other as conversations were not allowed at this point in the recruiting cycle. Next, the Husker coaches visited the principal, then the guidance counselor and finally left the high school after spending an hour and fifteen minutes.

Once in the car, Pierce figured he was about to drive to the next town, so he was surprised when Fisher said, "Pull over. That's the bank—pull over there."

Fisher walked into the small town bank and asked to see the owner. After fifteen minutes of small talk, they visited the insurance guy, the farm implement dealer and even the used car dealer. Confused and frustrated, Pierce finally asked, "Clete, how are we going to finish all these things in three days? We have twelve towns. If you're going to take this much time, we're in trouble. It's noon and we ain't left Humphrey!"

Fisher calmly responded, "Jack, I want you to understand, the kid's father banks at that bank. This is where he gets the insurance for his cars. That's where he buys machinery for the farm. Who the heck do you think is going to recruit this kid after we leave this town? I want this kid recruited twenty-four hours a day."

It was brilliant. Fisher was using the influential people in town to be his champions. Think about it. Every time the prospect or his family would run into someone in town, they would tell the family how wonderful Clete Fisher was and how wonderful it would be to play at the University of Nebraska.

Pierce got the message and learned the lesson. For the rest of his career, he was careful to build relationships with the people who influenced a prospect's decisions. He focused on building influencers and champions, people who loved him, believed in him and could trumpet his cause when he wasn't around. That young man couldn't go anywhere in Humphrey without influential locals saying things like, "Man, wouldn't it be great if you went to Nebraska?"

Observing a master salesman like Clete Fisher first-hand was probably a better learning experience for Pierce than anything he could have gleaned from a sales seminar. Mentoring relationships are powerful in any company and in any industry. Even if your company doesn't offer a formal mentoring program, you can always seek out an informal one on your own.

Mentorships are also advantageous for veteran salespersons as well. Serving as a mentor sharpens your own skills and causes you to reflect on what you are doing and how you might be able to do it better. Furthermore, serving as a mentor can reenergize a career that has become too boring and routine.

De-Recruit 'em

While sales leaders have many responsibilities, one of the least discussed but most important is the management of egos. Professional salespersons tend to be a self-confident and highly independent lot. What's more, they tend to be highly competitive. In many shops, there is great pride (and respect) that comes from being the number-one salesperson for the month, quarter or year. That competition is generally a good thing, but you do have to manage egos. Not everyone can be the number-one salesperson, which is tough when you have several outstanding ones.

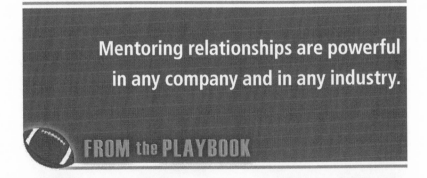

Mentoring relationships are powerful in any company and in any industry.

FROM the PLAYBOOK

Of all the salespersons in the world, college football coaches have got to be among the most competitive. After all, in addition to recruiting responsibilities, they are driven to coach football at the highest level and do what it takes to beat the competition. Their entire job security ultimately comes down to their team's ability to beat another team on the field of competition in a high-profile way, which leaves no doubt as to who wins or loses.

In managing egos, the head coach needs to be clear about his expectations and exactly what the selling expectations are for each assistant. The "team-first" philosophy that is so important for players to adopt must be sincerely believed and followed by the assistant coaches as well.

As far as who is the best recruiter on the staff, competitive people ultimately realize that competition itself answers the question. When you accept a coaching job at a big-time football school, you know the standards are going to be high. You know your colleagues on the staff are going to be ultra-talented and highly motivated. Unless you're naïve or unless the head coach has set up an unfair system, you know why you're the number two recruiter and not the best. The head coach's job is to keep encouraging and motivating the assistants to become better and better salespersons.

But managing egos goes much further than the sales staff. In some businesses, including college football, you need to manage the egos of clients themselves! It's much easier to manage egos of people you are paying (assistant coaches) than those of the clients.

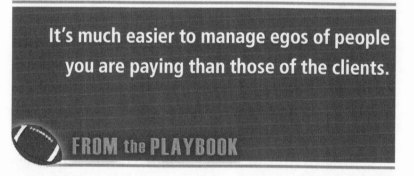

It's much easier to manage egos of people you are paying than those of the clients.

FROM the PLAYBOOK

Football coaches are selling their wares to elite clients: highly coveted blue-chip athletes. Less than one one-hundredth of one percent of the U.S. population ever plays major college football, and only a small percentage of those people are considered blue-chip athletes. It's a recipe for fat-headedness, cockiness and over-sized egoism. How does a football coach manage a team of big egos and teach them to be disciplined members of a finely tuned team especially after wining and dining them during the courtship process?

"From the minute they sign, 'til the minute they get on campus, you start de-recruiting them," Barnett explained.

"But you do it in a way in which you're talking to them constantly. You're getting them ready for school."

Barnett believes it helps when the incoming freshmen choose to attend summer school before their first season. Summer school allows incoming players to transition into college without the pressure of practicing. They only take two classes, so they experience what college is like. Because the course load is light, they can run home for a day or two if they start to feel homesick.

They participate in the informal summer workouts with the upperclassmen, so the new players start to understand how fast those guys move and how intensely they work. The newcomers ease into the process but are humbled quickly when they see how talented all the existing players are.

Former Minnesota coach Tim Brewster echoed Barnett.

"You gotta de-recruit 'em," he said emphatically. "So much smoke is blown at kids in the process, particularly with the Internet."

Brewster would tell all his newly acquired players to "keep it real." He explained how hard they will have to work to earn starting positions and that nothing will be given to them without first earning it.

"After a kid signs, it's like going to work. The fantasy world of recruiting is done and over," Brewster said.

In those industries where you have to "de-recruit" clients, do it carefully. People expect college coaches to act with authority, but they can't wield terror over their players like they could in times long gone.

Woody Hayes, the late, great Ohio State coach famous for his rough treatment of players in the 1950s through the 1970s, would not be allowed to use many of his tactics in current times. Nowadays, kids are more sensitive and less responsive to dictatorial leadership styles. Also, retention is important. Don't be so tough that you start losing people. If you de-recruit a player too strongly, he might transfer. If you de-recruit a client too zealously, he or she might "play" for your competition.

The person in charge of sales should be considered a sales "leader" and not a sales "manager."

Sales leaders must think quickly and take immediate action to mitigate any threat to the organization's ability to sell.

Successful sales leaders accept responsibility and accountability, but they realize a leader is not the same thing as a supervisor or a foreman.

One of a sales leader's single most important duties is resource acquisition—providing the sales force with everything it needs.

Be careful not to be blinded by great salespersons who might have fatal flaws and clients who are too good to be true.

When hiring staff, remember that frequent past behavior is the best predictor of future success.

Create a sales how-to book that is as detailed as a football team's playbook.

A quality mentoring program can make up for unsophisticated sales training.

Mentorship can be as beneficial for mentors as it is for the mentees.

In managing egos, sales leaders need to be clear about the sales expectations for each salesperson.

Chapter 9

DIAMONDS IN THE ROUGH
Prospecting and Qualifying

Anyone who has studied marketing and sales or has worked in those fields has probably heard of the "marketing funnel." It is also known as the "sales funnel," "purchasing funnel" or a handful of other names. Whatever you call it, the principles are the same. Picture a funnel in your head. The broad, wide top represents all persons who are demographically eligible to be your clients. Some call these people "suspects."

As you move down the funnel, its size becomes smaller and narrower. Just below the wide top of the funnel would be prospects—those people you know you can help and who have an initial interest in what you offer. As you continue down the tapering funnel, there are fewer and fewer people at each stage in the marketing and selling process. Finally, those people at the very bottom, the few who "drip" out of the funnel, are your "done deals," signed-up clients.

Prospecting is a top-of-funnel activity. Delivering sales pitches and answering objections are middle-of-funnel activities. Negotiating final terms and closing sales are bottom-of-funnel activities. What's more important? Top, middle or bottom? Most people would quickly answer "bottom!" But that question cannot be answered without further clarification. The degree of importance of each depends on where you are in your work. If you're just starting out, top-of-funnel activity is probably most important. If you're established in business, you're probably more focused on closing deals.

In general, the wise salesperson spends the majority of time with the most serious prospective clients who have worked their way down the funnel and are getting really close to signing their names on the dotted lines. The farther down a person is on the funnel, the more time you spend on him. This is only logical. But a problem can develop when so much time is spent with bottom-of-funnel people that no time is left for prospecting.

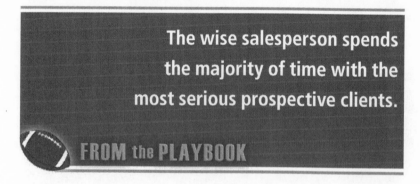

The wise salesperson spends the majority of time with the most serious prospective clients.

FROM the PLAYBOOK

Prospecting neglect usually occurs when a salesperson is enjoying an unusually large number of prospects who are arriving at the closing stage at about the same time. This is a heady experience when it happens. Such a situation creates a frenzy of activity and a rush of adrenaline as you do whatever it takes to bring the deals home while fantasizing about all the money you'll make as soon as everything is finalized.

Eventually, all those bottom-of-funnel people will flow out. You hope they become your clients. Some could ultimately choose to go a different route. In either case, the time will come when there aren't any more clients to work. If you haven't done enough prospecting during your busy times, you'll be left with a mostly empty funnel. You then have a long lag time before closing your next sale because it takes time to push new prospects down through each funnel stage. The trick is to work people at each stage constantly, so the flow of done deals is never really interrupted.

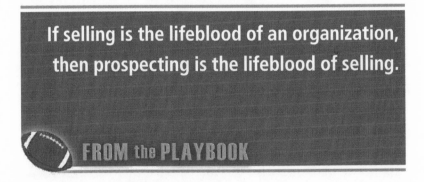

If selling is the lifeblood of an organization, then prospecting is the lifeblood of selling.

FROM the PLAYBOOK

No matter how busy you are, and no matter how successful you have been, never, ever stop prospecting. Make a perpetual commitment to be a great prospector, an originator of business, a generator of revenue. Be the type of person who other salespersons envy. If selling is the lifeblood of an organization, then prospecting is the lifeblood of selling.

Who Do You Want?

One of the first steps in prospecting is to determine who among all the suspects you want. Like all sales and marketing activities, prospecting must be in harmony with your strategic plan. That means you go after the types of prospects who will help you meet your mission and goals while being consistent with your vision and core values. Make sure your targeted prospects are the type of people who truly value what you can do. Make sure they have the problems that you are equipped to solve.

Now that you know who you want, make sure your branding and other marketing activities actually attract that kind of person. Branding sets the stage and establishes the selling themes. Portray yourself as the choice for the kinds of prospects you seek.

A football team that is known for its staunch, hard-nosed, impenetrable defense is going to appeal to great defensive players who are looking for a place that will set them up for a career in professional football. A team known for its pass-happy offense is going to have a much easier time attracting elite receivers and quarterbacks. A team that projects a brash, swaggering, bad-boy image is probably trying to pull in showboating, cocky, highly confident individuals. If done right, such a team can become an intimidating force with a cool mystique that helps sell incredible amounts of licensed merchandise. If managed poorly, such a team will end up on NCAA probation and be the target of public scorn and media disgust.

If your company has been around for a while, profiling potential prospects is easy. Just look at your most valuable current clients, identify what stands out about them and then search for those qualities among prospects. If your company isn't so established, it will require some trial and error as you search for those prospect qualities that are most in sync with your organizational purpose.

Those college football coaches who consistently sign highly rated freshman classes are great prospectors and know exactly what types of young men they should be targeting. Successful head coaches figure out exactly what they want their program to be and then go out and court those players who can make the vision come to reality.

> ## Just look at your most valuable current clients, identify what stands out about them and then search for those qualities among prospects.
>
> ### FROM the PLAYBOOK

When John Cooper was recruiting coveted players for the Ohio State Buckeyes, he searched for elite athletes who were "hungry." He liked hard-working kids especially if they came from challenging economic backgrounds.

"A lot of times those are the kids that are going to work the hardest for you," Cooper said. "I mean, you're their meal ticket. You're the only way they're going to get off the streets."

There was another criterion Cooper used when prospecting. He was careful not to target young men who were peaking too soon.

"We're not looking for a great high school player," he said. "We're looking for that kid who is going to keep getting better two, three, four years down the road."

Now that college coaches are forced to recruit players earlier and earlier in their high school years, there is a greater risk of a player plateauing long before he's ready to play in college. That meant that Cooper and his staff constantly studied how a young man would "project." They asked themselves how much potential does he have when he has better nutrition and a state-of-the-art weight program in college? Just how good can he become when he "grows into his frame"? How receptive will he be to coaching?

Over the years, Cooper was able to find some phenomenal athletes who were literally undernourished and had never benefited from decent strength and conditioning programs. After a few years at Ohio State, such kids sometimes evolved into All-Americans.

Legendary Texas A&M coach R.C. Slocum prospected almost exclusively in the state of Texas. Of course, he had the luxury of staying in his home state, considering that Texas boasts the largest and highest-quality high school football system in the country. Slocum preferred players from nearby, so they could stay close to and highly involved with their families. He believed that players with a strong support system nearby were most likely to succeed in his program.

"I wanted a young man who wanted his little brother and sister and Mom and Dad to be there at the games," Slocum said. "We recruited a whole lot in Texas, and we would invite those players and their families to our games, and that was the selling point we had. You can get in your car, drive to College Station, spend the day watching your son, go back home and sleep in your bed. You can still get up for church on time Sunday morning."

During the record-setting Tom Osborne era, Nebraska was obsessed with "fit." Especially during the 1970s and 1980s, Osborne and his staff were willing to take a lesser athlete if he was exceptionally intelligent and was capable of embracing the Huskers' culture of selflessness, hard work, diligent study and the pursuit of mistake-free football.

That's a very different target audience than Osborne's chief rival sought for Oklahoma in those days. Sooner head coach Barry Switzer put a premium on raw talent. He was obsessed with elite athleticism. His strategy was to stock so many world-class players on his team that he could "out-athlete" opponents in big games.

How to Find Them

Once you know the desired characteristics you are seeking in your prospects, the next step is to find them.

Regardless of industry, some prospect leads come from branding and advertising efforts. A prospect could be compelled to contact your company because of a long-standing, respected brand you have established in the marketplace. More directly, the prospect could be responding to one of your advertisements. Maybe the prospect stumbled upon your company's website or Facebook page. He or she could also be responding to a direct mail piece or email blast your company sent to a list of leads purchased from a company such as InfoUSA or Hoover's.

While the marketing department may have worked hard to build that brand and may have spent countless hours and dollars creating effective mass media campaigns, the prospects generated this way are "passive" from a salesperson's point of view. When would-be clients seek out the company on their own or as a result of marketing, the salesperson is merely a friendly order taker who is filling a customer service role. The only selling skills such a person would exhibit would be those necessary to avoid screwing up the opportunity or those necessary to upsell the already interested prospect.

While most salespersons happily accept passive sources for prospects, they don't count on them. Consider these call-ins to be pleasant surprises. The bulk of your prospects, and consequently the bulk of your income, will probably have to come from active sources—in other words, from your own efforts. As the old adage says, "Salespersons eat what they kill." The more proactive you are, and the more initiative you take in prospecting, the richer your diet.

To be a proactive, initiative-taking salesperson, embrace all facets of prospecting. That means you become a researcher, detective and tireless networker. You are constantly searching. If you have an assigned geographic territory, you must "own" it. You constantly touch base with people in your territory who can recommend people and give you tips on what possible clients are thinking.

> **Sometimes a client that doesn't look so promising at first can become a great one if you find a way to view him or her through a different lens.**
>
> FROM the PLAYBOOK

A proactive salesperson shows up at events, spends time on the phone seeking information and keeps up with those current events that can affect his or her industry. Creativity is important as well. Sometimes a client that doesn't look so promising at first can become a great one if you find a way to view him or her through a different lens.

To generate leads, coaches use sources that are analogous to those used by all businesses. Major football schools subscribe to a wide variety of recruiting services, which provide demo videos, ratings and scouting information on a myriad of players. Some of these services focus on a certain geographic area, such as Texas, New Jersey or perhaps the Southeast Conference states. Many of these services are thorough and highly sophisticated and provide scouting information and video online in high-quality format.

Leads also come from scouting work. A prospecting coach contacts all the high school coaches in his territory and asks them about his players. College coaches may ask their high school colleagues questions such as, "What Division I prospects do you have on your team this year?" or "Who has the most potential?"

During the spring evaluation season, college coaches will go visit high schools and talk to coaches about their best players. They also want to get the high school coach's opinions on other players in his district or conference. A good question would be "Who's the best kid you played *against* last season?"

Those college coaches who have built strong relationships with high school coaches often receive unsolicited leads. If a high school coach really likes one of the coaches at Notre Dame and believes one of his players is Fighting Irish material, he's probably going to go out of his way to make sure Notre Dame gets a shot at the kid.

If a college team has established a highly respected and widely recognized winning brand, players will seek the team out, sending inquiry emails and forwarding video links for the coaches to review. This is a more passive form of prospecting, but the better your team is, the more unsolicited leads you will enjoy.

Another form of football prospecting also doubles as an early selling tactic—camps. Major college teams hold several camps for different age groups of younger football players. Teenage boys come to campus, stay in the residence halls and work out with the college's coaching staff. Hundreds of boys attend camps each year at each college. The vast majority of attendees will never receive a scholarship offer from a college team. For them, it's a great life experience and helps them become better players during high school. But for some kids, the camps are a place to be discovered.

From a prospecting perspective, on-campus camps allow college coaches to evaluate prospects in person to see how they might fit in with the team. Just as important, the camps are sales tools. The NCAA doesn't allow overt selling during the camps, but it is a great chance for the school to show itself off. If a kid has a life-changing experience and is blown away by the coaches and the facilities, there's a good chance the team might earn his commitment and ultimately his signature on National Signing Day.

All of this prospecting requires an advanced client-contact management system, an electronic database that records info on each prospect and tracks him as he goes through the recruiting process. A good contact management program allows anyone on staff to update information and write documentation after each phone call or in-person contact.

Careful coaches log every conversation in the system, so they never go back on their word. The system has to be sophisticated because coaches are not only tracking many prospects, they're also tracking prospects that will be eligible to sign during different years. In other words, they're not just managing this year's incoming class. They're also tracking contact with promising eighth graders who can't enroll at their school for several years.

With several thousands of suspects and possibly a thousand prospects at any given time, the coaching staff can't possibly manage everything. Selling is only one part of their jobs. They also have to develop players, scout the competition, design plays, develop game plans and, of course, coach games. The support staff plays a key role.

At least one person will be responsible for maintaining the prospect database. At least one person will do nothing but identify, log and maintain prospect videos. Several people will be involved in the design and distribution of prepared marketing materials.

With a large and highly motivated support staff, coaches at the major football schools focus on prospecting, communicating and closing deals. They don't waste their time with minutia. Coaches only do what they have to do. Anything that can be done by an admin assistant or support staff member is delegated. This frees coaches up to do the high-value sales work (and of course the high-value coaching work)!

Then there's the "diamond in the rough," the prospective client that nobody has heard of. Such a prospect flies under the radar or may be a late bloomer, in that he or she only recently acquired or adopted the characteristics you are targeting. If you become adept at locating diamonds in the rough, you can guide those prospects down your funnel without the pressure of heavy competition. If the person is under the radar enough, your competitors won't even know about him or her until after you win the business.

> If the person is under the radar enough, your competitors won't even know about him or her until after you win the business.
>
> FROM the PLAYBOOK

In college football recruiting, the diamond-in-the-rough prospect is harder to find these days. That's because the process generates such incredible media coverage. Sports websites start tracking promising high school players when they are merely fifteen-year-old sophomores.

"If you're planning on going to Texas, Florida, OU or one of the other big schools, you better have played really well your sophomore year," said Joey McGuire, head coach of Cedar Hill High School, a powerhouse football program in the Dallas–Fort Worth Metroplex. "The big schools are almost through with their recruiting classes by the time it comes to your senior year. In order to get recruited as a senior, you just have to have a phenomenal year and still hope there's a scholarship available."

But there are still those players who physically develop later than others and those who play for small high schools in lesser-known districts in sparsely populated parts of the country. Some coaches are good at finding those under-the-radar or late-blooming guys. If they consistently find a lot of these prospects, they'll enjoy a lot of long-term success on the field.

Another diamond in the rough could be a kid who has played a different sport for most of his life but has highly transferable athletic skills. A football coach who is good at prospecting and qualifying can go to a high school basketball game, for instance, and identify which players would also be good at football.

As a position, tight end provides a good example of why a prospector needs to have open eyes. The tight end position requires a unique athlete who possesses a number of highly coveted traits—size, strength, speed, balance, catching ability and athleticism. He must be big and strong enough to serve as an extra blocker on the offensive line during running plays, but he must also quickly run precise routes in the passing game.

When prospecting for great tight ends, a coach looks for body control, athleticism, speed and change-of-direction ability. To find such players, coaches often look for wide receivers who appear to have a large frame they could fill out. They also like power forwards on the basketball team.

Switzer ran the wishbone offense when he coached at Oklahoma. In order for it to work well against talented defenses, the wishbone required a versatile athlete at quarterback, two fleet-footed half backs and a very special athlete at a less noticed, somewhat underrated position—fullback.

In the 1970s, Switzer saw an amazing young tailback at a high school in Texas. His name was Kenny King, and he was highly recruited. Though he was a touted tailback, Switzer saw potential as a fullback, the running back who lines up at the point of the wishbone.

"I knew Kenny could be a fullback as soon as I saw him line up in a four-point stance," Switzer said. "The jets he had! The speed he had! He would ricochet up through the line and outrun everyone. He had several 80-yard runs for us because he was so strong and so fast."

Referrals

One of the most effective prospecting sources ever known to exist is the referral. When current or past clients put their names on the line in advocacy of your business, you have instant credibility with prospects. But referrals do not come easily. They must be earned. You earn them by showing integrity during the sales process and by delivering after the deal is signed.

In college football selling, referrals come from many places. First and foremost would be current and former players. Anyone who has gone to the school and had a positive experience can provide powerful sales testimony for prospective players. If the current or former player was a star, the referral is even more powerful.

Parents of players are also referral sources. Keep in mind that some parents have multiple sons. Perhaps it's a genetic thing, but it's quite common for more than one good football player to come from the same household. If son number one is having or had an enjoyable experience at Dear Old State U., there's a good chance little brother will come too. The same principle applies to sons of former players when those sons are fortunate enough to inherit Dad's athletic ability and love of the game.

High school coaches, teachers, guidance counselors and principals are an absolutely essential source of referrals. That's why so many college coaches spend incredible amounts of their precious time meeting with high school coaches, calling them on the phone and building friendships with them. College coaches often invite their high school brethren to special coaching clinics and offer them the chance to assist at the college team's football camps. The number-one reason for doing this is to build relationships and trust that can lead to valuable referrals and recommendations. A relationship with a high school coach now could possibly lead to an All-American on your team years down the road.

When you make referrals a major part of your prospecting strategy, make sure you know the referrer. If you are familiar with the referrer's personality, you know how seriously to take the referral. Is the person an exaggerator? Is the person prone to minimizing things and making understatements? Or is this person's opinion rock solid and are referrals rare?

> **When you make referrals a major part of your prospecting strategy, make sure you know the referrer.**

FROM the PLAYBOOK

"There are certain [high school] coaches that are a little naïve in that they don't really know what you need at the major college level," said former Nebraska assistant coach George Darlington. "He might be a very sincere guy, and he might be talking about the best guy he's ever personally coached, but the kid's still not good enough to play at USC or Nebraska."

Darlington said some high school coaches become so effusive in their praise of their star players that you would think, "This is the greatest kid that's ever put on a jock strap."

On the other side of the coin, a small percentage of high school coaches are frankly jerks, guilty of dereliction of duty because they do such a terrible job of promoting their players. Such coaches don't return calls from college coaches, or they withhold information or give vague, unhelpful answers. When asked what a kid is like, such a coach might respond, "He's a normal teenager." For a college coach who is trying to prospect and qualify, that's a useless answer.

As a college coach, you have to gauge what kind of referrer you're dealing with. If he's an overly enthusiastic exaggerator, take half of what he says with a grain of salt. If he's a disinterested user of understatement, don't give up on the prospect too quickly. You might miss out on a talented player.

Just because you have a strong referral from a quality source doesn't mean that you can assume anything.

In the late 1990s, Mario Edwards was a starting cornerback at Florida State and helped legendary coach Bobby Bowden win his second national championship in 1999. Edwards went on to an NFL career, playing for Dallas, Tampa Bay and Miami. In the fall of 2011, his son Mario Edwards, Jr., was a superstar defensive end at Ryan High School in Denton, Texas. As an even more promising prospect than his old man, Rivals.com tabbed Edwards, Jr., as a five-star recruit and ranked him as the third best player in the entire nation.

You might think that Florida State had a high likelihood of landing young Edwards since his father had such a good experience there. You're right. He committed to the Seminoles in the spring of 2011, the end of his junior year of high school, according to Warchant.com.

But the story did not end there. As time went by, the younger Edwards starting having second thoughts. Was Tallahassee too far from his home in the Dallas area? Though he remained officially "committed" to FSU, he took visits to other schools and wound up saying he would decide among LSU, Texas and FSU.

Often when this wavering occurs, the original school is left holding the bag, watching the metaphorical tail lights as the prized recruit drives off to the competition. Florida State lucked out in this case. Edwards reaffirmed his commitment for good on February 1, 2012, and signed with Florida State. He was a huge catch, the highest-rated player in one of the highest-rated 2012 recruiting classes in the nation.

Although he had every reason to come to Florida State, Mario Edwards, Jr., was not a sure thing. He was the dream referral, but the Seminole coaches still had to earn his signature.

Qualifying Prospects

Perhaps more difficult than sourcing prospects is the art of qualifying them. Prospect qualification is one of the most significant factors separating highly successful dealmakers from mediocre ones and certainly from the poor performers. Qualification allows you to work efficiently, separating the suspects from true prospects. It allows you to spend your time wisely by identifying which prospects have the highest likelihood of becoming clients.

> ## Qualification allows you to work efficiently, separating the suspects from true prospects.

FROM the PLAYBOOK

When you qualify, you are determining the prospect's level of interest, identifying who influences them (or who the real decision maker is), thus establishing the client's time horizon and assessing whether the client would be sufficiently profitable if signed. The most successful sales professionals have developed advanced qualifying skills, most important of which are questioning and listening.

You qualify prospects by finding out as much as you can about them and their motivations and then honestly assessing if they are truly interested in you and whether or not you can properly serve them. Ask tons of questions. Do your due diligence by thoroughly vetting prospects. This means you research them through a variety of means often without their knowing it.

The earlier in the process you can qualify a prospect, the more efficient you will be with your time and money.

When Phillip Fulmer was leading the Tennessee Volunteers, he and his assistant coaches would try to qualify out-of-state players' willingness to leave home before expending significant resources on them.

"If we're recruiting a guy in Florida, and he's got Florida, Florida State and Miami and then us, the odds are we're not going to get that young man," Fulmer said. "If he's looking at Florida and Clemson and Penn State and Michigan and

Tennessee, you got a better chance. He's telling you he's willing to go out of state."

Once a prospect's proclivity for venturing far from home was established, Fulmer would ask questions designed to uncover the true decision maker. "Often times, it's not the kid," he said. "It's a parent, grandparent or coach—somebody that has a whole lot of influence on a young man somewhere."

Sometimes you have to get a little personally involved in order to discover the true decision maker, but be careful not to get so personally committed. That can make it hard to see possible signs that landing the sale would be unlikely and not worth your time.

In your business, ask questions such as, "Who are the other people who will weigh in on this decision?" "Who else in your company do I need to meet?" "How useful would it be for the two of us to meet with your boss sometime?" You must identify who is really calling the shots as early as possible.

Coach John Cooper followed a similar qualification strategy during his career.

"Don't spend time on somebody you don't have any chance of recruiting," Cooper said. "You may have a kid in Florida; his mom graduated from Florida. His daddy is a Florida grad, and his sister's a cheerleader there. You're probably wasting your time. Wish him good luck and find somebody else."

With only 365 days in a year and a limited number of waking hours per day, prospectors cannot afford to waste valuable time "chasing windmills" no matter how grand and glamorous such prospects might appear on the surface. Be aggressive and set stretch goals for yourself, but be brutally honest too. Can you truly solve the would-be client's problems? Can you provide great value to the prospect?

Remember that clients determine what is valuable—not you. If you are not convinced you are equipped to perform according to the prospective client's specific needs and values, you will most likely not get that client.

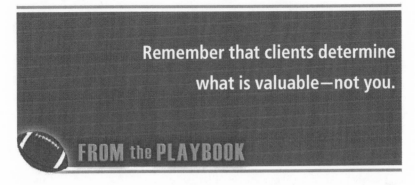

Remember that clients determine what is valuable—not you.

FROM the PLAYBOOK

When many sales professionals think of prospecting, they think only about the prospect's interest in their businesses. While that is crucially important, great care must be taken to make sure the prospect makes sense for you too. If you harbor any doubts about the prospect's likelihood of producing a profit for you, hesitate and do more study before bringing him or her on board.

Just as football coaches have to guard against being blinded by world-class talent, all businesses have to be wary of the client who is too good to be true. Too many times, businesses bring on a client who appears to be outstanding but ends up costing the company more than he generates. Such costs could include an actual loss of dollars, time, resources, reputation, goodwill or employee happiness and productivity. Factor in opportunity costs as well.

A client who is marginally profitable but causes you to miss out on other business is indirectly a money-losing client.

In a sense, prospect qualifying is essentially a form of risk management. Former Colorado and Northwestern head coach Gary Barnett believes that all prospects came with a certain degree of risk. It could be grades, behavioral issues, lack of size and strength, speed that's a step slow or a maturity issue. Whatever the deficiency, even the greatest players in the world came with at least some risk.

When a coach qualifies prospects, he must sort out who comes with what risks and determine how he could mitigate that risk. If you can't develop a reasonable way to minimize a given player's/client's risk, you should not take him.

In college football, character flaws and behavioral issues are the risks that pose the greatest threats to a team's potential success. These are also the risks that a coach—desperate to land a program-changing blue chipper—is most likely to overlook. It is so easy to be blinded by a star prospect when that client is one of the best-looking athletes you have ever seen. If that all-everything player has behavioral issues, he might be more trouble than he is worth.

Getting all star-crossed by a great athlete can be dangerous especially if it's the head coach who falls under the spell.

It's not as big a deal when assistant coaches are blinded by a player's overwhelming talent, Barnett said, but the head coach must be the gatekeeper who asks the tough questions in order to make sure the prospective player is really appropriate for the team.

There's an old football adage. "You don't want to play against a kid six days a week just so you can have him play for you one day a week," Barnett said. If a football coach has to lie awake every night worrying that his star player will drive under the influence of alcohol, start a bar brawl or be arrested for sexual assault, the player is not worth it.

It's similar to the role a sales leader must play when an eager sales rep hasn't done his due diligence on a client who superficially looks better than life. The person who has not been intimately involved in the prospecting process is generally a more objective judge of a client's value than the guy who has been working the relationship depth chart—rapport, relationship, trust—with him.

> The person who has not been intimately involved in the prospecting process is generally a more objective judge of a client's value.
>
> FROM the PLAYBOOK

To start the process, the sales professional must be personally involved and personally engage in researching and profiling the prospect. In college football, that means coaches personally evaluate a player's game film and personally watch him play at his high school or when he comes to campus for a summer camp.

"Don't get caught up in what some guy who's drinking iced tea in Southern California and has a recruiting service tells you is a five-star player," George Darlington said. "Same thing goes for some part-time evaluator in the Midwest or a so-called guru down in Texas. That's the key. You evaluate the film as a staff, talk to the high school coaches and then you end up getting kids that are, quote, 'Better than what the gurus said they are.'"

Because qualification is so important, you want to use any and all means at your disposal. Tom Osborne used to rely on his current players to help him assess the worthiness of prospects. When a high school player would officially visit campus, he would be matched with a current player who served as his personal host. Osborne and his staff would quiz the hosts about the visiting prospects after they left campus.

"We would oftentimes hear from a player, 'You know, coach, you really don't want this guy,'" Osborne said. "We figured there were things that the player had picked up on that we might not have seen as the player who hosted him took him to a movie or went out to dinner. Occasionally, we would not recruit a player based on what that host player would tell us."

What about ego? If you are targeting highly talented, elite prospects like big-time football players, you have to qualify for ego. But be careful, because some ego is good. If the ego is honest and based on a player's true ability, it's actually a positive thing. If it's a self-centered ego focused on self-aggrandizement, run away from that prospect and don't look back! In other words, great players know their abilities, but they find a way to channel that ego toward the good of the team.

In any business, qualifying whether a prospect is right for you can be difficult. It can be a real crapshoot in college football. Because of escalating competitive pressure, teams are forced to make offers earlier and earlier in a player's high school career. Although you can tell at a very young age if a person is athletically gifted, you cannot always tell how big and strong they will be. A big kid in middle school or early high school could be an early bloomer who is peaking. His physical growth could be about to plateau.

When professional coaches qualify incoming prospects, they look at what the players did in college, between the ages of eighteen and twenty-two, Slocum pointed out. The pros are allowed to put their prospective draftees through several batteries of physical, mental and social tests. Despite all that, they still make mistakes. You occasionally see the number-one draft pick who flames out and never makes an impact.

If that's the case, it's no wonder that college coaches miss on a lot of players. They are looking at performances between the ages of fourteen and seventeen from guys who have never left home and lived on their own. What's more, highly recruited kids are used to being the best player on their teams. Some of these young studs arrive at a powerhouse football school and have a hard time accepting that everyone else on the team was the best player on his high school team too.

Some high schoolers might be labeled as "can't miss" prospects because they did not play on very deep teams or competed in lesser leagues, allowing their athleticism to be exaggerated.

"I've seen kids that have been very highly rated, and I sit there thinking, Man, he'd have a really hard time playing for us," said McGuire, the Texas high school coach. College football prospect qualification comes with a much greater risk of failure than professional football.

Despite the risk, there are some players who you think are so talented and so successful that nothing could ever slow them down. Nevertheless, sometimes the greatest of the great still don't work out. There are a number of reasons for such monumental disappointment.

"Some kids, their whole goal is to get a college scholarship," Darlington said. "Once that happens, they never get any better. They don't reset their goals."

Darlington once had a player whose father enjoyed a successful NFL career. The kid was a promising, highly recruited prospect who never played much at Nebraska and ended up graduating in relative football obscurity.

"He never did *not* do what he was supposed to do in the weight room. He never got in trouble. He did all the minimum things we asked, but he never pushed himself to get better," Darlington said.

Sometimes the great prospect fails because, deep down, he's harboring a secret: he doesn't truly embrace the game. He doesn't have the heart necessary to achieve elite status in college ball.

"A lot of talented kids don't necessarily love the game," said former Minnesota coach Tim Brewster. "Football's a hard, tough game, and the commitment you've got to make to be a player at this level is amazing. It's a year-round commitment, and some kids aren't willing to do that."

Don't Dismiss Too Soon

Elimination is the primary reason for qualifying prospects. You want to discard those suspects who are least likely to buy so you don't waste time on them and don't allow them to pump you for information that will simply allow them to negotiate better deals with your competitors.

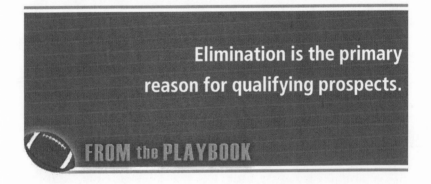

Elimination is the primary reason for qualifying prospects.

FROM the PLAYBOOK

That said, qualification is an art that requires a sense of balance and a heightened awareness. It requires you to become adept at reading emotions and uncovering motivations. Be a thorough detective when evaluating whether a client is right for you. Sometimes only a fine line separates an apparent suspect from a career-defining future client.

Former Nebraska off-campus recruiting coordinator Jack Pierce gets a smile on his face and shakes his head when he thinks back to a couple big misses he made while qualifying prospects. Perhaps the most famous was an undersized running back from Wichita North High School in south-central Kansas.

The high school coach kept pushing hard, trying to convince Pierce that the young player could turn into a great college player. The coach pushed so hard that Pierce became leery, a little suspicious. Pierce looked at the kid's film and was impressed with his speed and balance but thought he was way too small, absolutely tiny.

That young man was Barry Sanders, who signed with Oklahoma State and later went on to become one of the greatest running backs in history. While that was a huge miss, Pierce and his Husker colleagues could take solace in the fact that Sanders never beat them.

That was not the case with one of Pierce's other misses: Jamelle Holieway, a superstar option quarterback from Banning High School in Los Angeles. Pierce was blown away by how good Holieway was on film, so he stopped by his high school to see him, but Holieway was in detention that day, which caused him to be late for practice.

When Holieway finally did arrive, Pierce wasn't impressed with his attitude, so he left. Later that night, Pierce was watching more film of Holieway and started thinking, "Well, maybe I made a mistake on that kid." Just to be sure, he went back to up to Banning High the next day but Holieway was out sick.

Oh well, Pierce then drove down to San Diego to do some recruiting work before coming back to Banning one more time two days later. Holieway was late for practice again. At the end of the evaluation sheet, Pierce frustratingly wrote, "THIS KID CANNOT PLAY FOR US."

Holieway enrolled at Oklahoma, quarterbacking the Sooners to the 1985 national championship his freshman year. Against the Huskers, he ran up and down the field seemingly at will and beat Nebraska two years in a row.

"After the second time he whipped our ass," Pierce said, "somebody put a big picture on my office door of Jamelle Holieway with a message that said, 'Jack says this guy can't play for us.' I still to this day don't know who did that."

Don't dismiss too fast but know that sometimes you will simply miss. The sales game is a fast-moving target. Prospect constantly and qualify diligently. Do your best, but don't beat yourself up when you inevitably make an occasional miss. Even the greatest salespersons in the world are imperfect.

Don't neglect top-of-funnel prospecting even when you're busy closing a couple deals at once.

Your targeted prospects truly should be the people whose problems you are best equipped to solve.

Leads from branding and marketing efforts are nice, but, over time, your future depends on clients you go out and get.

A prospect who does not look so promising at first can become a desirable one if you see him or her through a different lens.

Buy prospecting lists but remember the best information comes from asking a lot of questions of many people.

Log every prospect conversation so you never end up going back on your word.

If you are blessed with support staff, delegate everything except those things that can only be done by a sales pro—you.

By targeting diamonds in the rough, you enjoy access to the prospect without the burden of heavy competition.

Keep an open mind. A prospect might be able to fill more than one client role.

Referrals work better when you really know the referrer.

Never take a strong referral for granted. You still need to earn the business.

The earlier you qualify, the more efficient you'll be.

Part of qualifying is determining if the client is right for you. Don't be star-struck by a too-good-to-be-true prospect.

Personally qualify instead of relying on second-hand information.

While elimination of suspects is the goal of qualifying, be careful not to dismiss too soon.

Chapter 10

POSTCARDS, PHONE CALLS AND SOCIAL MEDIA
Delivering Your Message

When Gary Barnett took over as head coach of the struggling Northwestern Wildcats in 1992, he realized he was accepting a monumental challenge. Northwestern, after all, was 3-8 the previous season, hadn't won a conference championship since 1936 and boasted the nation's longest losing streak (1979–1982). While his first three seasons ended with losing records, Barnett somehow turned the team around, winning the Big 10 Conference championship in both 1995 and 1996.

In addition to good coaching, a rock-solid commitment to recruiting was a big part of the turnaround. To attract quality players to a traditionally poor football team, Barnett and his staff had to work harder, smarter and more creatively. To stand out in an excessively competitive selling environment, Barnett's coaches started sending handwritten notes on a regular basis to their prospects. The hope was that a barrage of personal, handwritten messages would build a strong bond between the prospects and the Northwestern Wildcats.

It worked. Barnett dramatically ratcheted up the caliber of players coming to Evanston, Illinois.

Nowadays, every team writes handwritten notes to star prospects, but back then Barnett and his assistants were unusual. After handwritten notes became popular, teams started using the Internet in the mid-1990s. Then came text messaging. Then came social media.

Anytime there is a new communication medium or a new communication technique, enterprising marketers are going to capitalize on it. As you read this, some football coach is squirreled away in his office concocting a new way to reach players, make an impression on them and prove how much he values them.

Communication Plan

Communication itself is tactical but it grows out of your strategic plan. One of the things you determine when creating your strategic plan is your message—what information you will convey to your target audience. When you have thoroughly established your message, you design the communication plan, which is a list of tactics you will use to deliver the message to your constituencies.

Not only must communication be informative, it should paint a picture of how wonderful your product or service is in such a way that prospects can clearly envision themselves benefitting from it. Your communication must be persuasive in that you are building a case as to how it provides value and solves the prospective client's problems.

Powerfully effective sales communication must clearly address eight key concerns buyers have about products and services:

1. Saves money.
2. Makes money.
3. Reduces stress.
4. Saves time.

5. Is easy to use.
6. Provides security.
7. Boosts ego.
8. Makes them feel good about themselves.

> ## Communication itself is tactical but it grows out of your strategic plan.
>
> ### FROM the PLAYBOOK

Regardless of industry and regardless of a prospect's background, all buyers care about these eight items and expect all or most of them to be satisfied before making a given purchase.

The communication process strings through the entire marketing and sales process. Therefore, communication is a major tactic that salespersons use to climb the relationship depth chart to establish rapport, then develop a relationship that leads to trust and ultimately a signed deal.

Most organizations take a "mixed-media" approach to communication tactics, meaning they use a variety of media, or communication vehicles, to get their message across to prospects.

Mass Media

Use of mass media includes paid and unpaid messages. Of course, "paid" media is called "advertising" and can be print, broadcast, online, outdoor (billboards, bus benches), media sponsorship and product placement. Each organization has to determine which advertising methods are most cost effective for it.

While many companies rely on mass media advertising, college football recruiters generally do not need it. There are a couple reasons why they shy away from advertising. For one thing, the pool of prospective clients—elite high school seniors—comprises only a tiny percentage of the population. Even after segmenting down the audience by targeting select media, most college football teams would still be paying for way too many audience members who are not even close to the target audience. In other words, if you have to pay based on Nielson or Arbitron ratings that include females, adult males, and anyone who isn't a gifted athlete who loves football, you're wasting your money.

The other reason making advertising unnecessary is the incredible, phenomenal amount of earned media major college football teams enjoy. Earned media is coverage for which they pay nothing. Major teams are on television almost every week in the fall. Their games, practices and recruiting activities are covered in traditional and online media outlets.

Twenty-four-hour sports channels such as ESPN cover college football with great intensity. Every major city has at least one all-sports radio station if not several. Countless Internet sites exhaustively analyze every aspect of every major team in America.

Tens of thousands of people pay to watch their favorite team in person each week. Hundreds of thousands—and in some cases millions—of fans walk around wearing sweatshirts, ball caps and jackets with the team logo emblazoned upon them. Those same loyal fans purchase and display an incredibly vast array of other licensed merchandise such as flags, license plate frames and pin-ups. Earned media for college football teams is frankly an embarrassment of riches. Marketers at the typical organization would drool with envy.

Targeted Media

A football team's avalanche of earned media takes care of the marketing needs typically satisfied by advertising to establish brand identity and affinity. Advertising and earned media "soften the target," making it more susceptible to targeted media, which in turn further softens the target for sales efforts. The types of targeted media used by football teams provide a great analogy for any organization's communication plan.

When a high school football player makes contact with a college football team, his name and contact information are entered into a database. The contact can occur in a variety of ways: The high school kid could have attended a summer camp. He could have sent his information to the college football team seeking information. He could have been recommended by his high school coaches, or the college coaches could have found him as a result of their prospecting efforts.

Long before a young man's name and address are entered into the database, the college football team's marketing staff, working in conjunction with the head coach and the recruiting coordinator, created a detailed system of mailings, which includes letters, postcards, brochures and a variety of other skillfully designed communication pieces. Mailings are customized based on a given prospect's demographics such as in-state/out-of-state, class year, skill level, football position played, previous relationship to the team, and other segmentation.

Mailings are managed by a computerized tracker contact system. Based on the prospect's demographic profile and where he is in the selling process, the tracker will spit out mailings or alert someone to make an electronic or telephone contact at an appropriate time. By computerizing this process, football teams maintain and track communications with thousands of prospects at any given time.

Believe it or not, many teams ensure that the more promising prospective players receive a message—either in mailed, electronic or telephone-based form—on a daily basis. Jeff Ketron, coach of Douglas County High School in Castle Rock, Colorado, said he is continually amazed at the volume of daily mail his top players receive.

When it comes to the importance of selling a big-time, blueblood football team to blue-chip athletes, money is no object. Such teams can easily afford the cost of sophisticated and aggressive marketing campaigns. Needless to say, highly coveted high school players are absolutely inundated with mail. So are their parents and coaches. Many teams have extensive mailings that target a prospect's parents and high school coach. No stone is left unturned.

So what do the teams mail to prospects? The answer is simple: seemingly everything. First of all there are brochures, lots of colorful, glossy, expensive-to-produce pieces that trumpet the glory of the football team while painting a picture of the idyllic college life that a stud athlete will enjoy for four years on campus. Some brochures are thick; others are thin.

Detailed text isn't crucial, because (1) visual appeal is the name of the game when it comes to brochures—you want a lot of great photos, with a lot of the school's colors, casting the team in the most positive light possible; and (2) frequency and repetition are the focus. You want the prospects to be constantly reminded of the team and its key marketing messages.

To mix up the onslaught of printed items in a prospect's mailbox, teams will intersperse other items such as postcards, letters and videos. By varying the form of mailings, teams hope to catch attention, stay front-and-center in a prospect's mind and reinforce any brand messages prospects may have absorbed during earlier marketing contacts.

Because the young men receive so much mail every day from so many schools, it's hard to stand out in a kid's mind. He receives so much expensive-looking stuff in his mailbox that he becomes numb to it all and sick of it. Extremely rare is the prospect who would read more than 10 percent of the information he receives.

The marketing environment thus becomes very cluttered, loud and crowded. Because of that, college teams are constantly ratcheting up the creativeness of their mailings and the showiness of their glittering printed pieces desperately hoping to stand out among the sea of sameness that comes from brochures produced by a hundred different college football teams.

For instance, when Bill Callahan was head coach of Nebraska in the mid-2000s, the Husker staff decided to send their regular mailings via Federal Express. The thought was that a hand-delivered FedEx package was far more likely to make an impression. It was effective as Callahan's recruiting prowess exceeded his on-the-field success. Sure, the tactic was expensive, but when you have the marketing budget of a blueblood football team, such a cost is frankly irrelevant. It must have been a good idea, because the NCAA eventually clamped down on it.

Given the need to send so many marketing mailings, an obvious problem arises: What the hell are you going to say? After a handful of mailings, haven't you said all that you have to say? The answer is essentially "yes," so the trick is to say it in different ways.

While some mailings will be very broad and general, others are quite specific. They can also rehash the same information by repackaging it, putting a different spin or angle on it. Over the course of the recruiting cycle, a team could send multiple letters from each assistant coach. One letter might highlight his coaching philosophy; another could talk about how he has developed players; and still another could talk about each of the players he currently has at the prospect's position.

Just imagine all the letters the teams could write, then multiply that by nine assistant coaches, and they obviously cover quite a few days of mailings. This puts no burden on the assistant coaches because marketing staff write the letters for them.

Meanwhile, the coaches supplement the mailings with handwritten notes, personalized cards, phone calls, specialized websites and social media messages.

As it has in all professions, web-based marketing has rapidly ascended as a major communication vehicle for football coaches. Just as YouTube videos have provided great marketing benefit to many companies, persuasive promo videos are of utmost importance in selling the team to blue-chip players. Colleges are spending incredible amounts of money shooting and editing Hollywood-quality videos of their off-the-field amenities and their on-field glory.

Of course, the team's general website is a starting point, but specialized websites are also critically important. Teams will give their prospects personalized passwords granting access to private websites where they can actually see themselves dressed in the college team's uniforms with their last names pictured on the back of the jersey. They can see simulated videos of them running out of the tunnel ready to play their first game.

In a competitive selling environment, communication has to be high tech. If "painting a picture" is one of the primary goals of marketing communication, these websites are powerful tools.

The Internet is the greatest marketplace ever invented because it is available worldwide twenty-four hours a day, is so vast that every imaginable product or service is available, has low barriers to entry and is comprised of billions of prospective customers.

The Internet is also the worst marketplace ever invented because it is available worldwide twenty-four hours a day, is so vast that every imaginable product or service is available, has low barriers to entry and is comprised of billions of prospective customers. It's too loud and crowded, making it hard to stand out and be noticed.

While the Internet (and the social media that are a part of it) provides us with historically unprecedented access, it also provides us with unprecedented clutter. It is easy and challenging at the same time. It has the potential to bring riches but is filled with land mines. You can't afford to take missteps.

When using web-based communication methods or any of the other new media, your branding must be of value and stand on its own merit. In other words, nobody is impressed just because your company, organization or football team has a presence online. Prospective clients are impressed if your presence is interesting, fresh and provides value to them. In an ultra-crowded communication environment in an ultra-competitive market, the quality of your communication must be top shelf.

Each new technology not only provides a new way for coaches to communicate with prospects, it also opens potential loopholes in the NCAA recruiting rules.

Several years ago, text messaging changed football recruiting dramatically. While the NCAA has long had strict rules limiting the number of telephone calls coaches can make to each prospect, there were no limits on the number of times the prospects could call the coaches.

Similarly, there were no limits on text messaging. That meant a coach could text his prospects anytime he wanted.

Often the coaches, would text "call me" to get around the telephone limitations. If you remember, text messaging exploded in popularity several years ago. That meant almost every teenager in America had a text-enabled mobile phone and nimble fingers exercised in cranking out tons of cryptic, often misspelled shorthand messages with amazing dexterity and velocity.

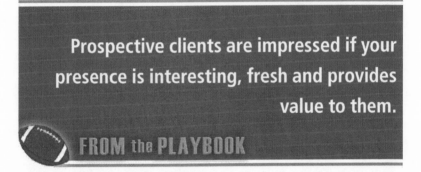

Prospective clients are impressed if your presence is interesting, fresh and provides value to them.

FROM the PLAYBOOK

Besides "call me," coaches used lengthy text threads to carry on detailed conversations. In other words, coaches were climbing the relationship depth chart with many prospects constantly through never-ending texting. Some coaches would wake up a couple times each night just to text prospects. God forbid more than a couple hours would go by in the middle of the night without hearing from your favorite school! During the heyday of texting, every coach on the staff would be sitting in a staff meeting talking football while simultaneously texting recruits.

Eventually texting became overwhelming for both players and coaches, and the NCAA banned it. Players couldn't focus on school, practice or family affairs because their cell phones never stopped buzzing. Coaches felt as if they could never set down their cell phones for fear of losing a prized blue chipper. Many parents of high school football players were horrified when they opened their son's cell phone bill and found hundreds of dollars in texting fees.

The demise of text messaging just happened to coincide with the rise of Facebook and other social media. Facebook doesn't have the same limitations as telephone and texting. Coaches go to prospects' Facebook pages and leave them messages such as, "How are you doing?" "Can you visit campus at a certain time?" "How are your practices going?" These messages are left through Facebook's private message feature.

By publicly posting the messages on a prospect's wall, the college could get into hot water with the NCAA. Several coaches have found that they can reach prospects faster through Facebook than using traditional email or phone calls. The young prospects appear to be more responsive to social media–based communication.

Of course, the football program created a Facebook fan page where the staff can post photos, videos and promote upcoming events.

Work the Phones

While the use of mass media and targeted marketing set the stage, more direct and personal approaches are needed to advance the process, to move the prospect up the relationship depth chart. In most businesses, college football recruiting included, the telephone still plays an important role in the sales process.

Prospects can call the coaches whenever and as often as they like, but each coach is limited to one phone call per prospect per week. Assistant coaches make sure they never miss calling each of their prospects each week, because the calls are so important for climbing the relationship depth chart and for simply staying at the front of the prospect's mind as he is peppered with sales messages from competing schools.

Because the calls are so precious, smart coaches prepare in advance. They make a plan for the call—what they want to discuss, questions they want answered and the general order of the call.

In early telephone contacts, the coach and prospect try to get to know each other and establish rapport. Coaches ask about family members, preferences, hobbies, use of free time and other basic questions, such as, "What other sports do you play?" and "How's your season going so far?"

Once past the basics, coaches deliberately try to build a relationship by going deeper with more meaningful conversations. Once that happens, the phone calls are less awkward, less like a job interview, and frankly less like a "sales call." If trust is established over the course of many conversations, the coach has a legitimate shot at earning the player's signature.

Each assistant coach on a staff is assigned a group of prospects. He "farms" those prospects and takes pride of ownership, working extra hard to climb the relationship depth chart with each of them. A player will often refer to the assigned assistant coach as his "recruiting coach" as he is typically not the coach who will be the kid's position coach once he enrolls at the college and officially joins the team.

Those assistant coaches who are star recruiters not only have engaging personalities, they are organized. They know everything about all their prospects and can instantly answer any question about those prospects when asked by the head coach or recruiting coordinator. Assistants that are also great recruiters are worth their weight in gold.

According to Rivals.com, the best recruiters in 2012 were D.J. Durkin, Florida; Lance Anderson, Stanford; Jerry Azzinaro, Oregon; David Beatty, Texas A&M; and Dameyune Craig, Florida State.

The head coach doesn't call players as often as the assistant coaches do. At most schools, head coaches expect their assistants to prep them thoroughly before making calls.

"I told my staff, 'Don't ever blame me for losing a kid,'" said former Ohio State coach John Cooper. "Whatever I need to do to help you recruit the kid, you let me know. If you want me to call him, you want me to write him, you want me to go see him, you tell me. So every Sunday afternoon, my recruiting coordinator would give me a list of kids to call that week. I'd start Sunday night. It might be a dozen; it might be fifteen or twenty. It might take me 'til Thursday to get them all contacted, but I would contact them sometime during that week."

When national championship–winning coach Phillip Fulmer was leading the Tennessee Volunteers, he wanted all calls to be of substance, so he had his assistants keep logs of their conversations with players. He would review these logs before he personally called the young men.

"I had every coach give me three [players to call] each week," Fulmer said, "so if there were nine coaches, that would be twenty-seven calls. We would have all the information on a sheet, so if a girlfriend was important, I would ask about the girlfriend. If Granddad was a part of the equation, then I would ask to speak to Granddad while on the phone. If the young man had an illness in the family, you be sure to ask about the family. You try to, as much as you can, make it personal to him, because the kids get tired of the calls, where they don't look forward to your call or won't take your calls."

Yep, just like the rest of us, football coaches sometimes have a hard time getting prospects to take their calls and an even harder time getting them to return voicemails.

Voicemail

Because of the rapidly increasing clutter and excessive communication in today's marketplace, the world is now suffering a serious epidemic. It's the highly contagious disease of blowing off and completely ignoring voicemails.

Are you frustrated about the lack of voicemails you leave that are never returned? If so, you're not alone. According to Brian Sullivan, author of the book *20 Days to the Top*, prospects only return 5 to 10 percent of all voicemails—fewer than one in ten! Despite the shockingly low response rate, Sullivan believes you must keep leaving those recorded messages. In fact, many of the most successful salespersons in the world regularly leave voicemail after voicemail until they finally get the prospect to call back or they actually manage to catch him or her live on the phone.

According to Jill Konrath, author of *SNAP Selling* and *Selling to Big Companies*, many professionals are having to leave ten or more voicemails before receiving a call-back from a C-level executive. Konrath doesn't believe this is a function of executive-level rudeness or arrogance, rather it's the fact that these people are "crazy busy" and simply can't get back to calls that don't fall into the "emergency" category.

Prospects are more likely to return your voicemails if you make them interesting. First of all, Konrath recommends you never say you're calling to "touch base" or "check in." Those are useless reasons to waste a prospect's time. Make sure you always say something of value.

Remember that the prospect you are calling defines what is valuable, not you. How do you know what they value? Sullivan recommends you do a little research on the person and reference something unique about them. Doing so will show that you cared enough to learn about the person and will grab their attention because you're talking their language.

Next, Sullivan advises that you hint what benefit the person will receive if they return your call and then spark curiosity by saying you have something to share with them that they will find valuable or interesting. If appropriate, you might want to offer a gift, something for free, such as a free report, counseling session or market advice. Then follow up with an assertive close encouraging them to call you back.

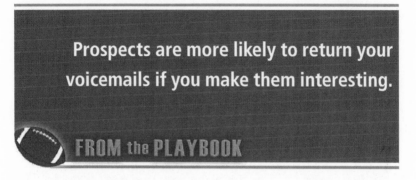

Prospects are more likely to return your voicemails if you make them interesting.

FROM the PLAYBOOK

After all that, you still might not hear from them. When that's the case, leave another message and be prepared to keep doing so. Because everyone has become so busy and distracted in our cluttered communication environment, it has sadly become acceptable to delete voicemails without returning the call because the prospect assumes you'll just call back. If you don't follow through and keep calling back, you'll probably never catch the person. When dialing for dollars on the phone, you have to keep dialing. Don't stop. Be assertive, because rarely do would-be clients call and volunteer to give you money.

While big-name coaches such as Urban Meyer, Chip Kelly or Lane Kiffin usually succeed in catching a prospect's attention when they call, lesser-known head coaches and assistants have a harder time. If a prospect simply isn't interested in their teams, and sick of excessive phone calls, even a Meyer, Kelly or Kiffin message might be ignored. Unless you're the Urban Meyer of your profession, plan on leaving a lot of voicemails.

Gathering Intelligence

In a competitive selling situation, communication is often not completely straightforward. Sellers and buyers sometimes don't see eye to eye, and while sellers are ideally supposed to see themselves as "buyer coaches" and "purchase facilitators," sometimes, the two sides find themselves at odds or in conflict.

In certain industries, sellers and buyers automatically operate in an adversarial setting. Both sides hold their cards close to the vest, not wanting to give up negotiation options. Some buyers keep one potential vendor on the line as a back-up plan, a decoy or as a means of gathering information they can use in negotiations with the real, preferred provider. To make the playing field even more treacherous, one provider may deliberately spread misinformation about another in order to sabotage the competition and confuse the buyers.

Competitive marketplaces can become perilous because there are so many moving parts, competing interests and hidden agendas to monitor and manage. The situation is somewhat analogous to the espionage, reconnaissance and counter-intelligence in which nations engage.

If you are going to play such a game, borrow a page from the Central Intelligence Agency. You better have your own intelligence and counter-intelligence plans as well as the intestinal fortitude to carry out those plans. Idealistic people, especially those on the outside of a given industry, find such behavior to be unseemly. Practical people realize that you sometimes have to play rough to win highly contested battles.

Football coaches use a variety of tricks to gather intelligence. Some are compliant with NCAA rules; others not so much. Most commonly, they will have a friend pretend to be a sports journalist and call prospects saying they need to do interviews for news stories. If they're not getting enough information from the prospective player himself, coaches have been known to call girlfriends and best buddies and ask, "What's so-and-so thinking? Where do you think he'll end up playing?"

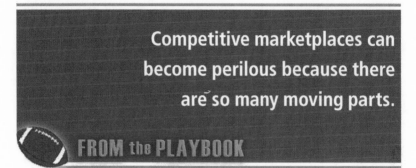

Competitive marketplaces can become perilous because there are so many moving parts.

FROM the PLAYBOOK

As an assistant coach at Colorado in the mid-1980s, Gary Barnett was recruiting Erich Kissick, a promising running back out of Kansas City. Barnett called Kissick's brother one night, and it became apparent that the brother didn't know who Barnett was.

"I said, 'Tell me what Erich's thinking, what schools,'" Barnett recalled, "and he said he really likes this guy from Colorado, and that was me, so I knew I was in."

Of course, those intelligence gathering calls sometimes yield bad news. The source might say, "He's hoping to hear from Notre Dame, or he's gonna go to SC or he ain't gonna leave home," Barnett said. "Somebody will tell you the truth because they're flattered you called them, that you got them involved in the process. A kid will always tell somebody the truth, and it's usually somebody close to them. You have to find out who that is."

Gathering intelligence helps coaches determine how much time and money to put into a given prospect. Only go after those prospects who have not mentally committed to someone else, have a strong interest in you and are willing to overcome any obstacles such as geographic distance between their home and the college campus.

Cooper had a favorite trick he would sometimes use on out-of-state prospects.

"I'd have somebody on my staff that wasn't recruiting him, maybe another coach, call the kid and tell him he was from another school," he said. "'Hey, I'm from Montana State' or Washington State or someplace way far off that you know the kid is not interested in. You say, 'Hey, we'd like to have you come out and visit, have you see our campus.'"

The kid might say it's too far away and that he has already narrowed his choices to a couple schools. If that was the case, Cooper's secret staff member would probe a little more. If the kid mentioned that he was seriously considering Ohio State, Cooper and his assistants would ratchet up their efforts.

"You have a third party do your dirty work," Cooper said, "and you find out if the kid is telling you the truth or not."

Sometimes, you can gather intel by guessing what you think might be happening with your prospect or competitor, calling them up and asking a loaded question. Let's say you manage a shopping mall. You and the manager of a competing mall tend to go head-to-head trying to attract the same retail tenants. Although you have been trying to attract Brooks Brothers to your mall, you have a hunch you're losing out to the competitor. You could always call the manager of the other mall and say, "Congrats, I hear you landed Brooks Brothers." After saying that, wait and listen. What the other manager says and how he or she reacts is a sneaky way to do reconnaissance.

Although it is often in their best interest to remain silent, most people can't help themselves. It's human nature to share and communicate. It's also human nature to brag, show off and be the person in the know. If you manipulate that natural tendency to your advantage, you can be one of the best-informed marketers or salespersons in your peer group.

Some people might not consider it ethical, but gathering intelligence is a necessary fact of life in highly competitive industries that operate in loud and crowded marketplaces.

A Personal Touch

No matter how well developed your communication plan is and how sophisticated your communication tactics are, always remember that conveying messages is ultimately a very human endeavor. The personal touch must be infused throughout the communication process in order to move your prospects up the relationship depth chart.

> Gathering intelligence is a necessary fact of life in highly competitive industries that operate in loud and crowded marketplaces.

FROM the PLAYBOOK

Find a way to personalize marketing. It touches a person's soul because it shows that you care and that they are important prospects worthy of your extra time and special effort.

As a powerhouse football feeder high school in Texas, Cedar High hosts more than its fair share of college coaches each year. Head coach Joey McGuire has a front-row view and an active role in the recruiting process. Those collegiate coaches who take the time to write thank you notes, especially handwritten ones, make quite an impression on McGuire.

Coaches who have a personal touch, good interpersonal skills and an obvious appreciation for other people really are the most successful football salesmen.

When McGuire thinks about all the famous coaches who have recruited his players, one in particular really stands out: Mack Brown. The University of Texas head coach is legendary for his personal touch and his diligent communication with anyone he encounters. Brown is master of the handwritten note.

"One time a graduate assistant at UNLV went and watched Texas practice for their bowl game, and Mack wrote him a note thanking him for coming," McGuire said. "People who are truly successful make you feel good being around them, and you want to do something for them in return."

Your communication plan should be designed only after you have established your message.

Communication tactics should address eight key concerns buyers have about your product: saves money; makes money; reduces stress; saves time; is easy to use; provides security; boosts ego; makes them feel good about themselves.

If you want to make an impression, your marketing-message frequency may have to be higher than you ever imagined.

To stand out among a sea of marketing mailers, try using an odd shape or size or even pop a letter in a FedEx envelope.

Just because you have new communication technology doesn't mean you can stray from proven, bed-rock principles of marketing.

During early sales calls, establish rapport. Focus on relationship building in later calls.

Because prospects return fewer than 10 percent of sales-oriented voicemails, make them interesting and never say you're calling just to "touch base."

Consider using a third party to dig up information in order to determine if your prospect is telling you the truth.

Chapter 11

PAINTING A PICTURE
The Sales Presentation

Andre Johnson was a blue-chip cornerback in the early 1980s at Forest Brooks High School in Houston. Legendary Oklahoma coach Barry Switzer, who had a long track record of pulling great players out of the Houston area, was hot on Johnson's trail and believed the young man was good enough to start for the Sooners as a true freshman.

Switzer dispatched one of his assistants to Johnson's house to meet the family, according to Switzer's 1990 autobiography *Bootlegger's Boy*. After being chewed out and ordered off the property, it became clear to the assistant coach that Johnson's mother hated the University of Oklahoma and had no interest in sending her young pride-and-joy up north to Norman. The assistant walked away with his tail between his legs and returned home.

When Switzer heard the story, he sensed a challenge.

On the return trip, Switzer accompanied the assistant. Upon seeing the men approach the house for an unannounced visit, Mrs. Johnson blocked the front door and just let them have it—shouting and cussing about every rotten thing she had ever heard about the Sooners as well as Coach Switzer in particular.

At that point, Switzer writes in his autobiography, "My nose picked up a familiar odor coming from her kitchen ... that took me back to my childhood."

"Is that cracklin' bread I smell? By golly, it is, isn't it, Mrs. Johnson?" Switzer said.

Cracklin' bread is a long-time tradition in some African-American households. The bread is baked with pork fat to give it a rich taste. Although Caucasian, Switzer grew up in an African-American community. After telling Mrs. Johnson how much he missed his "black grandmama's" cracklin' bread, Switzer kindly asked Mrs. Johnson for a taste. She obliged.

As the old saying goes, "If a camel gets his nose in the tent, his body will soon follow."

Before long, Switzer and his assistant were laughing with the family, sharing stories and painting a picture of how young Andre Johnson would become a star at Oklahoma. When the two coaches left the home, they not only had their fill of cracklin' bread, they had something even better: Andre Johnson's commitment. It was an impromptu sales presentation that ended up being highly effective.

While Switzer's cracklin' bread experience would not define the traditional corporate sales presentation, it worked for him. He found a way to disarm a skeptical prospect. He related to the prospect on a personal level. He was persuasive and persistent but not obnoxious or overbearing. He found what mattered to the prospect and his mother and focused on that as he shared the benefits of his product. He painted a picture so bright and vivid that the player and his family could all envision wonderful outcomes. He worked the relationship depth chart—rapport, relationship, trust and signed deal—in one single encounter. That kind of sales speed is rare indeed, but it's sure nice when it goes that quickly.

Purpose

A sales presentation is your pitch. More specifically, the presentation is your formal chance to present how your company's attributes are beneficial to the prospect. It's a chance to show how you provide value and how you can solve a prospect's unique problems. Sales presentations tend to occur after earlier preparatory sales work has been completed.

Before meeting in person, the prospect has probably been exposed to the company's brand through the mass media. The company has no doubt sent marketing materials via mail or electronic means and communicated over the telephone. Ideally, much of the detective work would have been completed before the formal pitch. During pre-meeting phone conversations, the salesperson should have asked the prospects numerous questions to find their points and determine what they truly value.

The presentation is another step in your quest to move a prospect up the relationship depth chart. Although the presentation is your chance to highlight yourself and your company, there is still plenty of opportunity to listen. That's important, because you can never know enough about a prospect and listening strengthens relationships.

In business, a sales presentation can occur at your office, the prospect's office or a neutral venue. Same thing goes in college football sales, but typically they occur on campus or at home in the player's living room.

"Going into a home, we want to first make sure everyone's comfortable," said Purdue assistant coach Donn Landholm. "It's a chance for us to meet parents face-to-face and grandparents, brothers, sisters—whoever the young man wants us to meet."

During the presentation, Landholm said he and his colleagues will go over a wide range of information, some of which is foundational in nature such as academic programs, degree plans, student housing and transportation to and from campus.

After the basics are covered, it's time paint a picture of what life is like as a Boilermaker football player. They'll talk about how the player will use the football facilities, game day environment, what position the kid could play and where he might fit as a freshman on the team's depth chart.

While the word *presentation* implies that the seller is delivering a formal speech to the buyer, a sales presentation should not be one-sided. It must be customized and adapted to each prospect's needs. As the inspiring Zig Ziglar once said, "People do things for their reasons, not yours."

Focus on what the prospect values during the presentation and take time to draw them in by asking clarifying questions and tying things back to what they told you during earlier communications.

The Sequence

There are many ways to structure a sales presentation, but it's always best to use those tried-and-true methods that have stood the test of time. Whether you're pitching a football team to an elite blue chipper or hoping to convince a *Fortune* 500 firm to bring you on as a consultant, the sales presentation must follow a logical format that feels right to the client and syncs with their sense of order. The approach needs to build a persuasive case efficiently and effectively. A sales presentation must conform to human nature, which has remained static for ages. If you use human nature in your favor, the presentation is more likely to be successful. If you fight human nature, you're engaging in futility.

> ## If you fight human nature, you're engaging in futility.
>
> FROM the PLAYBOOK

Back in the 1930s, Professor Alan Monroe of Purdue University essentially married the art of presentation with the psychology of persuasion. The result of his scholarly work became known as Monroe's Motivated Sequence, a concept that is still pertinent for modern sales professionals.

The concept was originally intended to help orators structure persuasive speeches, but it's equally applicable to sales presentations of all kinds, whether you're presenting to a large group or an audience of one single decision maker. As you plot your sales presentations, keep Monroe in mind.

Monroe's Motivated Sequence advises presenters to build their case using five distinct steps completed in exact order. First comes the attention-getter in which you introduce a problem by jolting the audience with something bold and unexpected—a story, quote, disturbing statistic or a big "bet-you-didn't-know" statement.

Step two is need. This is where you prove the problem is significant and worthy of the listener's attention. You also want to cast the need as something that won't be solved without the right approach by the right person or organization.

Monroe's third step is known as satisfaction. Here you prove that you have the solution to the previously mentioned problem. In step four, visualization, you paint a picture of how wonderful life will look in the future if they accept and implement your solution. You also portray how terrible things will be if they ignore your recommendations.

Finally, in step five, you tell the audience what action they should take. This is the big finish, where you powerfully and motivationally tell them to go do it!

Monroe's Motivated Sequence

1. Attention getter
2. Need
3. Solution/satisfaction
4. Visualization
5. Action

Think about your sales presentations and ask yourself how they fit into Monroe's outline. Are you skipping a step or two? Many salespersons start with step three, the solution, without making the case strongly enough that a solution is necessary in the first place. Don't fight human nature; structure your persuasive pitch in such a way that makes the prospect more acquiescent to what you are selling. Make them yearn for your solution intensely before you tell them about it.

Selling Softly

In the vast majority of cases, in the vast majority of businesses, hard selling simply does not work. Thank God! One of the reasons so many people fear a career in sales is the disdain they have for the hard sell. Don't worry, because chances are good that hard selling is actually counter-productive. One of the most liberating messages in this book is that selling softly works better than beating your prospect's head against the wall.

Although you want to avoid hard selling, that's not to say you should be passive and meek. On the contrary, you must be persuasive in your communication and persistent in your effort. Just don't be obnoxious and overbearing. Nobody should be the type of salesperson who would appear in a *Saturday Night Live* parody.

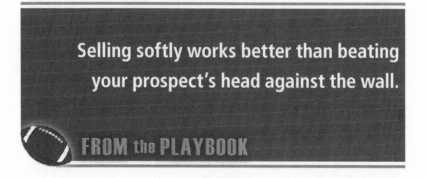

Selling softly works better than beating your prospect's head against the wall.

FROM the PLAYBOOK

Effective sales professionals climb the relationship ladder. They are interested in people and focused on providing valuable solutions. They are buying coaches. They are transaction facilitators who guide prospects to those products and services that provide the best value and solve the biggest problems. When you focus on coaching and facilitating your prospects, the hard sell is not necessary; in fact, it would feel very foreign and out of place if you tried it.

Preparation

"It's not the will to win that matters—everyone has that. It's the will to prepare to win that matters," said Paul "Bear" Bryant, perhaps the greatest head coach in football history.

Preparation is important in all walks of life, but in the game of football, it's patently obvious when you fail to do it. Just as he must prepare the team for on-field competition, a coach must prepare himself for every sales presentation. You should too.

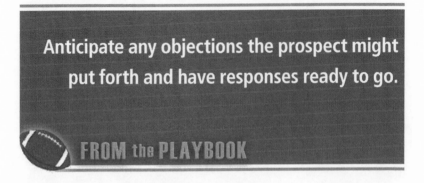

Anticipate any objections the prospect might put forth and have responses ready to go.

FROM the PLAYBOOK

When you consider what's riding on your sales presentations and how important a positive outcome would be, it makes sense to prepare diligently.

First, study your targeted prospect. Make sure you know everything you can about him or her. The better your background research, the more likely you will be to prove your ability to solve their problems and provide what they value. Go over all the notes you logged during your previous communications with the prospect to make sure you're not omitting anything important in the presentation. Figure out what critical pieces of information you still need to learn about the prospect and have a list of questions that specifically would yield such answers.

Anticipate any objections the prospect might put forth and have responses ready to go. Determine what parts of your sales presentations are just "boilerplate" material and which parts are to be customized. Spend time getting ready for the customized part, because you want it to sound natural and not awkward.

If you're new to sales, or you have become a little rusty since your last presentation, there's nothing wrong with practicing before a big meeting. You could always role-play with a colleague or friend. Of course, on-field success in football is totally dependent on practice, so it's no surprise that many new football coaches practice before their first in-person sales calls.

Casting a Vision

When you sit down in front of a would-be client for the big presentation, remember it's show time. Sure, a sales presentation should have some give-and-take, question-and-answer, but don't forget to put on a bit of a show. It's time to borrow a little from the theatrical world. All the hard work that you have invested in researching the prospect and preparing for the meeting is analogous to the rehearsals a theater troupe puts in before a live production.

When the curtain rises on your presentation, be ready to delight the audience. While we want to be genuine and honest, remember that show business sells. Sizzle sells. Excitement sells. Be energetic. Be positive. Be interesting. Paint a picture of how wonderful it will be to do business with you and your company. Cast a vision of how much the prospect's life will improve because you have the perfect solution to his or her problem.

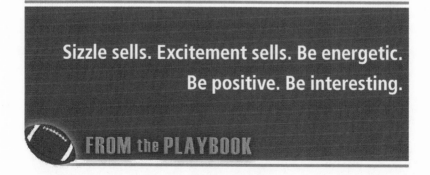

Sizzle sells. Excitement sells. Be energetic. Be positive. Be interesting.

FROM the PLAYBOOK

While you're putting on that great show, don't go too long. As they say in the theater world, leave them wanting more. Too much of a good thing is actually bad. You want your great presentation to end within a reasonable amount of time, so prospects don't become bored, and so you have enough time for questions and answers and casual conversation, which helps strengthen relationships.

If you are pitching more than one person, make sure to focus on all of them. It can feel natural to focus all or most of your attention on the supposed decision maker, but that can be a fatal flaw. For one thing, you never can be sure who will really make the decision. Just because the CEO is in the room doesn't mean that the vice president is automatically not the decision maker. The CEO may just be there out of curiosity and could be planning to have the trusted VP decide.

Just because the football player is in the room doesn't mean that the mother is not the real decision maker. If you focus too much on one person, the others present could feel slighted and disrespected. That never bodes well for you.

Men have to be particularly careful not to focus too much on the male audience members. Even in today's generally egalitarian business culture, it is still not uncommon to see male salespersons focus far more attention on the guys during presentations. In many cases, this could be a subconscious mistake as opposed to a deliberate one. Either way, it hurts your chances if a woman in the room is the real decision maker. Even if she is not, she may have tremendous influence over the decision maker. If she feels you are prejudiced or disrespectful, she just might sabotage your chances.

Spend at least some time highlighting value-added benefits during the formal presentation. These are things that aren't foundational to sealing the deal but can help "push it over the top."

For instance, a given blue-chip athlete could be focused primarily on going to a school where he has the best chance of winning a national championship. In his case, value-added benefits could be these: 1. Earn your degree; 2. Full-ride, four-year scholarship; 3. Tons of possible girlfriends on campus; 4. Shot at making an NFL team; 5. Enjoy the respect and admiration of millions of fans; 6. Being set for life, because so many influential alumni like to take care of former players from their alma mater.

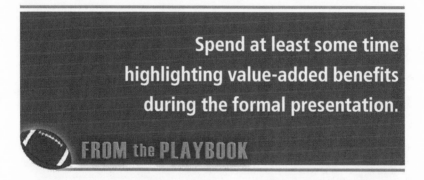

Spend at least some time highlighting value-added benefits during the formal presentation.

FROM the PLAYBOOK

If you plan to use audio-visual aids during your sales presentation, be very careful. Too often sales professionals will invest great effort in their PowerPoint deck and too little on the delivery. One of the biggest mistakes you can make is to sit there and read what appears on the screen. If you use PowerPoint or something like it, incorporate it into the pitch but don't make it the main focus.

Nothing is more dull, boring and awkwardly artificial than a sales presenter who simply goes over a PowerPoint, especially if you are presenting to a very small group of people. For more intimate sales presentations with only one or two prospects present, some reps are choosing to use an iPad or some other tablet device to illustrate key points.

The desirable picture you paint should linger in the prospect's mind long after you're gone. To provide a longer lasting vision, your message should be reinforced by a leave-behind packet that might include attractive materials designed specifically for use in sales presentations. These leave-behinds should have the same design as your website, videos and other printed materials, but are created with the intent that they will be viewed by prospects as they reflect on your in-person meeting. Leave-behinds can be electronic or print.

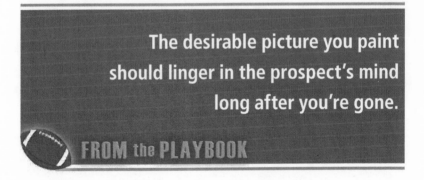

The desirable picture you paint should linger in the prospect's mind long after you're gone.

FROM the PLAYBOOK

Living Room Style

Whether he's making a pitch on campus or sitting down with a prospect and his parents in the family's living room, each coach has his own presentation style. While you put on a bit of a show during a sales presentation, it's still important to be your authentic self. If you aren't genuine, savvy prospects will probably pick up on it and become suspicious of you and your intentions.

When Tom Osborne and Barry Switzer were competing on the field and in prospects' living rooms throughout the 1980s, each man was true to his personal style. Switzer would dress in an athletic warm-up, sit down on the floor with the kid, have a beer with the dad and put his arm around the mom. Osborne was more business-oriented, more likely to focus on the important information and was generally dressed professionally. Both approaches worked just fine because they appealed to different prospects. The key is to avoid being someone you are not.

When sitting in a prospect's living room, most coaches try to strike a balance between plain-spoken honesty and enough showmanship to pique the kid's interest and entertain the parents.

As he visited players' houses over the years, former Colorado and Northwestern head coach Gary Barnett acknowledged that different types of families required minor adjustments in his approach, but he believed in being himself and telling the truth.

"I always told the family that most people can handle the truth," Barnett said. "They might not like what I said after that, but I always wanted to be honest with them. If I knew that a kid was probably going to be moved to tight end, I would tell them. It cost me recruits, and my assistant coaches were always on me for doing that. I just didn't want [players] to have any surprises. I didn't want anybody to ever come back and say that's not what you said in the living room."

An effective living room style means you are also capable of adjusting to different environments and thinking quickly on the fly. When delivering a sales presentation in a residential environment, you don't have the same tools and amenities that you have at your disposal in a properly equipped conference room. You are also subject to a variety of distractions in the house and in the neighborhood.

"Try to control the setting as much as you can," said Phillip Fulmer, who served as Tennessee's head coach from 1992 to 2008. "You say politely, 'May I turn the television down?' Turn the radio down if it's interfering. I've even asked to leave the living room and go to a table if there were kids playing, so you could have adult time."

Fulmer wanted prospective players and their parents to know that the visit was a business meeting focused on how the University of Tennessee could benefit the young man and how he, in turn, could contribute to the team. Much of Fulmer's pitch focused on social, academic and spiritual growth.

"It wasn't just about how many touchdowns he was going to score or how many tackles he was going to make or even about getting drafted," he said. "We were there to sell the total experience. That appealed to most people."

Whether you're trying to sign football players or land great clients for your business, sales presentations generally work better when you already have a relationship established. For coaches, that means you have talked to a student on the phone, via social media and perhaps hosted him as a participant in one of your camps. For other sales professionals, it could mean you were referred, met the person at a chamber of commerce networking event or had a promising telephone conversation.

That said, some sales presentations occur a little earlier in the process, well before you have made a significant climb up the relationship depth chart. In such a situation, take some time to get to know the prospect better and really work on the first two positions of the relationship depth chart— rapport and relationship.

When coaches visit the homes of prospects they don't know so well, it makes sense to find out what the player values and what aspects of the football team and school most interest them. The presentation would then be immediately customized to the player's interests.

If you keep an open mind, sales presentations can bring pleasant surprises. When Barnett was coaching at Northwestern in the 1990s, he came upon Bryan LaBelle, an intriguing prospect from Bellevue, Washington. LaBelle was a big, athletic blue chipper with limitless potential as a college offensive lineman. While he was a great-looking kid who would be a boost to any team that got him, Barnett didn't think he had any chance of landing him.

As he was preparing for the visit to LaBelle's home, Barnett thought, "Do I really want to fly all the way out to Washington to do this?" Despite the lingering doubt, he made the trip. Barnett arrived at the LaBelle family house and conducted the normal living-room sales presentation during which the parents commented about how "far away" Northwestern was. Such comments obviously concerned Barnett.

Suddenly, out of nowhere, young LaBelle said, "By the way, coach, I am coming to Northwestern."

It was such a shock that Barnett almost fell out of his chair. That business trip to Washington paid off for Barnett as LaBelle went on to play quite well for Northwestern and was drafted by the New Orleans Saints.

Role Playing

Sales presentations can be more effective when more than one representative of the selling organization present together. Presenting in pairs or maybe even trios can relieve the pressure on a given presenter and make the presentation more interesting for the prospect(s).

But remember that too many cooks in the kitchen spoil the dish. Don't have too many presenters. In most cases, you don't want more than three presenters because then the presentation can feel crowded and clumsy. When a half dozen presenters are involved, it feels as if the presenting company spends more time introducing staff members than focusing on the would-be clients.

Tag-teaming a presentation can allow you to play different roles: good cop versus bad cop; straight man versus clown;

cautiously reluctant versus overly optimistic. Football coaches do this all the time during in-home visits.

One coach will say, "You're going to have to work awfully hard to earn a starting position." The other coach balances it by saying to the first coach, "Aw, come on, of course, he's going to start! Tell me you ain't ever met such a great athlete!"

Such game playing can make the presentation more enjoyable and relaxing. Of course, role playing in a professional setting has to be more sophisticated than that done for seventeen-year-old boys. Dealing with sophisticated business people requires better acting skills, but in certain circumstances, role playing can be powerfully effective.

Some role playing is less overtly dramatic. Not everybody has to be a salesperson in order to sell. In other words, every organization needs at least some people who can be the stereotypically gregarious, assertive person whose picture ought to be printed next to the word *salesman* in the dictionary. Other people in the organization are role players. While the typical "sales" guy will probably lead the effort, other team members can be brought in for informational purposes or to reassure a prospect about the quality and depth of the organization's talent pool.

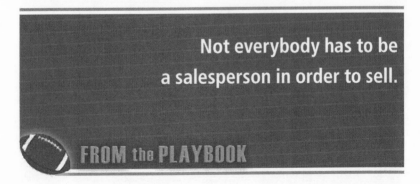

Not everybody has to be a salesperson in order to sell.

FROM the PLAYBOOK

Personalize It

Whether meeting a player for the first time in his home or on campus in the football complex, it's important for coaches to relate to the player and his family in a personal way. Prospects come from a wide variety of demographic and cultural backgrounds. A prospect's life experience is often vastly different from a coach's.

Because coaches at major football schools are famous and highly paid, they can be intimidating especially to low-income families in which nobody has ever gone to college. In such a situation, a wise coach will make damned sure he does nothing to make the prospect or any of his family members feel inadequate or embarrassed.

Even when you're not talking about big factors, such as socioeconomic status, a sales professional can do little things during a sales presentation to put prospects at ease and let them know that you care about them as people.

For example, during another recruiting effort at Northwestern, Barnett signed Ray Robey, a talented defensive lineman out of Rockford, Illinois. When Barnett arrived at the Robey family home, he noticed Ray's father had a foot injury requiring him to have his shoe off, foot wrapped and his leg propped up. To show solidarity with Ray's dad, Barnett took off one shoe when visiting. He wanted to make an obvious, visual point that he related to players and the people they cared about. Barnett believes the gesture had a huge impact on young Ray.

It is often the little gestures that make a big impact in the sales game. A personal touch or something special can make a sales presentation more memorable for prospects.

Hall of Fame former coach John Cooper built quite a reputation as a football salesman while recruiting so many star players to Ohio State in the 1990s. He used a number of techniques to make his visits more memorable.

On a couple occasions, Cooper would get a school picture of the prospect's kid brother or little sister. Any time he would come to visit the prospect's house, Cooper would show the younger sibling the picture and say, "Hey, I'm still carrying your picture around." The next thing Cooper would know, the youngster would be sitting right next to him. The mother and older brother would be thrilled, because he gave attention to the younger kids.

Cooper had a coaching friend who had an interesting way to put a memorable exclamation point on a home visit. The coach would pin a note on the kid's pillow: "Hey, Johnny, get a good night's rest tonight. I'll be thinking of you," and then the coach would sign his name. Little things can make a big impression when you're trying to get an edge in a brutally competitive environment.

A sales presentation is your formal chance to present how your company's attributes are beneficial to the prospect. It's a chance to show how you provide value and how you would solve a prospect's unique problems.

Before a sales meeting, do your background detective work and establish initial relationships via telephone.

Don't just focus on features and benefits. Think about moving the prospect up the relationship depth chart.

A presentation isn't all talk. Make sure to listen as well.

Structure your sales presentation logically and persuasively, taking advantage of human nature.

When you coach and facilitate your prospects, the hard sell is not necessary.

Determine what part of your sales presentation is boilerplate and which part is to be customized. Focus your preparation on the customized part.

Cast a vision of how great life will be with your product or service by using a little showmanship during the sales presentation.

Highlighting value-added benefits can be just enough to push the deal over the top.

Over-reliance on audio/visual aids is one of the biggest mistakes you could make.

Tell the truth, communicate earnestly and be yourself but be the most appealing version of yourself.

Two presenters are usually better than one, but three presenters can feel like a crowd.

Doing something a little special and out of the ordinary makes prospects feel as if you truly value them and their business.

Chapter 12

WHAT SIDE OF THE BALL DO YOU WANT TO PLAY ON?

Listening and Empathy

At the beginning of 1991, Marshall Faulk was a wanted man. He was wanted by many of the nation's most prestigious football schools. He had just finished a stellar senior season as a star player at George Washington Carver High School in New Orleans, and college coaches were camped outside his front door.

Faulk had a rough childhood, growing up in one of America's most notorious housing projects. As a youngster, football was his passion. From an early age, he was good at the game and caught the eye of several college scouts. Recruiters courted him as a junior, and by the time he was tearing up the fields as a senior, scholarship offers were pouring in.

It was obvious that football was not only his passion, it was his ticket out of New Orleans's infamous Ninth Ward. But the big question was what lucky school would land this athlete and his rare combination of speed, agility and balance.

As 1991 National Signing Day drew nearer, Coach Tom Osborne and his staff at the University of Nebraska were high on Faulk and confident he soon would be wearing the Huskers' scarlet and cream. After all, Faulk liked Nebraska.

So did his mother, his guidance counselor, and even his English teacher, who had a great deal of influence on him.

Husker recruiting coordinator Jack Pierce worked hard to develop a relationship with Faulk and figured out which people played a role in his life. Like all good salespersons, Pierce built a relationship with those who influenced Faulk. Several Nebraska coaches, including Osborne, stopped by to visit.

During the in-home visit, Osborne knew he made a connection with Faulk and his family. As an experienced football salesman, he could feel it when personalities clicked in a player's living room. There was no doubt in the coach's mind that Faulk and his mother felt good about Nebraska. In fact, Osborne admits that he thought it was almost a done deal—Faulk was practically on his way to Lincoln, Nebraska.

On National Signing Day, Marshall Faulk signed with San Diego State University, far away from and far less prestigious than the football powerhouses that were courting him. Osborne was shocked.

"It turned out we had been recruiting him as a defensive back, which most people had," Osborne said. "But Marshall deep down always wanted to be a running back." Of course, SDSU told Marshall they would be delighted to have him play running back, but with his 4.35 speed, Nebraska would have loved to have him in its backfield too. Faulk had the talent to play either side of the ball quite effectively.

"Although we had been very thorough, and we had done our homework," Osborne said, "we hadn't asked him a key question: 'Marshall, which side of the ball do you want to play on?' That's why it's really important to do a lot of listening. I think we could have had Marshall Faulk if we had just recruited him as a running back."

The rest, as they say, is history. Faulk flourished at SDSU, rushing for more than 1,400 yards and scoring 23 touchdowns in just his freshman year. During a thirteen-year professional career with the Indianapolis Colts and St. Louis Rams, Faulk amassed a whopping 12,279 rushing yards and scored 136 touchdowns, some of the most impressive running back statistics in NFL history.

Surely, it must have been frustrating for Husker coaches watching Faulk's career from afar, knowing that they came so close to signing him. It's a feeling that many coaches have been forced to deal with because they didn't do an adequate job closing the deal on a certain player.

It's a feeling that business people deal with as well. Like football coaches, professionals must listen carefully to their prospective clients. How many deals does a salesperson lose because he or she talks too much and doesn't respond to what the client wants? How many star employees does a hiring manager miss out on because he or she doesn't truly listen?

Don't be left wondering what could have been. Be sure to ask your clients, "What side of the ball do you want to play on?"

Listen and Truly Hear

Gary Barnett served as head coach of the Colorado Buffaloes and the Northwestern Wildcats. He holds the unique distinction of being a two-time coach of the year in both the Big 10 and Big 12 conferences. He is famous for taking the once moribund Northwestern Wildcats, one of the poorest programs in history, and leading them to the 1996 Rose Bowl. His 2001 Buffaloes won the Big 12 conference.

When asked what separates a good recruiter from a great one, Barnett quickly pointed to the art of listening. A great recruiter not only asks the right questions, he truly hears what a prospective player feels.

"A lot of young recruiters are just waiting to talk," Barnett said. "They don't really listen to what that recruit is saying and what that recruit's parents are saying. So they don't really know where they stand."

Often professionals will think they are listening more than they really are, because the natural tendency when selling is to just talk, talk, talk. While there are a few rare people who listen too much, most of us don't even come close to that.

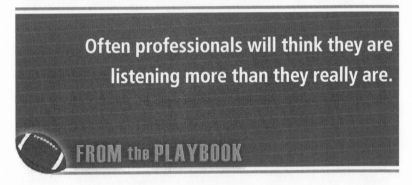

Often professionals will think they are listening more than they really are.

FROM the PLAYBOOK

When you're trying to establish a business relationship, focus on the other person. Listen with interest. Listen with intensity. Listen as if your business success depends on it.

An honest person will admit that he or she is his or her favorite discussion subject. It sounds horribly cynical to say that, but let's face it—it's true. People invest a great deal into themselves. They lie awake at night worrying about themselves. They worry about being successful and not being adequate. Even the most humble among us have at least some ego. Therefore, when someone shows interest in your "favorite subject," you can't help but like them.

How do you know if you listen enough? To be safe, follow the "rule of thirds." Two-thirds of the time in any conversation should be spent on listening, focusing on the other person's needs, wants, hopes and desires. One-third of the time is your chance to talk about yourself.

Now, some people go too far. They become so good at interpersonal communication that they become "total communication givers," meaning they give three-thirds of the time to the other person. If you are a communication giver, discussion partners will love you. They will think you are a sparkling conversationalist. But the problem is that conversation partners leave knowing nothing about you. How could a person ever do business with you or refer clients to you if he or she knows nothing about you? Remember to reserve your third.

In order to be an effective practitioner of the rule of thirds, you will want to be a forgiving person, for the better you become at interpersonal communication, the more you will realize how lousy the rest of us are. Forgive the other person when he or she wants to keep talking and shows absolutely no genuine interest in you. This can get frustrating. Good interpersonal communicators sometimes express frustration: "I listen all the time. I'm always showing interest in other people. Why doesn't anyone ever reciprocate?"

> Forgive the other person when he or she wants to keep talking and shows absolutely no genuine interest in you.
>
> FROM the PLAYBOOK

While others' lack of skill or interest in listening might be maddening, it's actually a blessing. If everyone followed the rule of thirds, the math wouldn't add up. It would be a fight to see who could listen more, and consequently, nobody would talk! If someone allows you to do the questioning, they are actually giving you power. The person who asks the most questions is the one who leads the conversations.

Attentive listening not only helps you find selling cues, it ultimately conserves your resources.

Former Tennessee coach Phillip Fulmer made sure he asked detailed, purposeful questions to find out whether a given prospect's interest in the Volunteers was high enough to continue spending time and money on him.

"You might hear, 'Well, my mother wants me to stay close to home,'" Fulmer said as an example. "And these other four schools are close to home, but you're five hundred miles away." Prospects often self-qualify themselves if the salesperson gives them some time and actually listens to what they say.

See the World through Johnny's Eyes

As it is in all professions, knowing where you stand is critical when it comes to the highly competitive and dynamic game of college football sales.

Former Texas A&M coach R.C. Slocum agrees that the ability to listen is critically important, calling it the number-one skill set a football coach must possess. As the winningest coach in A&M history, Slocum would know. He was a prolific salesman who put together several solid teams. His Aggies lost only four home games during the 1990s.

Slocum had a saying he often used to remind his assistant coaches to listen and empathize: "If you want to sell what Johnny buys, you need to see the world through Johnny's eyes."

Too many recruiters miss the boat, Slocum believes. Such coaches meet with a player and his family and spend all their time talking about what they believe and what they think is best for the young man instead of going slowly at first, asking probing questions and getting the young man to open up. This gives the coach a better understanding of what the player is all about and what he really wants from a college and his future football team.

By failing to be a careful listener, a college coach lacks the information necessary to build rapport with the prospect.

"An example of that is a guy who goes in and says, 'Your high school coach and I have been great friends for years. He's my buddy,'" Slocum said. "But the young man and his family may feel like the high school coach hadn't done a good job of utilizing him on the field. Just by saying that, you took a step backwards in the process."

A number of other pitfalls can burn a coach who doesn't listen before leaping. Slocum preached to his assistant coaches that they should sit back, listen and gather intelligence. This would allow them to choose the best selling points later in the courtship.

"Early on in the recruiting process, you should go very slowly down any road, and don't go down any roads unless he takes you there," Slocum told his assistants. "And even then, go slowly until you find out just exactly what's down that road, and then little by little, try to get some areas that you are comfortable you can talk about. Don't just take off charging in some direction saying, 'We've got a great engineering school.' Well, he may not really want to study engineering. That just may be what his mother wants him to major in. You better find out before you go too far what he really wants and what's important to him."

A coach could think he's building rapport by talking about a player's girlfriend, telling the prospect that "she can come be with you and watch you play if you go to school close to home."

However, the player may be looking forward to getting away from her and starting a new relationship in college. A careful salesperson won't go too far down any path until the prospect has given a clear indication of how he or she feels.

In order for listening to be effective, one needs to ask the right questions, the kinds of questions that yield important and useful answers.

When Coach Slocum prepared for phone conversations and personal visits, he would first formulate a plan. He identified certain questions or discussion areas that he wanted to explore.

> **In order for listening to be effective, one needs to ask the right questions, the kinds of questions that yield important and useful answers.**
>
> **FROM the PLAYBOOK**

Before each meeting, Slocum knew what information he wanted and was prepared to get it.

"Don't just get on the phone and say how you doing? How was practice today?" Slocum said.

"You're not finding out anything. That's just chit chattin'. You should always have probing questions. It's okay to have some chit-chat, but while you're doing that, ask questions to find out what he's all about."

In addition to providing selling cues to the coach, these probing questions also help him determine whether the player is truly a fit for the team.

"If you ask a lot of questions, you might find out that football is not all that important to him,"

Slocum explained. "Maybe he just played 'cause his dad wanted him to do it. You might think this guy down deep isn't burning with the desire and willing to make the sacrifices you have to make to be a big-time football player."

Probing questions are important in any business, not just football recruiting. Too many salespersons, executives and entrepreneurs go to networking events just for the sake of networking. They grab a cocktail, enjoy the free appetizers, say "hi" to a few people and then go back to the office.

Many of us simply "chit-chat" instead of deliberately seeking valuable information from our conversations. If you sell copiers, you need to move beyond small talk and ask questions that lead you to businesses that must replace their aging machines. Insurance brokers must probe to find out who is experiencing a life-changing event or is about to expand their business. Real estate agents need to ask, "Who do you know who's thinking about moving in the next year?"

Many of us simply "chit-chat" instead of deliberately seeking valuable information from our conversations.

FROM the PLAYBOOK

Having a plan before you start conversations makes your interactions with other professionals more fruitful. But regardless of what information you seek, and regardless of how much you learn from a given person, it is paramount that you focus and truly listen to each person. Showing deep and earnest interest in a person is a critical part of listening.

When a savvy professional spends time with a prospect, client or colleague, he or she listens actively and makes that person feel like nobody else matters, that for at least one moment, nobody else exists in the whole world. If you can do this, the results are powerful.

Who Da Ball Got?

In the early 1980s, two Nebraska assistant coaches touched down in the Louisiana bayou at the Lafayette Regional Airport, about 135 miles west of New Orleans. Off-campus recruiting coordinator Jack Pierce and receivers coach Gene Huey made many trips to Louisiana looking for blue-chip talent.

Upon checking in at the local Hilton, Pierce and Huey walked right into the hotel's patio happy hour—all the Louisiana shrimp and crawfish you could eat. Pierce struck up a conversation with a woman working at the hotel.

"This is pretty nice," Pierce said, "but where can we go and get THE best shrimp and crawfish in this area?"

The woman responded, "Oh, there no talkin', man. No talkin'. Henderson, Louisiana. And da best restaurant in Henderson be 'Roband's.'"

The two Midwestern coaches hurried fifteen miles down the highway in search of the best bayou food Cajun country had to offer. They exited at the Henderson sign, drove along the main drag and discovered a small town with only a couple rows of buildings on either side of the road. That was it. Pretty much the whole town was visible at just a glance. They drove all over and found a handful of restaurants, but no Roband's.

Frustrated, they stopped at a gas station, and Huey suggested Pierce go inside and ask for directions.

"Hey, man, we're looking for Roband's Restaurant," Pierce told the cashier standing behind the counter. He looked at Pierce and replied, "Boy, what dat sign say across da street?"

"Robins," Pierce said.

"Dat say Ro-BAND's, crazy," he corrected Pierce in his French-inspired local accent.

Pierce shook his head, thanked the man and walked back to the car, where Huey was waiting. "So where is it, Jack?"

Pierce couldn't pass up the opportunity. "Boy, what dat say?"

"What do you mean?" Huey responded.

"What dat sign say over there?" Pierce asked again.

"Robin's."

"No, man. Dat say, Ro-BAND's," Pierce said fighting back laughter.

The two coaches went in wearing Husker garb and championship rings on their fingers. They talked to a bunch of locals and had one of the best meals of their lives. Pierce formed a friendship with the owner/chef Lionel Robin. In fact, when the Huskers played the Louisiana State Tigers at the Sugar Bowl in New Orleans a couple years later, Pierce gave Robin two of his allotted tickets.

Suffice it to say, when you're in a different culture, another part of the country, or are doing business internationally, you not only have to adapt to the local way of doing things, you need to embrace it. As the old saying goes, "When in Rome…" Communicate the way your prospects communicate. A great salesperson knows how to empathize, to see the world from his or her prospect's point of view.

During his tenure as the Husker's off-campus recruiter, Pierce spent a great deal of time in Louisiana, a hot, boggy state that consistently sent star players north to Nebraska's cornfields. Over time, he fell in love with the culture, and he eventually learned the language!

He remembers one time when he visited Louisiana's St. Martinville Senior High School. The high school coach asked, "Where ya be from?"

"Nebraska," Pierce responded.

"Oh, man. That Nebraska. That 'I' formation," the high school coach said. "Come on, man, let's go back here. We see what you gonna wanna do."

The two went to the high school coach's office to talk football and watch film with a couple of the high school assistant coaches. As the group talked about the Husker game file Pierce brought to show off, Pierce felt like he was visiting a different country.

"Who da ball got?" one of the high school coaches asked Pierce, who responded with a confused, "Beg your pardon?"

"Who da ball got?" the high school coach asked again. "Run it back. Who da ball got?"

Confused, Pierce said, "Coach, what are you talking about?"

Suddenly, the high school coach remembered he was dealing with a northerner and said, "Oh, how you say dat ... 'Who *got* da ball?'"

It's the little things that make cultural and language differences so interesting.

Empathy

If salespersons are good at empathizing and adapting to their surroundings, they will actually enjoy and savor the differences. Those who can transcend any cultural, religious or language differences are the ones who are best at establishing rapport, building relationships and eventually achieving trust with their prospective clients.

Just because it's important to relate to your prospects doesn't necessarily mean it's easy. How does a coach, especially a head coach, relate to teenage players? How does a guy who is frequently on television and is typically the highest paid person at the university relate to some poor kid in a violence-riddled urban ghetto?

Phillip Fulmer believes the ability to adjust to different people and surroundings is one of a salesperson's most important skills.

"I used to say a coach is a migrant worker disguised as a millionaire," Fulmer said. "You adjust to all settings and situations, and there are some scary places out there." It's not enough to simply *deal* with a different or "scary" situation, Fulmer said. You must make yourself part of it in order to make prospects and their families feel comfortable around you.

One long-time assistant coach, who wishes to remain anonymous for purposes of this story, remembers recruiting a talented young man whose mother was a prostitute. During an in-home visit, the coach was sitting in the family living room talking with the prospect and his mother when two guys, half drunk, knocked on the door. She ended up taking the drop-in clients to the back room.

The kid was humiliated. The coach, dealing with simultaneous feelings of pity and revulsion, had to carry on with the conversation and help the young man feel as dignified as possible.

Next time you find yourself in an uncomfortable business setting, just remember that story!

"If you do [recruiting] for a while, you see every situation—inner-city Los Angeles and the south side of Chicago to rural Kansas and Nebraska. You're all over the place," Tom Osborne recounted. "You're recruiting kids from affluent situations and kids from abject poverty. You're recruiting quite a few kids who have no one in their family who has ever gone to college or has any knowledge of what it's like to go to college. You just have to get used to it."

Even when a college coach is recruiting a youngster whose parents and older siblings went to college, they still must work hard to relate. A coach is much older than his players.

He is most likely married and a father. He travels the nation recruiting players, is interviewed on television and works in a high-profile profession that millions of people follow obsessively. Any time he goes out to dinner, other restaurant patrons request autographs.

On the other hand, a recruit is a teenager. Even though he is incredibly gifted athletically, he worries about the same things as every other teenage boy—grades, girls, social life, trying to figure out who he is and what he will make of himself as an adult. Like all teenagers, football players mature at different speeds. Some are ready to accept adultlike responsibilities. Others aren't even close.

Somehow, these two totally different people—coach and prospective player—have to find common ground and build a trusting relationship in order for the coach to close the deal and sign the kid.

Coaches can better relate if they deliberately think like teenagers. That means they have to know what television shows teens watch, what movies are popular, what video games they are buying and what slang words are in vogue.

"It keeps you young," Gary Barnett said. "You're constantly trying to see the world through a seventeen-year-old's eyes. That means every couple of years you have to 'retool your computer,' because seventeen-year-olds are thinking differently. There are new things out there."

In the mid-1980s, Barnett was coaching in remote southwestern Colorado for the Fort Lewis Skyhawks, a small liberal arts college located in Durango. After a couple of years there, he got a big break. Up-and-coming head coach Bill McCartney hired him as an assistant, coaching running backs at the University of Colorado in Boulder.

Making the jump from Fort Lewis to the high-profile Big 8 Conference tested Barnett's ability to adjust to different people and surroundings. That first year, he was concerned about his ability to recruit African-American athletes because he had no black players on the small college team and coached none during his eleven years as a high school coach.

"I played in college [at the University of Missouri] with a number of black athletes, but I had not coached around that culture. I was worried about adjusting," Barnett admitted. "I think my personal desire not to be embarrassed, and not to lose, made me learn and be very observant and watch everything."

During his first year as a recruiter, Barnett did not sign one single African-American player. After that he had great success. He was able to adjust to nuances of African-American culture after he learned about it and came to appreciate it.

Relating to black athletes, especially those from low-income backgrounds, was never a problem for Hall of Famer Barry Switzer. Long before he was coaching national championship teams at Oklahoma, Switzer grew up as the son of a bootlegger in a black community in tiny Crossett, Arkansas. After Switzer's mother committed suicide, his father had black girlfriends, and Switzer was essentially raised by Erma Reynolds, a woman he refers to as his "black grandma." He buried her at age 102 and delivered the eulogy at her funeral.

When Switzer started coaching at OU, many schools—especially those in the old, corrupt Southwestern Conference—were on the quota system, which meant in part that African-American athletes were typically recruited only as receivers and running backs. On the contrary, Switzer was starting a black quarterback at Oklahoma as early as 1972. That was significant because, in recruiting, Switzer primarily battled against the Texas Longhorns and other Southwestern programs.

"I told my staff when I first became head coach, 'We're going to recruit the best players in all positions,'" Switzer said. "They understood what I meant. There's no quota system at Oklahoma."

Switzer's open mind and ability to relate to all cultures gave him a tremendous recruiting advantage in those days. Because of that, it took years before the Texas schools could truly compete toe-to-toe with Switzer when they were all battling to recruit a given African-American player.

"When I played against Texas, the black community, the brothers, all wanted Oklahoma to win," Switzer said. "Because why? They knew my story, and they knew I was playing black athletes at all positions. I was playing black quarterbacks. I was 'black Jesus' to the black community in the early seventies."

That reputation gave him instant credibility and a nice head start when he visited African-American homes. His background and actions as head coach made it easier for him to establish the rapport, relationships and trust necessary to sign any athlete especially an African-American who may have grown up in a low-income home in a segregated community during the 1960s and early 1970s.

Switzer was proud of the relationships he formed with these families. In fact, he says one of the greatest compliments he has ever received came from the mother of an African-American player when she said, "Coach Switzer is the only coach who made me feel comfortable in my own home."

Making someone feel "comfortable in his or her own home" ought to be the number-one priority of anyone who has something to sell. It is only through relationship building and ultimately the establishment of trust that a healthy, long-term business relationship can exist.

Now, Switzer had the benefit of growing up in a black community, but what if you don't have much in common with your prospects? How do you relate then? What about the coach who grew up in a middle-class or privileged background who has to recruit kids from an impoverished background?

The first piece of advice from former Georgia and Marshall coach Jim Donnan is to break down the barriers that may exist. Make the prospects understand that you feel comfortable in their environment.

"One of the first things I tried to do is walk into the kitchen and see what they had to eat, just to let them know I felt good about being in their house," Donnan said. "I didn't care what it looked like, you always go in and ask Momma for something to eat. She would always like that."

Current University of California head coach Jeff Tedford agrees. "Some environments are tougher than others," he said. "Regardless, the people are nice and try to put their best foot forward. You go into some houses, and they put on a lavish meal. At others, it's a bowl of peanuts or potato chips. Whatever it is, it's awesome."

Donnan was convinced that families could sense if a coach was uncomfortable. If that's the case, chances are the mother would be uncomfortable with that person coaching her son. If he isn't blessed with the natural ability to be comfortable in all situations, like Switzer was, a good football salesman trains himself to be that way.

By having a positive attitude, by telling himself that people are people, and by genuinely trying to understand others' perspectives, the introverted salesperson can become one who adjusts and empathizes with great skill.

Not only is meeting your prospects in their own surroundings good for your selling success, it also helps you serve them better once they become your client (or coach them better when they're actually on your team).

"That's why I make sure I go into every single home of every single player we recruit," Tedford said, "because I want to know their background. I want to know where they came from."

If you don't ask the right questions, you might be operating under flawed assumptions.

When establishing a business relationship, focus on the other person. Listen with intensity.

You can't fully connect with your prospects until you can see the world through their eyes.

When doing business in a different culture, don't simply adapt to it; embrace it.

Sometimes your success depends on your ability and willingness to relate to people who are very different than you.

Making someone feel comfortable in your presence is one of the most basic requirements in developing a profitable client-provider relationship.

Chapter 13

WE'RE GETTING READY TO PLAY NOTRE DAME
But All I'm Thinking about Is You

Tucked away in the extreme northeast corner of the Lone Star State is the sleepy town of Hooks, Texas, population 2,900. Located just outside Texarkana along Interstate 30, Hooks isn't known for much and certainly doesn't stand out on the map.

But that wasn't the case in the fall of 1974. That's when a star running back at Hooks High School was tearing up the football fields of East Texas. His name was Billy Sims, and he was one of those once-in-a-lifetime athletes. Having rushed for nearly 8,000 yards in his high school career, Sims was coveted by all the big-time college football schools.

Three hundred miles to the northwest, University of Oklahoma coach Barry Switzer had his sights set squarely on Sims, having identified him as the Sooners' "number-one recruiting priority" that year. Switzer was practically obsessed with Sims. Almost every Friday afternoon after practice, Switzer would board a private jet and fly down to Hooks to see Sims play. Then he would quickly return home to coach the Sooners the next day.

Although he doggedly pursued his top prospect, Switzer was still worried. He wanted to do something that would truly impress Billy Sims.

Now, you need to know about a trick college football coaches use when recruiting players. When they're in their office or hotel room before a game, coaches call their best high school prospects and say something like, "I'm here in South Bend getting ready to play Notre Dame, but all I'm thinking about is you and how much I'd like to have you on our team." Of course, Switzer made these types of calls, and in 1974, Billy Sims's phone number was always on the list.

Coaches hope the phone calls will make recruits feel important, but the young men see right through it. They know coaches are calling a bunch of players.

Switzer got the chance to do something special one Saturday when his Sooners were in Boulder playing the University of Colorado. At halftime, the Sooners were leading the Buffaloes 28-0. Needless to say, Switzer felt pretty good as he entered the locker room at half, so he wasn't worried about tending to the team. He spied a pay phone on the locker room wall, picked up the receiver and called CJ's Conoco Station in Texas. When the manager answered the phone, Switzer said, "This is Coach. I wanna talk to Billy."

Sims had been listening to the game on the radio while pumping gas for his job at the service station. He was flabbergasted that Barry Switzer would take the time to call him during halftime.

"Coach, you're supposed to be at the game!" Sims said.

"Well, you're listening to the radio aren't ya?" Switzer asked. "Then you know it's halftime!"

Switzer deliberately kept Sims on the phone for the entire halftime period. Switzer even told Sims the plays Oklahoma would run on Colorado during the second half so Sims could listen for them. The two talked so long that the referee eventually came over, tapped Switzer on the shoulder and said, "Coach, it's getting late. You got to get your team back on the field."

Switzer smiled and said into the phone, "You heard the ref, Billy. I gotta go finish this ass whippin'. Wish you were here!"

By the end of the conversation, Sims knew he was special. Switzer had spent the entire halftime with him and no other prospect.

What's the moral of this story? Make the people in your life—clients, prospects, colleagues—feel special. Make them feel like they're the only ones who matter to you. Give them your entire focus while you're with them. Lavishing attention on others will close more sales and earn you more business opportunities.

It certainly worked for Coach Switzer, because Billy Sims eventually did sign with Oklahoma, where he became a two-time All-American and the 1978 Heisman Trophy winner. His likeness is now immortalized in a bigger-than-life bronze statue that stands proudly on the OU campus.

In today's ultra-competitive, fast-paced economy, salespersons and marketers must take the time and do the things that make their prospects feel special. If you fail to do this, especially with the biggest and potentially most profitable clients, there will likely be a line of competitors ready to do it.

So who's your "Billy Sims" and when are you going to call him? What are you going to do to show him how much you would value his business?

Personal Attention

Just like the most desirable prospective clients your company is chasing, star football recruits expect college coaches to treat them as if they're the only player in the world. Those who are so gifted and talented are in demand, so a school wishing to sign them needs to treat them like gold.

Aramide Olaniyan plays linebacker at the University of California–Los Angeles. Rated by Rivals.com as a four-star prospect in 2010 coming out of Woodberry Forest School in Virginia, Olaniyan had many scholarship offers. He turned down Michigan, Clemson and North Carolina, among others. Why did a Virginia kid choose to play football 2,600 miles away in Los Angeles? One of the big reasons was the way the UCLA coaches made him feel.

While UCLA's then–head coach Rick Neuheisel created more than his fair share of controversy, he was a cunning recruiter. When Olaniyan took his official visit to UCLA, Neuheisel personally conducted the campus tour. An alumnus of UCLA, Neuheisel shared stories from his own college days and painted a picture of what campus life would be like for a future Bruin.

Throughout the tour, Neuheisel asked the young prospect questions and listened carefully to the responses. The time and personal attention made quite an impression. Olaniyan visited several campuses during the recruiting process, but no other coach spent so much time and rolled out the red carpet the way Neuheisel did.

Coaches devoted much more personal attention to hot prospects years ago before the NCAA greatly regulated the amount of contact. In the free-for-all-days of the 1970s, Nebraska's Tom Osborne would travel to see top prospects on a weekly basis or even more frequently.

One of his top quarterback prospects during the early 1970s was David Humm, a blue chipper from Las Vegas. Osborne remembers flying to Nevada to visit Humm every single week, fourteen weeks in a row. In the end, it paid off as Humm was a three-year starter at Nebraska and went on to a long NFL career.

At about the same time, Osborne recruited Ed Burns, a coveted high school quarterback out of Omaha. Burns, who eventually signed with Osborne and went on to play a couple years for the New Orleans Saints, had a part-time job at his neighborhood K-Mart. One day as he was stocking shelves, he noticed a commotion with customers and employees gathering in the aisle behind him.

That's when he saw a tall, red-haired guy walking toward him. It was Tom Osborne, who popped into the K-Mart just to say "hi." That surprise, along with Osborne's multiple visits to Burns's home and high school practices, made the young prospect realize he was truly valued by the famous man who was chasing him.

Salespersons often gain great benefit from hosting prospective clients at the office. It's a chance to better explain a company's products and services by getting a prospect on your home turf. You can introduce him or her to colleagues and give tours of the operations. In certain situations, as appropriate, there may be value in entertaining a prospect in your own home.

In-person visits are similarly useful for coaches selling their programs to blue-chip players. In his book *No Ordinary Joe*, author Michael O'Brien describes Saturday night dinners during official on-campus visit weekends taking place years ago at Penn State. That's when the late Joe Paterno and his wife, Sue, would invite the parents of prospects over for a dinner personally prepared by Sue.

There wasn't much football on the discussion docket. Instead Coach Paterno would entertain the parents and work hard to make sure everyone was comfortable. He made sure that everyone got his or her fair share of attention. Parents typically left the home feeling good about the man who would be taking care of their son if he were to sign with Penn State.

We Want Vince!

As you search for innovative ways to make an impression and let your prospects know they are special, you might want to employ the efforts of others. Your clients, fans and champions out in the business community can play a huge role as you market to new prospects. Because of strict NCAA recruiting rules, college football teams have to be careful about orchestrating such efforts, but they're perfectly fine if they happen without the direct involvement of the school.

Because fans follow recruiting so closely on the Internet, they tend to know a great deal about the kids their favorite football teams are recruiting. That means they usually know when prospective players are visiting campus especially if it's game day. It is fairly common at the blueblood schools for fans to introduce themselves to the prospects, welcome them to campus and hold up signs imploring them to say "yes."

Spontaneous adoration from 15,000 fans helped Tim Brewster land one of the nation's biggest recruits when he was an assistant coach at Texas in late 2001. That's when he was engaged in a tremendous battle to recruit an all-everything blue chipper from inner-city Houston by the name of Vince Young. Brewster starting tracking Young when he was a high school sophomore and worked hard to build a strong relationship with him.

During an on-campus visit, Brewster and Young were about to take in a Longhorn basketball game. Before the game, coach and prospect talked one-on-one downstairs in the bowels of the Frank Erwin Center at the University of Texas sports arena. To give Young a taste of the campus buzz, Brewster took his prized recruit upstairs so he could walk on the court and take in the pre-game atmosphere.

Immediately, upon stepping on the basketball floor, fans recognized Young. The news whipped through the arena quickly. The crowd started chanting, "We want Vince! We want Vince!"

Brewster was blown away by the sudden public adoration. He walked Young back into the locker room where the recruit turned to Brewster, tears streaming down his face, and said, "This is where I need to be. I'm a Longhorn."

Of course, Young starred at Texas, achieving All-American honors and leading the team to its first Associated Press national championship in thirty-six years. He was a first-round pick of the Tennessee Titans in 2006.

Game Day

Coaches who really want to sell prospects on their universities often pull out one of the most powerful weapons in their sales arsenals—a game-day visit. This is akin to a car salesperson getting the prospect to take a test drive or the real estate broker convincing the would-be buyer to go on a showing or the haberdasher helping a man try on the expensive suit.

Game-day visits are powerful especially at the blueblood schools, where more than 80,000 fans fill stadiums wearing the team colors. You would be hard-pressed to find a more exciting, electric environment than a large university campus on a football Saturday. Exploiting emotion is certainly one of the most important and effective sales techniques that exists; big-time college football stadiums are absolutely bursting with emotion. For most teams, bringing an impressionable young prospect onto campus on a game day is a no brainer.

But to cash in on a game day's selling power, coaches have to make the player feel special. It can be a challenge for a coach to give prospects a great deal of one-on-one attention when he is dealing with the stress and jitters that are common during pre-game. In addition to focusing on the game and reviewing his game plan, the head coach may have to do pre-game media interviews, meet with alumni, greet dignitaries and keep an eye on the team's collective mental condition.

Given that, it can be a challenge to lavish enough attention on recruits. Nevertheless, an effective coach-salesperson digs deep, "flips the switch" and gets the job done.

"We would occasionally talk to a young man who went to visit some other place, and the head coach or the coaching staff didn't pay much attention to him," Tom Osborne said. "Of course, he wouldn't be going there. You can't do that."

Whatever business you're in, Osborne's advice applies. If you're going to invite prospects to your big event, you must somehow take the time to make them feel special even if that means taking time away from your more immediate responsibilities. And, really, if a coach had done his job during the week, he actually does have enough time to sell the program to the visiting Friday night stars on game-day Saturdays.

"I always felt like this: the hay is in the barn Thursday night," said former Georgia and Marshall head coach Jim Donnan. "There's not a whole lot you can do except just relax and go over tips and reminders, but there is a lot you can do on Saturday with a young man who comes to your campus."

In fact, Donnan thinks it's ridiculous that some coaches say they can't recruit on game days because they need to concentrate, because they're worried about the game. By the time Saturday comes, there's nothing you can do about the game, he said, "But you sure as heck can recruit some players, and whether it's walking their momma out on the field, letting her see what it looks like or taking the dad inside the dressing room … whatever it might be, you have got to spend time with all those players and make sure you get to know them all and make them feel like it's important for you to know who they are."

That personal attention is particularly important when it is an "unofficial" visit, meaning the prospect is paying his own way. Furthermore, a player must feel special on every one of his unofficial visits even if he visits campus several times—even if he comes to every single home game. Those visits are important because a head coach can only visit a player's home once. The more unofficial on-campus visits, even game-day visits, a coach gets, the more opportunity he has to build a relationship and eventually trust.

"I think people are whistling Dixie if they think that they don't need to spend time with a kid on game day," Donnan said. "I think you can really get some valuable, quality points with him."

If that's the case, then Ohio State "whistles Dixie" quite a bit. Former Buckeye recruiting coordinator John Peterson said his team tries to avoid having players in on game day. It's not because of worry about the game or concentration; Peterson believes it's a matter of logistics.

"Typically, these kids are coming off a Friday night [high school] game, and they're arriving late," Peterson said. "Even though the atmosphere and emotion of a Buckeye game is unlike any place else, we would rather spend a full weekend with him during a December visit."

One would be hard-pressed to criticize Ohio State for that sales strategy, because they have boasted some of the nation's finest recruiting classes in recent years and have fielded some of the nation's best teams. Whether or not you believe in game-day visits, the law of personal attention remains the same. Whenever or however your prospective clients visit you, spend copious amounts of time with them and treat them like gold.

When the Client Takes Control

No matter how badly a salesperson wants to roll out the red carpet and make an impression on the prospects, sometimes the best way to make a would-be client feel special is to simply leave him or her alone. For a confident, proactive salesperson, it's a terribly foreign feeling, but some clients need a little air. If you press them more than they want, they may simply eliminate you from consideration. Keep your sales radar on and adjust your approach and intensity level based on the client's personality and preferences.

With the right attitude, salespersons will likely be more successful if they allow self-confident clients to make decisions on their own terms.

Over the course of his coaching career, former Texas A&M head coach R.C. Slocum pursued hundreds of prospects and encountered about every sales situation you can imagine. He considers the recruitment of Terry Price in the mid-1980s to be one of his great sales successes.

Interestingly, Price's family took control of the process in a way very few families ever had. The family was so proactive, confident and organized, that Slocum considers them to be a model other players and their families should follow.

Slocum remembers calling Price's home early in the recruiting process. His father answered the phone and said in a pleasant but assertive voice, "Coach, Terry's involved in football right now. We don't want him being called and spending all his time on the phone with college coaches. We're going to go through this season. When it's all over, you can call back, and we will set up appointments for coaches to visit our home."

"Fair enough," Slocum thought. He waited for several weeks. As soon as Price's team played its last game, the A&M coach called the Prices again. He was granted an appointment to meet Price and his parents at their home, showed up and gave his best Aggies sales presentation.

"Okay, Coach, we have heard your story and your pitch," the father said. "We're going to have all these coaches in, and then we'll pick out the five schools we're going to visit. We'll let you know if you're one of the five."

Sure enough, Price's father called Slocum about a week later and let him know Texas A&M made the cut to be one of the five schools that would get an official visit. He further informed Slocum that after the final visit, the family would sit down and make a decision.

"There wasn't anything I could do to speed up the process," Slocum said. "We were the last visit, so I was a nervous wreck. They went home on Sunday and I waited and waited."

The waiting was agonizing and eventually Slocum felt as if he could take it no longer. But what could he do? He promised to leave the family alone until they announced a decision. In situations like that, good selling professionals get creative.

Slocum and his then-assistant Bob Davey were sitting around at a Dallas hotel and were growing anxious because they had heard nothing from the Price family. Davey picked up the phone, called the Prices and said he was a reporter from *USA Today* doing a story on blue-chip players and wanted to know if Terry had reached a decision.

"We're having a family meeting right now," Mr. Price responded to the fake newspaper reporter. "We're probably going to make a decision this evening. You can call back tomorrow."

Davey hung up the phone. "They're doing it right now!" he told Slocum.

Shortly after that, Slocum received a phone call. "We've reached a decision, and Terry's coming to A&M," the father said.

Of course, Slocum was thrilled with the news. That was the end of it. The family was so deliberate, and so orderly, that Slocum knew he didn't have to worry about young Terry backing out of his verbal commitment. It was a final decision, a done deal.

In the end, the coach's patience paid off. Price had a stellar playing career with the Aggies and went on to play professional football for a few years. After retiring from the NFL because of an injury, Price returned to A&M as a graduate assistant coach. Today, he serves as a full-time assistant coach at the University of Mississippi.

Slocum honored the Price family's wishes and gave them space, room to breathe. That's hard to do when you want the prospect so badly, but you have to read your would-be clients and gauge your response accordingly. In such a situation, you have to trust that the prospect will thoroughly consider what you are offering and make a decision that's good for both of you. Ultimately, you have no choice when you find yourself in such a selling situation. While you risk losing the prospect by stepping back, you will surely lose him or her if you push too hard. In such situations, make a person feel special by honoring his or her wishes.

Your *Real* Business

No matter what you do for a living, success ultimately comes down to your ability to deliver great value for the money your clients invest.

But how do you define value? You don't. Value is determined by the client. Value lives in the client's mind. By making your clients feel truly special, you make it easier for them to see the great value you can provide.

The greatest football salesmen understand that value is critical. They know what matters to their prospective players. They realize they're not really working in the "football business." In reality, they're working in the "I'll-help-you-grow-into-a-man" business. They're in the "I'll-make-you-a-success" business. They're in the "I'll-get-you-to-the-NFL" business.

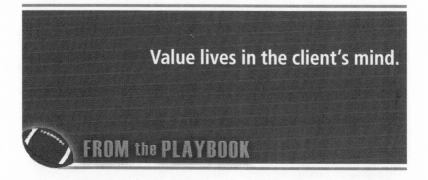

Value lives in the client's mind.

FROM the PLAYBOOK

Similarly, real estate agents are in the "help-you-get-your-dream-house" business. Insurance brokers are in the "keep-you-safe-and-secure" business. Financial advisers are in the "make-you-wealthy" business. Professional consultants are in the "keep-your-company-solvent" business.

Prospective clients feel most special when the would-be provider convinces them that it's all about them. The successful vendor is the one who is in business to make someone else's dreams come true.

Make prospects feel special, like they're the only ones who matter to you.

The most coveted clients have a right to demand red carpet treatment.

Incorporate emotion into your marketing, because it is one of the most powerful selling tools.

Even if it is a sacrifice, include prospective clients at your premier events.

Don't set up a meeting with a prospect unless you can devote adequate attention to him or her.

Assess your prospect's personality and then decide whether to lavish attention or give him or her some breathing room.

Value exists in your client's mind, not yours.

Chapter 14

MOMMAS PACK
THE SUITCASES

Identifying Your Influencers and Champions

Extraordinary talent is a double-edged sword.

Those uncommon human beings who are blessed with world-class athletic abilities have access to rare opportunities that regular folks can barely imagine. On the other hand, those extraordinary athletes unavoidably end up disappointing an awful lot of people.

When you are one of the nation's very best high school football players, everybody wants you but only one team can have you. That means you say no to scores of schools and literally millions of fans. Turning down his number two school can be the most difficult thing a player has done so far in his life, especially if he has climbed the relationship ladder with the coaching staff.

Such was the case for T.J. Yeldon, a star running back from Daphne High School in far southern Alabama. Rated as an elite five-star prospect by Rivals.com in 2012, Yeldon had offers from Alabama, Auburn, Florida, Florida State, Oregon and many other big-time programs. How on earth does he decide on one when so many are throwing themselves at him?

It just so happened that Yeldon wasn't the only player on Daphne's team to make the Rivals Top 100 list of 2012 recruits. Yeldon was rated as America's fourth best high school player, and his teammate, four-star linebacker Ryan Anderson, came in at number 98. According to TideSports.com, Anderson committed to the University of Alabama in April, near the end of his junior year of high school. In somewhat of a surprise, his teammate and close friend, Yeldon, announced in June that he would play for Alabama's bitter rival—the Auburn Tigers.

Alabama fans, hoping to get a two-for-one deal from Daphne, were disappointed. Anderson was disappointed; he didn't like the idea of playing against his friend in the state of Alabama's famous Iron Bowl every November.

Though Yeldon committed to rival Auburn, Anderson did not give up. He kept lobbying his buddy to switch allegiances to Alabama. Anderson vigorously recruited Yeldon on behalf of the Crimson Tide. They attended a couple 'Bama games together. Anderson eventually enlisted the support of other guys who had verbally committed to 'Bama.

Eventually, Anderson's efforts paid off, and in December, six months after committing to Auburn, Yeldon switched his commitment to Alabama. While the decision thrilled Anderson and a whole lot of Tide fans, Auburn fans had to be disappointed to lose such a promising running back, a guy who can run the 40-yard dash in 4.4 seconds.

One of the biggest reasons T.J. Yeldon decided to switch his commitment was that a person who had a lot of influence on him was a champion for Alabama. The story perfectly illustrates the power that influencers and champions play in a persuasive selling process. Yeldon's talent was so incredibly immense that he had his pick of schools. Any coach would have bent over backwards and performed somersaults to sign him. Yeldon probably felt a great deal of pressure.

When you have so many choices, and consequently so many people to turn down, decision making is not easy—especially for a high school kid. Most people in such a situation turn to an influencer or a champion. Whichever team has the influencer or champion in its back pocket has the edge.

Influencer vs. Champion

Not all influencers are champions and not all champions are influencers, but often one person can play both roles. Influencers and champions play important roles in a sales effort that is so important that selling organizations work hard to identify them and manipulate them. Selling organizations can win over influencers, but they have to create champions. What's the difference between the two terms? Quite a bit, even though they often work hand-in-hand.

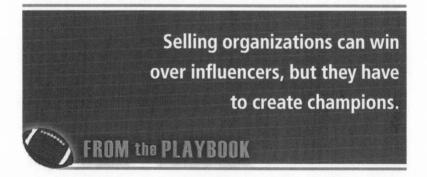

Selling organizations can win over influencers, but they have to create champions.

FROM the PLAYBOOK

An influencer is someone who helps a prospect make decisions and often sways that decision. The influencer is someone special or important in the prospect's life to whom he or she turns for advice, guidance and sometimes even accountability. Some influencers are neutral and objective, preferring to play a listening and counseling role, helping prospects come to their own decisions. Other influencers have definite opinions and try to talk the prospect into making a certain buying decision.

In college football recruiting, an objective influencer would do a lot of listening while the prospect weighs his options. Such an influencer would only offer advice when asked and wouldn't care which team the prospect chooses as long as he is happy and has a high likelihood of academic and athletic success. The biased influencer has a definite opinion and attempts to persuade the prospect in a certain way. A biased influencer essentially becomes somewhat of a champion for his or her preferred choice.

Champions are biased by definition. They champion a cause or organization in which they believe. They are advocates. They are cheerleaders. They endorse and give testimony for those they believe in. For many possible reasons, they are loyal to one organization above all its competitors. The more champions you have, the more successful you'll be in whatever you are trying to accomplish.

Marketers and sales professionals need specific strategies for developing and deploying champions as well as how to identify and win over influencers.

When you encounter an influencer, you want to turn them into a champion. If you can get the person who influences the buying decision, especially if the influencer is particularly influential, to become your raving fan, your chances of landing the business are outstanding.

Whether you're selling college football scholarships to blue chippers or any other service to any other audience, one of the single most important things you must do is identify who is the primary decision maker. Almost as important is the need to identify which people will have the greatest influence on that decision maker and to assess whether you can win their favor. Once you convert an influencer into being your champion, you then use that person for two reasons: to help you sell and to gather intelligence.

A won-over influencer can help you tailor your conversations with the prospect. If the influencer is close to the prospect, he or she can tell you what really matters. An influencer could probably tell you if a blue chipper is most focused on education, early playing time, preparation for pro football or winning championships. That same influencer can warn you every time the kid receives a phone call or hosts a competing coach.

> **A won-over influencer can help you tailor your conversations with the prospect.**
>
> FROM the PLAYBOOK

"The main thing we had to do once we identified the kid was to find out who the hell was really going to make the decision," said former Nebraska off-campus recruiting coordinator Jack Pierce.

That real decision maker could be a player's girlfriend, head coach or one of his teachers. Sometimes it would be the dad. Most often it was the mother.

"Mommas pack the suitcases," said Hall of Fame coach Barry Switzer, who led the Oklahoma Sooners to three national championships. Switzer, like all good football salesmen, realized that true decision-making power belonged to the mom in almost all cases. If you don't win her over, your odds are slim and slimmer.

The legendary Don "Fox" Bryant, sports information director emeritus at Nebraska, can verify the importance of mothers and how much work coaches would put into wooing them. Bryant remembers a line that the late great Husker coach Bob Devaney liked to use as a joke during football booster banquets: "We've found in recruiting it's been very helpful to work through the mothers. But it doesn't always work. One time we were trying to recruit this kid through his mother, and she liked us so well, she enrolled in the university and the kid went to Kansas."

Moms tend to be especially important decision makers in single-parent and ethnic minority households.

"I think I recruited ten or twelve kids that had both parents in the house," Pierce said reflecting on his long career with the Huskers. "Most of them were single-parent homes and sometimes the kid didn't even live with either of his parents."

When dealing with sometimes confusing family dynamics, it's even more important to find the true decision maker and zero in on that person. The earlier you can identify the influencer, the better. That way, you have both intelligence and a positive influence on the prospect right from the start.

"Once you made that identification," Pierce said, "there's no sense in spending a lot of time with anybody else." Finding influencers and engaging champions makes you far more efficient. That's important for salespersons dealing with a number of highly contested prospects and insufficient hours in the day.

One of the true values of an influencer/champion is that they can continue to work the prospect even when you are not around.

"Try to get as many people around him that you have had conversations with," said former Texas A&M coach R.C. Slocum. "As a recruiter, you might get a canned answer from him, but you'll go talk to his counselor, and she'll say, 'Coach, I'll tell you what that young man really wants.'"

If a coach talks to enough of the prospect's influencers, he will start to build a true profile of who the kid is and what it will take to sign him.

> One of the true values of an influencer/ champion is that they can continue to work the prospect even when you are not around.
>
> FROM the PLAYBOOK

"If you turn over enough stones, you start to get a picture of what's really important to him and what it's going to take to get him committed," Slocum said.

Discovering Influencers

As you do your detective work, it usually starts to become clear who the primary and secondary influencers are in a prospect's life. Former Ohio State and Arizona State head coach John Cooper preferred the direct approach. He would ask prospects, "Who are the most important people in your life?" "Who's the most influential person in your life?" It was almost always the mother, Cooper said, especially in African-American families.

Phillip Fulmer, who led the University of Tennessee to a national championship in the late 1990s, also asked direct questions. As the prospect would answer the questions, Fulmer paid close attention to the body language.

"If a young man brightens up when he talks about his coach, then obviously, he's got a part in [the decision]," he said.

One of Fulmer's favorite questions was, "Who's going to help you make this decision?" Typically, high school players would mention their mother, high school coach, older brother and father if he was in the picture. Once Fulmer knew the identity of the powerful influencer, he would build just as strong of a relationship with that person as he would with the player.

Sometimes a prospect will be vague and non-committal when asked to name his influencer. In the business world, a mid-level person might not want to give up control or admit that he or she lacks decision-making power. That person could also be protecting C-level executives from interruptions from salespersons.

In college football, a prospect could be very private or be worried that naming the influencer will mean the recruiting relationship will grow deeper before he's ready. When you're having trouble drawing information out of a prospect, be patiently persistent. Keep asking, digging and researching.

You can also look at precedent: What kind of influencers did previous prospects have?

During George Darlington's thirty-year tenure as an assistant coach for Nebraska, he was tremendously successful recruiting the West Coast. As the guy who recruited primarily in California, Nebraska's undesirable weather and distant location made the recruitment of moms more important than ever. After many years of signing West Coast blue chippers, he also noticed that mothers were almost always more influential in the decision-making process than fathers even when the parents were happily married and the dad was fully present in his son's life.

When Darlington looks back at all the recruiting he did, he believes he lost only one prospect when the Huskers had the mom in their pocket but not the dad.

One time, Darlington was pursuing a star prospect from San Jose. Colorado had done an effective job selling the father, but Darlington had the mom in his corner.

"The father naively thought he was going to convince the kid to go to Colorado, but he wasn't," Darlington said. "It was almost comical because you sat there and knew that the father thought he was going to pull the strings, but I knew darned well the lady there already had made her decision and we were home free."

Darlington knew to focus extra attention on mothers because his experience taught him to do that. But that same body of experience taught him to adjust his focus when dealing with certain cultures. In addition to the West Coast, Darlington recruited Hawaii and the Pacific islands. In Hawaiian and Samoan cultures, he discovered, the man of the house made decisions.

"In those cultures, the patriarch is going to be the key to whether a kid comes or not," Darlington said. "If he doesn't give his blessing, you're fighting windmills, because the kids are very respectful of the person in authority."

Of course, strong influencers can exist outside the immediate family.

"Every kid's got someone in the community he looks up to," Switzer said, "especially if he's from a single-parent family, the mother is uneducated and doesn't know anything about going to college." Such a player may rely heavily on his high school coach or someone in the community who has served as a role model or mentor during his childhood. If Switzer could identify such a person, he would try to sell him or her just like a close family member.

But be careful of false influencers. There are those people who get some sort of psychological payoff pretending to have influence over the buying process, especially if the actual prospect or one of the real influencers is a high-profile person.

Recruiting services, advisers, analysts and journalists have more and more influence over the players they promote, highlight or cover in the media. Some of these people cross the line and become personally involved with the players. In some cases, they might be doing this for altruistic reasons. On the other hand, they might be steering a player to their favorite team, or perhaps more nefariously, they could be accepting payment from someone to sway a star player's decision.

Because blue chippers tend to be famous and highly desirable people, many outsiders want to be a part of their lives in the same way groupies want to associate with famous actors and rock stars. Just because someone is a star-struck hanger-on doesn't mean he has any real influence.

Winning 'em Over

The best football salesmen climb the relationship depth chart with influencers just as they do with prospects. Winning an influencer's favor requires a similar approach. First you establish rapport, then build a relationship, which leads to trust, which makes deal-making possible. An influencer must trust you in order to become your champion.

As you begin climbing the relationship depth chart with an influencer, start with good communication.

"It's really important to keep the parent, be it mothers or fathers or both, in the loop when it comes to recruiting," said University of California coach Jeff Tedford. "We make sure we educate [parents] the best we can to make sure it's a good decision and the right fit for the player."

One of the quickest ways to ascend the relationship depth chart is to take the time to explain things. Never assume the influencer knows the process as well as the prospect and certainly not as well as the salesperson. Take time to find out what the influencer does not know and show them how it all fits together.

Another way to prove yourself is to go out of your way to make a personal connection, to put extraordinary effort into your relationship with an influencer.

In 1995–1996, college football teams nationwide were hot on the trail of Mike Brown, a star defensive back from Saguaro High School in Scottsdale, Arizona. Brown was Mr. Everything that year, one of the best players ever to come out of the state of Arizona. Ron Brown, an assistant coach at Nebraska, pulled out all the stops in his pursuit of young Mike Brown.

As it turned out, Mike lived in Arizona with his mother and stepfather. His biological father lived in Gainesville, Florida. Not realizing that Mike was very close to both his parents and stepparents, most teams didn't bother talking to the father in Florida. Coach Brown figured this out early in the courtship process and therefore deliberately climbed the relationship depth chart with the father too.

NCAA rules limited coaches to one visit per week with family members. What's more, a visit to one family member had to occur on the same day you visited any other family member. In other words, if you wanted to visit the prospect, mother, father and grandparents, all those meetings had to take place within the same twenty-four-hour period.

On a couple occasions, Coach Brown would fly to Florida to spend time with Mike Brown's father. Then he would catch a flight, taking advantage of the three-hour time difference between Gainesville and Scottsdale, and spend the late afternoon and evening with Mike and his mother.

Coach Brown's due diligence and strong dedication made quite an impression on both sides of Mike's family. He won the parents' trust and turned them into his champions. It paid off too as Mike Brown did end up at Nebraska where he played on a national championship team his sophomore year and earned first-team All-American honors his senior year. He eventually went on to a ten-year career in the NFL, making the Pro Bowl as a defensive back with the Chicago Bears.

Honor the Influencers

Working with influencers takes work. Some salespersons resent having to take the time with people who aren't the primary prospect. Don't fall into this trap. Holding animosity toward influencers or even feeling annoyed because of them is dangerous. If you don't embrace those who influence your prospect, you run the risk of scaring off both the influencer and the prospect.

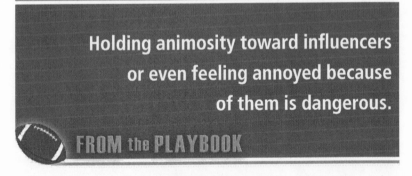

Holding animosity toward influencers or even feeling annoyed because of them is dangerous.

FROM the PLAYBOOK

Ultimately, working with an influencer is in your best long-term interest. When prospect and influencer are both sold on an organization, the prospect has a higher likelihood of being a good client and a greater chance of being retained for an extended period of time. For college football coaches that means they ought to feel happy when family members and other influencers are involved. It's actually an encouraging sign for the future.

Coach Slocum was always amazed when a parent took an overtly hands-off approach to the recruitment process.

"Your child is born, and all the way through you've helped him make big decisions," Slocum said. "Then they get to be seventeen, and they've got to make their biggest decision up to that point in life, and the parents say, 'Well, Coach, it's up to him. It's his decision.' As a parent, you don't want to make the decision for him, but be involved, guiding the process. Make sure he's looking at all the right issues and don't just turn a group of professional recruiters loose on your son. The son is young, and you've got coaches, professional salesmen, who have been doing this for a living for a long time. They're going to push and pull and twist your son in every kind of way."

The smart coach *wants* the family to be involved. It means the young man will be more likely to stay in school, stick with the team and become an outstanding player. The smart salesperson in any business wants a relationship with influencers for essentially the same reason.

Developing Champions

Not all champions have a pre-existing relationship with a prospect. Some of them are people in a certain community who professionally love you and your company. They are your fans, the people who would run through a brick wall for you. They could be personal friends, distant admirers, current or former clients, current or former referrers. They could also be influencers of past clients whom you converted in champions.

Suffice it to say, you can never have too many champions. Those organizations that have raving fans out in the world do more business. A large group of champions on your side is like having a huge marketing and sales staff without having to pay the salaries and benefits.

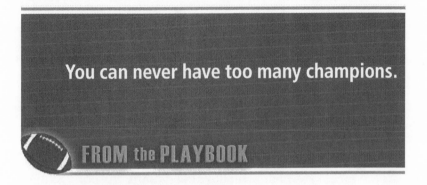

You can never have too many champions.

FROM the PLAYBOOK

But champions don't just appear out of thin air. They are developed. They must be created and then maintained. That means an organization should have a part of its marketing plan focused on how to deliberately develop and maintain champions. Part of that plan would be an ongoing communication plan for champions that would include mailings, electronic communications, phone calls and, most importantly, personal visits.

The most successful blueblood college football programs have humongous networks of champions. To start with, big-time schools have thousands and thousands of alumni spread across the nation, and many of these former students remain rabidly loyal to their alma maters. Chances are, in any given year, that some of the alumni will have personal relationships with blue-chip football players.

In addition to alumni, current students play an important role in championing the school and its football team. Students wear the school colors, show up at games and go back home over breaks and inevitably run into high school kids thinking about college plans. Some of these kids are friends with or related to high school athletes.

Most football teams have a "hostess program" in which nubile sophomore and junior women are carefully chosen to give campus tours and put an attractive face on a prospect's campus visit. There have been cases where hostess programs at some universities have been linked to inappropriate behavior, but most of the time the programs are legitimate, at least from an official-university-policy standpoint.

Current varsity football players are probably the best salesmen of all. If they are happy and enjoying a great collegiate experience, they will help sell the team whenever asked. Prospective players and parents can sense when the existing players are cohesive, engaged and enjoy being part of the team.

Although students, alumni and fans make up the majority of a team's champions, there are others who play critical roles. Some of the best champions are high school football coaches, junior college coaches, owners of recruiting services, teachers, guidance counselors and leaders of youth programs. These champions are located in the various towns and cities around the country where the team goes to recruit players.

To develop these champions, coaches spend time with them on a regular basis, build relationships and establish trust by never letting them down, never going back on their word and treating every prospect they refer with the utmost of respect.

College coaches absolutely relish strong, long-standing relationships with those high school coaches who tend to pump out a lot of prospects each year. Most high school coaches try to maintain some neutrality as their players choose among competing colleges, but that doesn't prevent them from pointing out positive things about their favorite college coaches. It also doesn't prevent them from being secret intelligence sources for their collegiate coaching buddies.

It's against NCAA rules, but some crafty college coaches like to show up in the hometown of one of their favorite, most trusted high school coaches, call him on the phone and say, "Hey buddy, I'm in town, and I've got a case of beer. Let's sit down and show me film of everybody in your area."

It is in these off-the-record meetings that a collegiate and high school coach can talk openly. This is when a high school coach can tell the truth and say things off the record to help his friend: "This guy's dad is in jail and has big problems" or "This guy's on drugs" or "This guy is the best we played against all of last year." When you have a true champion in your corner, you can get information like this from someone in the know who is willing to keep it discreet.

Joey McGuire is head coach at Cedar Hill High School, a powerhouse talent-producing football program in the Dallas–Fort Worth Metroplex. McGuire is a successful coach who looks out for his players and takes great pride in helping them decide which school is right for each of them individually. He never makes decisions for his players, but he's there as an adviser and a source of support.

College coaches know McGuire is not the type of high school coach they can manipulate, but they like him. They respect him. That's because they know he'll treat them fairly and do what he can to make the college-selection process as positive as possible for college coaches, high school kids and their families.

But sometimes McGuire will have a late bloomer or some other guy on his team who has great potential but for some reason isn't receiving much recruiting attention. In this case, McGuire will go to bat for the kid and go out of his way to make sure colleges know about the young man. In such a case, it is only logical that he would likely seek out colleges where he has healthy relationships with the coaches.

Even with a highly ethical and objective coach like McGuire, it makes sense for the college-level guys to build strong relationships with him. And McGuire appreciates and values those relationships.

"The best college coaches come in here and make you feel good about your program," McGuire said. "It's not all about them; it's more about you. After they walk out of here, you think, *Man, I just had a two-hour conversation with a guy I feel like I've known all my life!*"

Don't forget the junior college coaches. They can be some of the most important champions of all. It is not uncommon for one or more members of a given recruiting class to come up short in their efforts to meet NCAA eligibility requirements. In many cases, these students are referred by the college that recruited them to a junior college or a community college. While there, they can take classes to build up their GPAs and play a year or two of football. After that, they can transfer to the four-year university they originally chose.

There's one problem, however. Once a player enrolls in a junior college, he becomes fair game. Every four-year college can start recruiting him again, and he can go wherever he wants. He has the right to change his mind. That means that the four-year school needs to be careful where they recommend he goes to junior college. The blueblood school wants him at a school where the coach is a champion, a guy who will encourage the kid to stick with his original commitment.

In the early 1980s, Nebraska placed its future Heisman Trophy–winning, All-American running back Mike Rozier at Coffeyville Community College in southeast Kansas. Nebraska made an agreement with Coffeyville's coach that no other university would talk to Rozier while he was there fulfilling his academic requirements before transferring to NU. Knowing that Rozier was a phenomenal talent, the head coach at one of Nebraska's chief rivals tried to force his way into Rozier's dorm. The Coffeyville coach literally stood in the door and physically blocked the opposing coach from entering.

Now that's a *loyal* champion.

Building a Pipeline

In the early 1980s, a coach from San Diego's Lincoln High School traveled to the Midwest and paid a visit to the University of Nebraska. Husker coach Tom Osborne and his staff were very gracious to the high school coach, sharing information and touring him around the football complex. The visiting coach said to himself at the time, unbeknownst to anybody else, "If I ever have a player good enough to come to Nebraska, that's where he's going to go."

Eventually, the coach had an outstanding quarterback/running back at Lincoln High by the name of Steve Taylor. He broke many of the records the legendary Marcus Allen had set at the same school several years prior. Remembering his warm feelings toward Nebraska, the coach pushed Taylor in that direction.

At the same time, current LSU head coach Les Miles was then an assistant coach to Bill McCartney at Colorado. Miles was trying to convince Taylor to play in Boulder for the Buffaloes. According to George Darlington, Miles would write scathing letters about the supposed evils of going to school at Nebraska and send them to Taylor. Taylor's high school coach was actually intercepting all those letters and, just for fun, mailed them to his friends on the Nebraska coaching staff. Apparently, some of them were quite humorous.

"Les didn't realize that there was no way Steve was going anywhere but Nebraska," Darlington said, "because the coach had great influence on Steve. So, Les's penmanship and literary skills were really a waste of time."

Of course, referrals—especially like the rather strong one Steve Taylor received—are one of the most important benefits from having established a large group of champions spread across the country.

Purdue assistant coach Donn Landholm stressed the importance of building a pipeline from various high schools into your college team. You make sure the first guy you sign from a given school has a great experience along with his family. If that happens, the coach will recommend another player the next year. After you get a couple of players from the same high school, and all are happy, you have built a pipeline. If you manage things properly, that pipeline can deliver prospects for years and years.

Building a successful pipeline typically requires a territorial management system by the selling organization. That's why it usually makes sense for businesses to keep sales reps in the same territories for many years. Valuable equity exists in long-standing relationships inside your territory.

If you manage your territory right, you'll have champions all over the place, and they will be so loyal, they'll do much more than just refer people. They may actually start to think of themselves as "extensions" of your company. When that happens, you have true selling power indeed.

There's one last thing to mention about champions: develop those relationships before you need them. You will enjoy far more success calling in favors and seeking referrals from people who have already fallen in love with you than you would when you quickly patch together a relationship right at your moment of need.

Find the real decision maker. Sometimes it's hard to tell.

Identify your prospect's influencers and turn them into champions.

You can win over an influencer, but champions must be created.

A champion will continue selling for you even when you are not around.

One of the easiest ways to identify influencers is to simply ask the prospect.

Be wary of false influencers.

Develop a trusting relationship with the influencer just as you would with the would-be client.

Turn influencers into champions by thoroughly explaining complicated matters. Give extra value and spend extra time.

When prospect and influencer are in agreement, you have a higher likelihood of retaining the prospect once he or she becomes a client.

Implement a plan that deliberately develops champions.

Use your champions for intelligence, not just influence and persuasion.

If you are fortunate enough to have champions, keep your mind open to their suggestions.

Reward your most loyal champions.

Ideally, champions should see themselves as extensions of your organization.

Chapter 15

RAPPORT + RELATIONSHIP + TRUST = SIGNED DEAL

Hayden Fry grew up in the 1930s on a dusty ranch near Odessa, Texas. Too poor to own their own land, his family leased 2,000 acres and scratched out a living during the Great Depression. As a boy, Fry developed a work ethic on the farm and learned life lessons the hard way, often reinforced behind the woodshed with the crack of his father's horsewhip thwacking his backside.

It was a life of discipline and a time when kids learned to respect authority as well as their peers. When he wasn't laboring on the farm, Fry excelled in school, and like a lot of Texas boys, he loved football. He was pretty good at the game and eventually went on to play quarterback at Baylor University. After earning a master's degree and completing a stint in the United States Marine Corps, he began a long career as a college football coach including successful tenures as head coach at Southern Methodist, North Texas State and the University of Iowa.

At all three of those schools, Fry inherited losing football programs and turned them into winners. As head coach at Iowa, he led the Hawkeyes to three Big 10 Championships and three Rose Bowl appearances. He retired in 1998 after amassing 232 wins and was inducted into the College Football Hall of Fame in 2003.

When he coached at SMU in the mid-1960s, Fry recruited Jerry LeVias, the first African-American player to receive a scholarship in the history of the Southwest Conference. LeVias had other scholarship offers, so it was quite a coup to attract him to a school that had such an entrenched culture of racial exclusion.

So how did Hayden Fry convince Jerry LeVias to join a school in a conference that never before had signed black players?

The answer is simple: Trust.

"I never even mentioned football to Jerry," Fry said. "We talked about his educational objectives. What he would become after graduation. We talked about personal things. It was obvious he was a great football player, so there was no need to talk about football."

Fry signed LeVias because he built a trusting relationship with him. When trust exists, football coaches don't have to "sell" their prospective players anything. Neither do sales and marketing professionals who work in any other profession. Prospective clients believe the trusted providers will keep their best interests in mind and provide them with the best products or services for their unique needs. When you achieve a level of trust with someone, deal-making is easy.

In order to build trust, you must climb the relationship depth chart. At the bottom of the chart is rapport, which leads to the second level—a relationship. After that, trust blossoms, ultimately leading to a sale or a done deal. With each prospective client you meet, start at the bottom of the relationship depth chart and work your way up.

Coaches climb the relationship depth chart by listening to their prospective players, empathizing with them and getting to know all the important people in their lives.

"I instructed my coaching staff that if the young man they were recruiting had a dog named Spot, then you better get to know Spot," Fry said. "In other words, you needed to know the family, their background, their goals in life, religious beliefs. A lot of other coaches just talked about X's and O's, but our first priority was to talk about education and what they were going to do after graduation. That was a big selling point with not only the recruit but also the families. They knew we had a sincere interest in the young man and his future rather than seeing him as just a football player."

Football coaches must climb the relationship depth chart quickly and do so under extraordinary competitive pressure.

Ki-Jana Carter graduated in 1991 from Westerville South High School in suburban Columbus, Ohio. A *Parade* magazine high school All-American, he caught the attention of all the big-time college football programs not the least of which was Ohio State located right there in his hometown.

When asked about the "biggest fish that ever got away during his career," then–Ohio State head coach John Cooper quickly identified Carter.

"Gosh, we spent a lot of time with that kid," Cooper recalled. "We had him over to our campus probably twenty-five times on unofficial visits. I sure thought we had him, but at the last minute, he changed his mind and went to Penn State."

How did OSU lose the battle for the hometown hero? Relationships and trust. The Buckeyes assistant coach who had been personally recruiting Carter took a head coaching job elsewhere, right in the middle of the process thus forcing Cooper to assign a different coach to Carter. There could have been other factors, including a "pull" factor from Penn State, but in Cooper's mind, the reason Carter went on to become consensus first-team All-American at Penn State rather than at Ohio State was the sudden loss of a trusting relationship.

When a trusting relationship is lost, so goes the deal.

On the other hand, steadily strengthening trust seals deals.

Whether it was *USA Today*, ESPN, Rivals.com or nearly all the other media organizations that cover college football recruiting, the consensus number-one player in the nation during the 2012 recruiting cycle was Dorial Green-Beckham, a six foot, six inch, 220-pound wide receiver from Springfield, Missouri. During his senior year at Hillcrest High School, he caught 119 passes for a staggering 2,233 yards and 24 touchdowns. Despite his size, he runs the 40-yard dash in a blazing-fast 4.4 seconds.

Green-Beckham received scholarship offers from just about every major college in the country from coast to coast. He eventually narrowed all the suitors down to his final three: Arkansas Razorbacks, Missouri Tigers and Oklahoma Sooners. All three schools had good football programs and were located within a few hours' drive of his home.

On February 1, 2012, Green-Beckham stood before a press conference inside his high school gym and placed a black-and-gold ball cap on his head, thus announcing that he was enrolling at the University of Missouri. Just how did Mizzou beat out the other teams for the number-one high school football player in all of America? The answer is easy: a trusting relationship.

According to PowerMizzou.com, Green-Beckham endured a tough childhood, moving from home to home and living with drugs, alcohol and adult family members going to jail. When he finally found a stable home with the Beckham family about five years before high school graduation, it took a while for young Green-Beckham to learn how to trust adults.

Over the course of a four-year courtship, starting when he was merely a high school freshman, Green-Beckham built a trusting relationship with Missouri offensive coordinator

David Yost and head coach Gary Pinkel. Because of trust, Missouri landed the most celebrated recruit in school history.

When Cal head coach Jeff Tedford thinks about his greatest recruiting victories, DeSean Jackson is at or near the top of the list. Jackson was an outstanding wide receiver with 4.3 speed and incredible athletic ability. He graduated from Polytechnic High School in the Los Angeles area. He ended up winning Most-Valuable-Player honors during the 2005 U.S. Army All-American Bowl, a famous all-star football game featuring the nation's best high school seniors.

As is typical with such a phenomenal athlete, Jackson was at the center of a feeding frenzy. Everybody wanted him. His recruitment eventually narrowed down to a ferocious battle between Cal, which is located in northern California, and USC, which was located just a few miles from his house.

"As Southern California player of the year, there was tremendous pressure for him to go to school down there," Tedford said. "For him to step outside all that pressure and come up to Cal says a lot about our assistant coaches. There was communication and a high level of trust. That helped DeSean to understand that we were the best fit for him."

Trust facilitates decision making. Trust is what makes business possible. It makes business easier. When trust exists, deal-making is simply more fun, because participants endure far less stress and tension. In his 2008 book *Speed of Trust*, Stephen M.R. Covey shows us that even the most complicated business transactions can move quickly and freely if trust is present. Huge purchases are still sometimes made verbally and sealed with a handshake when both parties trust each other without reservation.

As a marketer or salesperson, you can just feel it when trust settles into your relationship. That's a great sign; it tells you that things are progressing toward a likely agreement.

Trust facilitates decision making.

FROM the PLAYBOOK

Donn Landholm, an assistant coach at Purdue, was heavily involved in his team's pursuit of a prospect from Georgia during the 2011 recruiting cycle. About halfway through the process, the recruiting secretary said to Landholm, "You know what? I think that mother really trusts you now." Sure enough, the prospect ended up signing with the Boilermakers. When a high level of trust is established, people have a difficult time turning you down.

Throughout this book, trust appears as one of the key themes. In order to succeed in sales and marketing, you must climb the relationship depth chart with each of your prospects as well as influencers and champions.

The relationship depth chart is sequential and therefore must be followed in exact order. First, seek to establish rapport. This simply means that after acquaintance is made, mutual affection exists between two people—I like you, and you like me. We have found some commonality and our personalities jibe.

Once rapport is in place, you can proceed to a relationship, which is a deeper commonality that implies a longer-term friendship, mutual respect, empathy and loyalty. When two people have a healthy interpersonal relationship between them, they tend to enjoy reciprocating—that is, giving each other items of value and doing nice deeds for one another.

Once the relationship is firmly in place, trust springs forth naturally. The stronger that trust, and the longer it has been in place, the more likely the two parties—buyer and seller—can come to a deal. Strong levels of trust lead to enduring business relationships, which can be almost impossible for a competitor to break.

Constantly climb the relationship depth chart with everyone you encounter. Wherever you are with any given person at any given time on the depth chart, the focus is only on advancing to the next highest rung. Your goal is to move every prospect to the top of the chart, but focus on one step at a time. In other words, you're unlikely to have trust if you skip the relationship part. You're unlikely to sign a deal when you haven't passed the rapport stage.

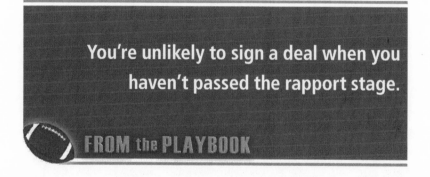

You're unlikely to sign a deal when you haven't passed the rapport stage.

FROM the PLAYBOOK

Trust-Building Techniques

A few key beliefs and behaviors contribute to the creation and maintenance of a trusting relationship:

- Mirror the other person's actions, voice and mannerisms.
- Put aside your own interests to focus on what the other person cares about.
- Tell the truth.

- Treat people as you would like to be treated.
- Be empathetic and consequently respectful to the other person's feelings and beliefs.
- Establish a long track record that shows you always do the right thing.
- Be a rock, the type of person upon whom others can always rely.

One of the reasons Tedford has been able to bring in several highly rated classes over the years is his interpersonal style. He is down to earth and tries to be honest with prospective players and their family members.

"I don't try to sell them anything," Tedford said. "I just give them information, and they get a gut feeling as to whether they come or whether they don't. I want them to walk away with a feeling that we weren't trying to sell them a bill of goods, but that they could trust what I was saying."

Gary Barnett, who took perennially bottom-dwelling Northwestern to the Rose Bowl before taking a head coaching job at Colorado, also believed in playing it straight with prospects. He would tell them that playing college football was going to be the hardest thing they ever did in their lives and that they shouldn't come to his school if they didn't fully trust the assistant coach who would be in charge of their future positions.

"I told every player that if you don't love the game, you won't succeed," Barnett said. "Then I told them the most important guy you're going to be with is not me. It's your position coach. That's the guy that's going to take you where you want to go. You've got to trust your position coach enough to put yourself into his hands and let him mold you for the future."

Trusting relationships are fostered when you go out of your way to relate to people, when you respect someone who is different than you and never ever make them feel inferior.

Let's face it, a disproportionately large percentage of promising football prospects come from households with low income and educational attainment levels. Highly paid, famous football coaches have to work hard to climb the relationship depth chart when people are so different from themselves. To be successful, they have to find common ground, a way to relate to each other.

Former Texas A&M head coach R.C. Slocum grew up poor in Orange, Texas, on the Gulf Coast immediately west of the Louisiana border. He was the first person in his family to attend college.

"I grew up in a family where my folks weren't formally educated, so I know the benefit of education and how it changes lives," Slocum said. "Knowing my background, it meant more to people from those kinds of homes when I told them 'I'm going to do everything I can as a coach to see that this opportunity is valuable for *your* son.'"

Slocum sincerely relished the role of playing "surrogate parent" to his players, especially those who came from disadvantaged homes. He enjoyed preparing young men for life after football. Because those feelings were genuine, prospects and parents picked up on them, which helped establish trust.

"I'd go into homes where the parents were just old country people like my mother and dad," Slocum said. "They didn't know a whole lot about college schedules, courses and degrees. They knew nothing about it. I wanted them to know I was a whole lot more than just a football coach."

Hall of Fame coach Tom Osborne had a fairly normal childhood, growing up in idyllic Hastings, Nebraska, in the 1940s and early 1950s. But his upbringing didn't prevent him from relating to people of vastly different backgrounds. Whether you were a rich kid from a tony Dallas suburb, a poor kid from inner-city Los Angeles or a big old farm boy who played eight-man football in central Nebraska, Osborne made you feel as if you were important, and it was obvious he cared about you as a person.

Years ago, Osborne and one of his assistant coaches, Jack Pierce, ventured into a remote swamp in the Louisiana bayou to visit a prospective player and his family. The home was a rusted double-wide trailer. The whole family was present for the big visit and warmly welcomed the two Nebraska coaches.

As the head coach, Osborne was treated as the guest of honor and was therefore seated in the center of a plastic-covered, nine-foot couch. On the wall above the couch hung a 1970s-era, black velvet picture of a shipwreck. The entire family—mom, grandma, brothers, sisters and the prospect himself—sat with Osborne on the coach, each one touching part of the famous coach's clothing or his hand. After a while, Osborne spread out his arms behind him, so as to gather the entire family in a big group hug.

It was quite a scene to see for Pierce, who sat by himself on a plastic-covered chair on the other side of the living room. Pierce would have normally been amused by such a spectacle, but the home had a funky smell, and he was seated next to a blazing space heater. Pierce was sweating, hotter than hell, feeling a little nauseated. Meanwhile, Osborne was sitting with the family as if the conditions were perfect.

Suddenly Pierce started to feel a little woozy, and the picture above the couch seemed to be moving—the ship was moving!

I can't believe it. The picture is moving, Pierce thought to himself. "Well I gotta go outside and get some air, I'm about to pass out," he recalls. "But then I realize there was a huge cockroach crawling behind the picture making it move."

You may be familiar with those over-sized flying cockroaches down in the bayou. They generally live outdoors in the trees but are known to enter warm houses when it gets a little chilly outside. Well, eventually the six-legged invader flew off the wall picture and landed on Coach Osborne. Pierce's jaw dropped.

"Tom just glanced down at it—and it was bigger than my hand—but never even broke his sentence," Pierce said. "He just kept right on talking. It was like nothing at all to him."

Pierce was amazed. At that moment, he suddenly had newfound respect for the boss he already respected immensely. Osborne casually flicked the bugger away and pretended not to notice. Making a scene over a cockroach wasn't an option. Making his hosts feel badly about their home was the last thing in the world Tom Osborne would ever want to do.

Osborne also built trust through a long track record of focusing on what was best for players.

"I think it's important that you have sincere interest in the well-being of the student athlete," Osborne said. "We talked quite a bit about education and their interests."

In the early 1980s, Osborne and the Huskers were locked in a recruiting battle with Oklahoma over Spencer Tillman, a talented running back out of Tulsa.

"I asked him, 'What are you looking for in a school?'" Osborne said. "He wanted to major in petroleum engineering. We didn't have petroleum engineering at Nebraska, so I told him, 'Spencer, you better go to Oklahoma, because they've got it and we don't.'"

Tillman earned All-American status at Oklahoma and interestingly ended up majoring in journalism instead of engineering. After several years in the NFL, he went on to become a nationally known sports journalist.

Would you be willing to recommend such a great client go to your direct competitor? In most cases, you probably should not, but a willingness to do right by people, even at the expense of your own benefit, will earn you a great deal of trust.

Ultimately, one of the best ways of developing trust it to take the initiative, take a risk and decide that you will put your trust in someone else. Ralph Waldo Emerson said, "Trust men and they will be true to you; treat them greatly, and they will show themselves great."

Ernest Hemingway said, "The best way to find out if you can trust somebody is to trust them." You can stick your neck out and trust someone. There's a bit of a risk to it, but if it works, you will have sped up the process.

Earning Your Trust

Just as you must earn your prospects' and champions' trust in order to sign deals, they should earn yours too. Trust should always go both ways. Trust ought to be reciprocal because that means the business relationship can move forward with speed and ease.

The nature of college football recruiting forces coaches to trust their prospects. The process is structured around non-binding verbal commits. Starting his junior year of high school, a prospect can verbally commit to a team. Because the recruiting calendar continues to speed up, those verbal commitments are coming earlier and earlier in the process. Once the college coach receives the verbal commitment from a young man, he may stop recruiting additional players for the position. If, after a while, the prospect reneges on his promise, the college can be left in quite a bind.

Jim Donnan, who coached at Georgia after leading Marshall University to a lower-division national championship, used to be rather blunt in talking about trust with his recruits. "I'd always tell a kid, 'If you're telling me you're coming, I'm going to count on it,'" he said. " 'If you're still looking, we're still looking.'" Essentially, this means that Donnan didn't count on a prospective player unless he trusted them.

Ask yourself a question: Why is your best client your best client? Think about that. When most sales professionals answer that question, they quickly say "trust!" That's a great answer, but enjoying a highly trusting relationship with a client means you can tell the client whatever they need to hear without worrying that they'll dump you for your competitor. Your best client is your best client because so much trust exists, which in turn allows you to say no when the client needs to hear it.

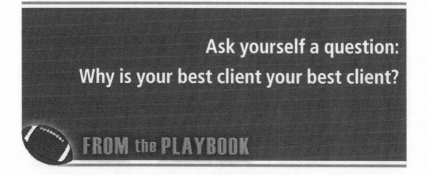

Ask yourself a question:
Why is your best client your best client?

FROM the PLAYBOOK

When a college coach has established two-way trust with a high school coach, things turn out better for all involved. Donn Landholm appreciates the honesty that exists when coaches at two levels trust each other unreservedly.

In such a situation, a high school coach can say, "Donn, I really like this guy. I think you should take a look at him." You could look at the guy and say without fear, "Well, he's not quite a fit for us." The high school coach in this situation is not offended because he knows his college-level colleague is honest, has been at his high school before and will be back again in the future.

"You want the high school coaches to know if they do send a guy to your school that he will be treated right," Landholm said. "He might not be an All-American, he might not go to the league, but he gets a fair chance. He gets a chance to get his degree and has a positive experience. All of that is critical when earning trust from high school coaches."

Former Nebraska assistant coach George Darlington's territory was the West Coast, and as would be expected, he spent much of his time selling the Huskers in the greater Los Angeles area, one of the most fertile recruiting grounds in the United States. Over his three decades at Nebraska, Darlington built rock-solid relationships with so many high school coaches. Because of mutual trust, many of these California coaches became fervent champions of Darlington and Nebraska.

As an example, there was an outstanding track coach at Hawthorne High School, an inner-city school located just minutes from Los Angeles International Airport. Hawthorne's athletic program was so strong that students from all over L.A. enrolled there to run track. The school almost always fielded one of the two or three best teams in the entire state of California.

Over the years, Darlington befriended the track coach as many of his athletes were also talented football players. Darlington knew the track coach was one of the guys he could count on to tell the truth.

"He was originally an East Coast guy, kind of abrupt and very honest," Darlington said of the Hawthorne High track coach. "I would always go visit him before talking to the football coaches. I walked in one day and asked him about this top recruit. The guy said, 'Don't touch him.'"

Darlington asked, "Why?"

"Can you trust me?" the high school coach asked.

Darlington nodded, "Yes."

"I'm telling you, don't touch him," the coach emphasized. "I'm not going to go into it; just don't recruit him!"

Darlington shook his hand and thanked him. "I turned

around and walked out of the school and never contacted the kid again, because when you have a guy that you can trust and you know is not going to do anything to hurt you, then you better listen," Darlington said.

Trust is a two-way street. Not only does it make business easier, it frankly makes it worthwhile. Those who flourish in a sales and marketing career for many years endure because they put a premium on people. They build trusting relationships not just because they help others make more money but because it's also the right thing to do. The elite sales professionals are in business for their clients. Ordinary ones are in business for themselves.

Trust facilitates and speeds up purchasing decisions.

Be attentive so you can sense when an aura of trust settles onto a relationship.

The relationship depth chart (rapport, relationship, trust and signed deal) is sequential and must be followed in exact order.

Establish a long track record of doing the right thing. Be the type of person upon whom others can rely.

The truth builds trust.

Trusting relationships are fostered when you go out of your way to relate to people and never make them feel inferior.

Put clients before profits.

Sometimes you have to take a leap of faith and just decide to trust someone in order to find out if he or she is trustworthy.

Your best client is your best client because you are comfortable saying no when he or she needs to hear it.

Chapter 16

SOONER OR LATER YOU HAVE TO ASK FOR THE ORDER

Overcoming Objections and Closing Deals

Ask an inexperienced sales professional to name the most difficult and stressful part of the sales process and the answer will likely be "the closing." Chances are the second most stressful part would be "overcoming objections."

That really shouldn't be the case. For if you do everything right earlier in the process, objections are merely clarifying questions, and the close becomes an anticlimactic formality. When you know what you're doing, and you are confident in your abilities, objections and closings are just two steps in a long process.

"The longer you do it, and the more situations you've found yourself in, the better you are. You learn not to panic," said former Texas A&M coach R.C. Slocum.

Any salesperson can become worried about a deal not closing. After all, most people who sell for a living "eat only what they kill," meaning that missed sales mean you're not taking any money home. Every time you climb the relationship depth chart with a prospect and establish trust, you're opening yourself up. It hurts when a prospect says "no." The fear of not making money and the risk of emotional pain together make some salespersons, especially young ones, nervous about overcoming objections and closing deals.

Sometimes a college coach will be turned down by a prospect even when a fair amount of trust has been established between the two.

"As a young guy, you're heartbroken," Slocum said. "You put in all that time and you feel terrible hearing those words."

When a more experienced football salesman hears such news, he responds carefully. Just because a prospect makes such a statement, it does not necessarily mean the deal is dead. You have to play your cards right and proceed skillfully.

"You can actually seal the door shut by your reaction," Slocum said. "You might make a mistake and say, 'Man, I'm so sorry to hear that. I've put in all this time, and I was really hoping you would come.'"

Defensive or poor-me responses make the situation uncomfortable for the kid. Some coaches actually react with anger. A prospect says he's going to a different team, and the coach says, "How can you do that to me?" And then he starts attacking and cutting down that school. A coach who does that is indirectly attacking the young man, telling him how stupid he is for making such a sorry decision.

Salespersons who respond in such an unprofessional way end up driving a wedge between themselves and the prospect and essentially kill any hope of ever making a deal.

"I learned over the years to not allow the prospect to slam that door tight," Slocum said. "I remember one particular young man told me, 'We are right in the middle of a deal with another school.' I said, 'Look, I can understand that. Man, you're under intense pressure, and I know people are pushing you and pulling you in every direction. I can understand why you would just want to get this thing over with, but I'm just going to hang in here with you and let you see how everything feels. All the reasons that we're recruiting you are all still true. Those reasons why I really think we're a good fit for you, we're close enough where your mother can come see you play and she can be here every week, a chance to come in and play early. You know what? Everything is still out there, so I'm just going to keep visiting with you."'

Slocum was careful to say nothing negative about the other school that was located far away. He simply remained calm, kept the relationship going with the kid and emphasized his positives. As it turned out, Slocum was right. The prospect was stressed out from the hectic recruiting process and just wanted to make a decision. After a couple days, he settled down, and interestingly, he ended up at A&M where he had a successful career.

Tennessee's Phillip Fulmer agrees with Slocum.

"No means 'not yet,'" Fulmer said. "A lot of people will just take no for an answer and get concerned about being in a bad place rather than continuing to sell. You got to find out when a no really means no. If a no is actually a *maybe* in disguise, then you still have a chance."

If you want to be a good closer, the first rule is to refrain from overreacting when you hear an objection. Don't give up too quickly. You can avoid overreacting by mastering all the other steps in the process.

> If you want to be a good closer, the first rule is to refrain from overreacting when you hear an objection.

FROM the PLAYBOOK

More important than the close is the need to climb the relationship depth chart. Prospects are not likely to turn down a vendor with whom they have developed a pleasant, trusting relationship. Focus early on discovering the prospect's problem by asking probing questions and truly listening to the answers. Remember that the client determines what is valuable, not you. When you know the problem and you know what they truly value, your job is to show how you do a great job of taking care of them. Each step in the process is essentially a mini close that gets you closer to the finish line.

The purpose of a close, at least within the relationship depth chart paradigm, is to confirm the decision, spur the prospect to take action and finish the deal. When you take the time to do all the steps properly, you will close more than your fair share of deals.

Objections

There are three main reasons for objections: one is good, one is neutral, and the third is bad. Fortunately, the vast majority of objections, especially if they occur later in the process, are good.

Bad objections are barriers or roadblocks used by the prospect to get away from the salesperson or to stop the process. Typically, these objections are used to convey that the client is turned off by the product, scared of doing the deal or flat-out uninterested. These are reasons or arguments as to why a person does not want to work with you. When you receive this type of objection, it's usually rather obvious. These objections are telling you that the deal has a low likelihood of happening and that you may be wasting your time to pursue this client any further.

Sometimes, an objection can sound bad but really isn't. It's actually neutral. A prospect might want to delay the decision until a later time for a very legitimate reason. A prospect might be interested in what you are selling but just doesn't have the time to deal with it right now. They might give you a soft no just because they are under too much pressure to deal with you.

Any no that comes out of these situations should be taken with a grain of salt. Give the prospect some space by asking when you should meet again. Then be sure to follow up.

The lion's share of other objections are positive. To a sales neophyte, they might look and sound bad on the surface, but they are really quite encouraging. In fact, good objections are so important to the selling process that you ought to be concerned if you don't receive any. It may be a sign that the prospect is not as interested as you think.

Good objections are actually concerns and questions dressed up as problem statements. Prospects use these objections to make sure they are receiving all the information they need from the sales presenter. They also use them to reassure themselves about a decision they have already made.

In other words, the prospect likes you and your service and believes you can provide value by solving their problems. At that point, prospects just want to be 100 percent sure that they understand exactly what you'll do. These good objections are last-ditch efforts to verify that everything is as great as they think it is. Assuming the salesperson answers the objections reasonably, it's a done deal.

Whether the objective is bad, good or neutral, avoid acting annoyed, troubled or irritated by it. Try not to be flustered by the objection. If you are caught off guard, you can always look up the information or bring in a colleague for assistance. Never be patronizing or condescending in your answers. It's a good idea to prepare for a wide variety of objections and rehearse your responses. Have answers ready to go that can either reassure prospects, reverse negative feelings or nudge them across the finish line.

Overcoming Objections

Several years ago, Fulmer and his assistants were trying to sell Tennessee football to a hotshot blue chipper from Dallas. Like many prospects, he and his parents were concerned about the long distance. After all, many eighteen-year-olds have a hard time leaving home and going to college hundreds of miles away.

The Tennessee coaches anticipated the concern based on past experience. To comfort the kid and his mom, they printed a list of every flight between Dallas and Knoxville to show them how many were scheduled and how affordable they really were.

There are an infinite number of possible objections a prospect could throw at you, and there are countless ways of responding. That said, you will probably have a list of five to ten most common objections. Have answers and rationale ready to go for each of the most likely ones. Preparation means you know what to say and also allows you to be more relaxed and confident as you sell.

"We usually have an idea about objections before we talk to kids, so we can be proactive," said Purdue assistant coach Donn Landholm. "Typically, distance is a concern. We do recruit in Florida quite a bit. If they mention distance, we'll come back with an example: 'Well, let's say you go to college some place close to home, and when you graduate you get a job offer halfway across the country, you'll have to move then.'"

If a prospect from the Sun Belt brings up concerns about West Lafayette, Indiana's cold winters, Landholm will focus on the school's indoor practice facility. A few other northern teams use a very impactful answer when a southern kid is concerned playing in the cold: "What are you going to do if you're drafted by Green Bay someday? Not play? Stay out of the NFL just because it's cold?" That one gets them thinking!

Landholm will also hear objections about Purdue's depth chart. Perhaps a linebacker recruit will see that Purdue has a large number of freshman and sophomore linebackers, making him worry he won't get early playing time.

Landholm responds to depth-chart objections with, "Well, we do have very high-quality players there, but if you're going to a program where they're guaranteeing you instant playing time, you need to be careful, because in another year, they might be saying the same thing to a player coming in behind you. Go to a place that has good players, because that's how you know it's a successful program.

One of the single biggest objections in college football recruiting involves girlfriends. If a prospect has a special young lady in his life, it can be tough to convince him to venture far off to play college football.

"Girlfriends are a pain in the ass," said Nebraska's George Darlington. Darlington said he typically lost one or two prospects a year on the West Coast because girlfriends convinced them to stay close to home.

Bob Hayes of Bakersfield, California, was the second player Darlington ever recruited to Nebraska. He had a girlfriend who was a junior. To convince Hayes to come to Nebraska, Darlington said to the girlfriend, "Look, if it's meant to be for you two to get married, it will work out even though he's in Nebraska and you're in Bakersfield. And sure enough, they ended up getting married and have been together for probably forty years or more."

When Fulmer as head coach was about to visit a prospect, he expected his assistant coaches to prep him. Assistants are the ones who work with prospects throughout the entire process. An assistant should be so versed on his assigned prospects that he could easily prepare the head coach by briefing on the players' likes, dislikes, concerns and challenges. This could help the head coach head off some concerns before the prospect even brings them up.

Perhaps one of the most common bad objections occurs when a prospect is interested in the competition. When Jack Pierce was off-campus recruiting coordinator at Nebraska, he became very adept at answering when one of his prospects said he was leaning toward a different team: "You're going THERE?" he would ask with an incredulous voice tone. "You're going to send your kid THERE?"

He wouldn't disparage the competing school. Instead he would confidently lay out three to five factors in which he felt Nebraska bettered the other program. The approach was very effective.

"I'm not going to talk bad about that school, but match those four categories," Pierce would tell parents. "Go visit that other school and look at those four categories. Then come to our school and look at the same four. That's the only thing your son needs is those four things."

Some objections can come as a big surprise especially if they happen late in the selling process after you have already climbed the relationship depth chart and achieved trust.

At Oklahoma, Jim Donnan was pursuing an in-state prospect in the late 1980s and had built a strong, trusting relationship over a year-and-a-half recruitment period. The prospect looked and felt like a sure thing for the Sooners.

Shortly before National Signing Day, a school from Florida contacted the young man and asked him to come to campus. For whatever reason, he did. They took him fishing, and he loved it. He loved the fact that he was fishing in January when it was cold back home in Oklahoma. The young man had such a great time visiting the warm-weather school that he came home and told his mother he was thinking about switching his commitment and going to college in Florida.

The mother was terribly distraught as she was totally sold on OU. She was absolutely beside herself when she called Donnan on the phone to tell him of this disturbing change of heart.

As an experienced football salesman, Donnan did not overreact. Because he knew the kid was visiting another school, he had a visit set up that night at the family home, and he was bringing head coach Barry Switzer along with him.

Donnan told the mother, "When he says in front of all of us tonight that he wants to go to that other school, I just want you to start crying, sobbing about how you won't be able to see him play very much. This isn't fake; this is the truth. I can hear how upset you are today. Just show it in front of him."

Donnan knew that the kid deep down wanted to be a Sooner and that he was simply enamored by the warm weather during a fresh-in-his-mind trip down south. He used the chief influencer in the kid's life (his mom)—who happened to be a big champion for OU—to overcome the objection for him.

Objection busting works best when you stay calm and think about the most effective way to answer the concern. Emotional, knee-jerk reactions tend to blow up in your face. Think quickly and go back to what the prospect values. Answer the objection in an understanding, common-ground-establishing way that reassures them, addressing the root concern while reinforcing those benefits that provide the best value and solve the most pressing problems. If the objection is complicated or technical, you may have to bring in the appropriate experts from your organization to make a convincing argument.

Seek confirmation that your answer was adequate. It's a mistake to assume that your objection-busting answer worked if the client just sits there and says nothing. You may want to ask, "Does that make sense to you?" "Does that answer your question?"

> **Objection busting works best when you stay calm and think about the most effective way to answer the concern.**
>
> FROM the PLAYBOOK

Closing

A closing can occur at any time in the process but usually doesn't happen until after you have climbed the relationship depth chart and established trust. Every once in a while, you get those wonderful surprises when someone swoops into your office and asks you to sign them up. In most industries, that seldom happens. Instead of waiting for pleasant surprises, go out and find prospects. Ask them questions. Discover what causes them pain and bring value to them by solving their problems.

While closings tend to be foregone formalities when you have worked the selling process properly, you normally do need to go ahead and ask for the order. Even if they're really interested, most clients will wait for you to initiate the close. If you don't, they might end up going with a competitor because you didn't say, "Let's fill out the paperwork."

Because you have done a thorough job with all the steps leading up to closing, all you have to do is just ask.

"Sooner or later, you have to ask," Fulmer said. "I don't know if some salesmen are afraid of the answer or just can't bring themselves to do it, but I was a guy who would make the ask."

Pierce did a fabulous job of building a trusting relationship with both mother and prospect when he was recruiting Neil Smith out of a rough neighborhood in New Orleans in the 1980s. Of all the mothers Smith worked with during the years he recruited players for the Huskers, he developed the closest friendship with LuTisha Smith. In fact, to this day, decades after her son finished his All-American Nebraska career and more than ten years after he finished his Pro Bowl NFL tenure, Mrs. Smith calls Pierce every year on his birthday and thanks him for bringing Neil to Nebraska. Pierce and Mrs. Smith are dear friends.

So how did Pierce close the deal with Neil Smith and his mom?

"I sat in front of her and said, 'LuTisha, you're the greatest woman I've ever met,'" Pierce said. "'You are the woman that raised these kids in all this adversity. You worked your behind off. You showed him right from wrong. You brought him up. You have taken care of him and taught him everything for the last seventeen years. You're the one who's given him seventeen years of guidance. Let us take the next four years. He'll always have you, and now we can do great things for him too. We can finish what you started.'"

Donnan liked to have fun with one of his favorite closing lines: "Hey, my wife wouldn't have married me if I hadn't asked her. What do you think? I mean, this is what you want to do isn't it?"

It's okay to have a little fun with your close but be strong, never timid or apologetic. While you might not be the most self-confident person in the world, be squarely confident in the thing you're selling. Product confidence can mitigate insufficient personal confidence. If you truly believe that you are peddling value, then there's no need to be a reluctant closer.

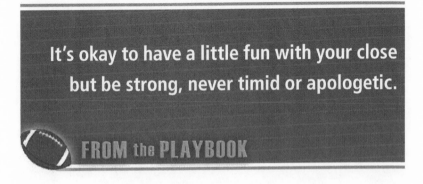

It's okay to have a little fun with your close but be strong, never timid or apologetic.

FROM the PLAYBOOK

Other than the "just ask" close, sales professionals have many from which to choose. Some of them are tried and true, while others might only work in certain situations and for certain personality types.

One is the "forced-choice" close in which you give the would-be client two choices, both of which would mean a sale for you. A football coach could say, "Well, Jimmy, are you going to be a defensive back or a receiver for us next fall?"

The "assumptive close" is one of the most commonly used. When using this close, you act so confident that the issue is essentially a done deal and you say something that conveys this assumption. A coach might say, "When are we going to mark you down as an official commit?"

The "emotional" close plays on one's feelings: "Picture how you'll feel the first time you run out of that tunnel and onto the field for that first game. Imagine what it will be like the first time you score a touchdown and 90,000 fans are cheering for you and chanting your name."

In the "pros-and-cons" close, you sit down with the prospect and make a list of plusses and minuses about going to your school. You just make sure the process is rigged so that far more plusses are obvious.

The "yes-yes-yes" close doesn't work as well for big-ticket items unless you have the right relationship for it. The salesperson asks the prospect a series of questions that you know end in yes such as, "Do you like our tradition?" Yes. "Do you think we can prepare you for pro ball?" Yes. "Would you like playing in front of 100,000 fans each Saturday?" Yes. "Are you going to commit today?" You hope the last one is a yes.

Landholm occasionally uses a version of this close. He will first ask a series of leading questions designed to end in yes. After the last one, he'll say, "Hey, we're ready for you to say yes. Are you ready to say yes?"

The "scarcity" close is quite effective when you are selling only a limited number of spots or a time-sensitive product. A coach could say, "We only have two scholarships left for this year" or "We know you're looking at other schools still, but we have to make a decision quickly."

You don't want to be too harsh in your language unless you are truly in the dominant position when it comes to supply and demand. If it was getting close to National Signing Day, Donnan would sometimes say, "Look, if you can't tell us tonight that you're coming, we're going to probably have to go in a different direction."

Then there's the "take-away" close to be used when you know a prospect would benefit from what you offer, and you know the prospect is sincerely interested, but for some reason, he or she is hesitant to pull the trigger. This close plays a little psychological trick on the would-be client. After all the time and resources you have invested and the relationship that has been built, it can be effective.

You say to the prospect, "Maybe you're not the right candidate for this product" or "I'm starting to think this might not be right for you." You're taking a bit of a risk with this close, but you hope that the possibility of not having this wonderful product or service is a jarring thought and will spark the prospect's initiative.

The list of closes goes on and on, but most of them are gimmicky and should be used sparingly or not at all. If you are selling very expensive items, intellectual property or a service that requires a major commitment on the part of the buyer, gimmicks are a turn off.

> **If you are selling very expensive items, intellectual property or a service that requires a major commitment on the part of the buyer, gimmicks are a turn off.**
>
> FROM the PLAYBOOK

Nevertheless, there are occasionally personality types involved in a relationship that might work. One assistant coach from a major football school had built a trusting relationship with a blue-chip running back from Dallas. The coach was almost positive the kid was going to end up signing with him but wasn't able to get him to verbally commit. Apparently, the coach was really good at making trick basketball shots.

One day, the coach and prospect were playing a game of horse in his high school gym. The coach stood at the half-court line and said, "Tell you what. If I make this shot, you commit … Deal?"

The kid laughed and said, "Sure. If you make that shot, I'm going to your school." The coach dribbled the ball a couple times, took a deep breath and nailed a perfect shot. Swish! The kid smiled, shook his head and said, "Okay, I'm in."

There's an old adage in the sales profession "A.B.C. Always Be Closing." This does make sense. Although you should always focus mainly on the next level of the relationship depth chart, in the back your mind, you want to look for little clues and signals that the prospect is ready to sign. To gauge this, try incorporating "test closes." It's like floating a weather balloon to test the atmosphere. Test closes help you figure out just where you stand.

Ask questions such as, "How are you feeling so far?" "What's the likelihood that you will make a purchase this month?" "What would it take for us to do this deal?" "If I was able to get you X, would you be willing to Y?"

When you're trying to close a highly competitive sale, it can help to bring in a designated closer. This person is usually a highly experienced salesperson with a level of power or authority and who has not worked much with the prospect up to that point. In college football, for many reasons, the closer is almost always the head coach. The NCAA allows assistant coaches to have more contact with prospective players. The assistant works with the prospect building the long-term relationship and developing trust.

At the end, when it's time to seal the deal, the famous, highly paid head coach comes in and dazzles them. The big boss comes in and says, "We want you. We know you can be a huge success here. Let's get it done."

Closing Signals

One of the best signs that a person is interested is questioning. When buyers start to ask several meaningful, probing questions, you know you have a live one on your hands. Questions that show the prospect is personalizing the product or service to her unique needs are tremendously encouraging. Of course, the best questions of all are, "What's the next step?" and "When can I sign up?"

Prospects will exhibit a number of verbal and non-verbal signs to let you know they are interested. While some of these signals are overt, many are subconscious. Be encouraged and try a test close when the prospect takes ownership indicating that he's already psychologically on board. A great sign is when he refers to your organization as "we."

Keep an eye out for growing friendliness, more joking around and increasing agreeability. The more she starts to express agreement with your statements, the more likely she is going to make the leap. You should also be encouraged if the client shares something with you in confidence or makes you privy to one of her company's competitive trade secrets.

Watch for the body language and facial expressions. If the prospect leans forward, has alert eyes, talks with his hands and seems to be energetic, you're doing well. Crossed legs and folded arms can be a negative sign.

Be wary of false closing signals. Sometimes a client will mislead you either deliberately or unknowingly. False signals can really disappoint you if you get your hopes too high too fast.

> Be wary of false closing signals. Sometimes a client will mislead you either deliberately or unknowingly.

FROM the PLAYBOOK

Pierce worked hard to attract the great Emmet Smith out of Escambia High School in Pensacola, Florida, in 1987. Of course, Smith ended up having a phenomenal career with the Dallas Cowboys and became the NFL all-time career rushing leader. In high school, he earned *USA Today* and *Parade* magazine All-American honors and caught the attention of college coaches coast to coast.

When Pierce and Nebraska head coach Tom Osborne visited Smith's home, Smith asked his dad to take a picture of him posing with the two coaches. In college football, that's considered a strong buying sign. *Damn, we got him!* Pierce thought to himself.

Pierce ended up going back to Smith's home a week later and was in a different room. There he noticed that photo framed and hanging on the wall along with similar photos with about forty competing coaches. "I then realized that picture wasn't all that special," he said.

Smith was one of the first players to announce his college choice live on ESPN (now it's quite common). Rumor had it that Smith was going to wear the colors of his future school to the press conference. He walked into the room wearing a red shirt and white pants.

Pierce was watching from a hotel room in New Orleans. *Oh my God, he's coming to Nebraska!* Pierce thought. But how quickly joy can turn to disappointment when Smith announced he would attend the University of Florida, where he went on to become an All-American.

Though the Smith story provides a good example of two false closing signals, you still have to look for them. In many cases, closing signals are entirely accurate. It is normally better to pounce on a false closing signal than to allow a true signal to go by unaddressed.

Contested Closes

Closes are easy when the prospect has a trusting relationship with you, but what happens when the prospect has climbed the relationship depth chart with you and your competitor at the same time? Even more confusing, what if he or she loves you both? This is a contested close.

Such situations are common when chasing the most desirable and coveted clients. Recruiting a top-100 high school football player is a perfect example. Blue-chip prospects sometimes build very strong relationships with several teams at the same time. The choice can be painfully difficult for them and a nail-biting experience for the college coaches involved.

When you find yourself in a contested close, be prepared to go into battle and fight until the very end.

During the 2011–2012 recruiting cycle, the University of Maryland had a superstar prospect right in its own backyard, a wide receiver by the name of Stefon Diggs. Rivals.com gave him a five-star rating and positioned him as the eighth best player in the nation.

According to TerrapinTimes.com, Diggs's choice came down to four suitors: Maryland, Auburn, Florida and Ohio State. In the end, Diggs chose Maryland even though the other three schools are bigger names with greater traditions. Diggs didn't make his decision until ten days after National Signing Day, which is unusual. Maryland coach Randy Edsall didn't sweat it out; he worked it out. He kept doing everything in his power up to the last minute to close the deal.

We're Engaged So No More Dating

One other thing about closings: keep on closing until the deal formally closes. In college football recruiting, teams seek verbal commitments from prospects before they formally sign. These "verbals," as they're called, often come several months before National Signing Day. During that time period, other teams keep calling, trying to convince players to switch or flip their commitments. That's why successful teams keep working their verbal commitments just as hard as those who have not yet committed.

There's also the concept of buyer's remorse in which a client regrets or starts to have second thoughts about a buying decision shortly after he or she commits.

In December 2010, blue-chip linebacker Dante Fowler, Jr., a consensus top-100 player, verbally committed to Florida State. The Seminole coaches were surely excited as Fowler had tremendous athletic ability and a great deal of upside potential. But as his senior year of high school progressed throughout 2011, as reported by InsidetheGators.com, Fowler started to waver on his promise. Rumors started circulating.

Despite stating publicly that he was "100 percent committed to Florida State," he took visits elsewhere. On National Signing Day, February 1, 2012, after being committed to FSU for fourteen months, he suddenly switched and signed with the Florida Gators.

Commitment-flipping stories have become common in college football recruiting. The official term is "decommitment." They comprise a small minority, but there are some players who knowingly commit to more than one school to keep their options open and then keep that secret from the colleges involved.

Although it's frustrating for coaches and fans, most of the blame belongs on adults, not the high school hotshots. Jeff Ketron, head coach of Douglas County High School in Castle Rock, Colorado, believes the increasing prevalence of decommitments shows that "adults are not doing their jobs."

In our culture as a whole, a person's word is not as sacred as it once was, and social consequences for breaking one's promises are not as severe. Adults who work in college football don't set a very good example as it is becoming common for coaches to job-hop, seeking millions of dollars from a more glamorous team before the multi-million-dollar contract has expired with the current team. Kids figure that if coaches can do it, they can too.

Another reason for a rash of decommitments is the push to make kids verbally commit too early before they are ready. Finally, once a young man verbally commits to a school, other coaches keep calling, so it's no wonder that many of these kids have second thoughts.

Most coaches work to convince their competitors' verbal commitments to decommit and join their teams, but as they do so, they kind of hold their noses. Many of them have an uneasy feeling as they do it. It's become an ugly but necessary part of the business.

During his career, former Colorado and Northwestern coach Gary Barnett lost his share of commits to other schools but convinced his share of guys to decommit from somewhere else in order to join his team. When he looks back at it, he still has an uneasy feeling about it, calling it a slippery slope. Over the course of time he became desensitized to it and accepted it as part of the game.

"You have to be a little leery of a guy who is willing to change his mind either to leave you or to come to you," he said. "That can be an indicator of past behavior that could be a predictor of future behavior."

Barnett concedes that players should have this right. After all, coaches come and go, teams can go back on their offers and rescind a scholarship offer, and sometimes players find out that a coach has lied to them. If that happens before National Signing Day, there's a good chance the kid will decommit.

Joey McGuire, coach of Cedar Hill High School in the Dallas area, has the right idea. He advises the blue-chip athletes on his team not to commit too early before they are completely sure.

"I always tell them do not commit on campus," McGuire said. "Wait until you get home. Give yourself a little time to think about it, because I don't want my guys decommiting. Once you commit, it's like a marriage. You don't need to be looking around. You don't need to be shopping anymore."

It makes sense that a high school coach would advise young prospects in such a way, but waiting to commit is probably good for the college coaches as they would be wise to make sure a prospect is good and ready before pressuring him to commit.

In other words, college coaches should make sure the prospect is genuinely committed before putting him in the "sure-thing" category. One of the ways they can do this is to emphasize that they expect this to be a serious, permanent, sincere commitment.

"When you commit, it's like getting engaged with our wedding scheduled for February [National Signing Day]," said former Ohio State recruiting coordinator John Peterson. "When you're engaged, you don't date other girls. If you're going to commit, let's make it right and cut off all recruiting activities and just focus on getting better, enjoying your senior year and getting ready to be a Buckeye." If a prospect wasn't ready to agree to the no-dating requirement, then Peterson would not consider him committed.

In order to minimize the chances of decommitments or buyer's remorse, make sure you hit every step of the selling process and climb the relationship depth chart. Make sure you truly can deliver value as your client defines it. Be honest from the beginning. Don't lie just so you can tell prospects what they want to hear as opposed to what they need to hear.

Don't take commitments lightly. When prospects say they are ready to become clients, let them know that you're counting on it. Finally, never assume someone is a sure thing. Keep promoting your products or services and keep progressing the relationship until you receive payment. Even then, you want to keep closing them in perpetuity so that they persist as your long-term clients.

As the master of malapropisms and self-contradictory quotes Yogi Berra famously said, "It ain't over 'til it's over."

If you react angrily or defensively when a prospect says no, you could be slamming the door on future opportunities.

"No" sometimes means "not yet."

Don't panic or overreact when you hear an objection.

Bad objections are barriers or roadblocks used to get away from a salesperson or to stop the process.

Good objections are actually so important to successful selling that you might want to be concerned if you don't receive any.

Good objections are usually questions dressed up like problem statements.

Have answers and rationales ready to go for your ten most anticipated objections.

Even when they are really interested, many clients will wait for you to initiate the close.

If you truly believe you are peddling value, then there's no need to be a reluctant closer.

To close a highly competitive sale, it might help to bring in a dedicated closer, an experienced person of authority who has not worked with the prospect up to that point.

Be wary of false closing signals. Clients can be very misleading.

It is better to pounce on a false closing signal than to allow a true signal to go by unaddressed.

In order to minimize buyer's remorse, make sure you hit every step of the selling process and every position on the relationship depth chart.

Chapter 17

SELLING AGAINST YOUR COMPETITION

The young upstart and the living legend clashed in battle back in 1979.

It wasn't on the field of play, rather inside a high school guidance counselor's office.

The young upstart was Jim Donnan, a brand-new assistant football coach at Kansas State University. The living legend was none other than Paul "Bear" Bryant who was fresh off winning his fifth national championship at the University of Alabama.

Both men were recruiting the same star high school football player. Donnan was hoping to lure the kid to Manhattan, Kansas, while Bryant wanted him to play in Tuscaloosa, Alabama.

Donnan had an appointment with the player and the high school football coach and was just about to sit down in a small conference room to begin his pitch. But before he could start, the high school coach nervously shared some news.

"Coach, Alabama just called and said Coach Bryant wants to see this guy, but he doesn't have an appointment. Would you mind him going before you?"

Whoa. This was an awkward situation. Donnan wanted to make a name for himself in his new coaching career, and Bryant was someone every young coach wanted to impress. Disrespecting the Bear was not good for a young coach's career. But Donnan had things to do to. He took a deep breath and protested.

"I gotta go somewhere else after this," Donnan said. "I have an appointment with a kid at another school. It's not my fault that his secretary didn't make an appointment."

The high school coach went back to the phone and told Alabama they would need to find a different time to visit. Problem solved. Conflict over, or so it seemed. Just as the conversation was warming up, Bear Bryant walked through the door.

Donnan stood up, shook the Bear's hand, and said, "Coach, you know I respect you, and I've always admired you, but I had an appointment with this young man, and I gotta go to another school after this. I won't keep him long."

Bryant wasn't too happy. After all, this meeting was taking place inside the state of Alabama where most people bowed down and traffic halted whenever the legend passed by. The Bear was not accustomed to waiting.

"Well, that's okay," Bryant growled in his famously deep voice, "but doesn't make any difference. I'm gonna get him anyway."

Sure enough, Bryant was right. The kid enrolled at Alabama and starred for the Crimson Tide.

Donnan referred to it as a "bitter reality pill." It's hard to compete with a living legend, especially in his own backyard. While he lost this battle, Donnan benefited from the experience. He showed confidence. He stood his ground. He didn't lose face or compromise his pride as a coach.

Donnan's run-in with the Bear is a common experience in college football sales. Most colleges have a national selling strategy and target prospects nationwide. Coaches end up chasing the same players, especially the highly coveted blue-chips, so they inevitably cross paths out on the road.

Some of these encounters are awkward or hostile, but most of them are cordial or even downright pleasant. Like professionals in many lines of work, coaches are cut-throat competitors but personally they are collegial. The profession is often defined as a fraternity. The trick is to balance your need to be competitive and beat the competition both in recruiting and on the field, while at the same time building relationships with fellow coaches in order to advance your career.

No matter what your profession, sales and marketing never occur in a vacuum. The selling of products and services takes place in the same world where your competitors live, work and play. Even though you do your best to achieve client control and protect your trade secrets, it's hard to fly under the radar in today's world. Many sales are contested. Even those that are not are probably closely observed by your competitors as they look for ways to gain an advantage on you in the future.

It is and will always be a competitive world. Given that, all marketers and salespersons must develop a tolerance for the competitive environment and an ability to balance the need for competitive confidentiality with the need to build meaningful professional relationships within the industry.

Camaraderie and Secrecy

It's touchy. As a coach, you want to be part of the coaching fraternity, but you don't want to compromise your competitive position. NCAA rules allow coaches to engage in an evaluation period each spring. That's when college coaches can visit high school coaches, look at film, evaluate transcripts and interview high school coaches about their players. Coaches might watch kids work out or run track, but they're not allowed to talk to the high school kids at this point.

Because there's no on-site selling going on during spring evaluation time, believe it or not, many coaches from competing schools will actually travel and evaluate together. They'll even watch film together and share thoughts on the most talented players they see. In the fall, during football season, competing coaches will often watch high school practices together and share their thoughts on the players they see. Of course, when you get into the strategy time and the actual communication with players, things get very hush-hush.

While some coaches enjoy the group evaluation approach with colleagues from direct-competitor schools, some can't stand the idea.

When Donnan worked his way up to head coach at Marshall and eventually Georgia, he wasn't thrilled when his assistants got too chummy with competing coaches while out on the road prospecting or selling. He would urge his assistants to be very secretive. Many times those innocent-sounding, small-talk questions can provide just enough information a competitor needs to get a leg up.

The cagey, more experienced coaches out there may pump a younger guy with questions particularly during spring evaluation period: "Where all have you been?" "Where are you finding players this year?" To be safe, Donnan would recommend his assistants be vague or tell a fib by simply saying they're just getting started with their first school.

"Respect the fact that these guys are fellow coaches," Donnan said, "but you wouldn't tell them what your game plan is if you're getting ready to play them in a football game. It's the same thing in recruiting."

Nebraska recruiter Jack Pierce used to take quite a bit of ribbing from competing coaches when he was out on the road because he refused to watch film of prospective players with anyone else.

"I didn't want some guy from Alabama or wherever sitting there with three or four other guys talking the whole time," Pierce said. "I wanted to concentrate on it. I wanted to be alone to watch it over and over. A lot of coaches thought I was stuck up as hell, but I was very serious about creating my own thoughts about players."

Friendships can be powerful and long-lasting in the coaching world. That sometimes compels coaches who could be adversaries into becoming advocates, who give and share advice.

Long before Hayden Fry was leading the Iowa Hawkeyes, he started out as a high school coach in Odessa, Texas. During that time, he became friends with Bryant because Alabama would sometimes recruit his players. A few years later, Fry became head coach at Southern Methodist University. He ran into Bryant at a coaches' convention and sat by him for a while.

Eventually, he worked up the nerve to ask a question that had long been on his mind: "Coach Bryant, just how did you win all those games?"

Bryant gave that infamous stare to the young Fry and responded in his low, Chesterfields-cigarette-graveled voice, "Son, just remember one thing. If the other team can't score, you can't come out worse than a tie." From that moment forward, Fry would generally put his best players on defense.

It doesn't hurt to build relationships with those salespersons who chase clients who are out of your league. A client that is not good enough or big enough for a larger business might be great for a smaller business. By friending the right people, the small guy can easily survive on a big guy's table scraps.

Long before he was recruiting future All-Americans to Ohio State, John Cooper coached at the University of Tulsa, a private school in northeast Oklahoma. Cooper knew he worked in the Oklahoma State Cowboys' and especially the Oklahoma Sooners' shadows. Tulsa really wasn't in contention for the same types of players that Oklahoma targeted. In such a situation, it made sense to work with the Sooners as opposed to being smashed by them. He built a working relationship with Barry Switzer.

"I would ask Switzer what in-state kids he was offering," Cooper said. "For the most part, we didn't waste a lot of time and effort recruiting those guys. Tulsa ain't going to be the same as Oklahoma in most kids' minds."

Switzer might say to Cooper, "There's this kid over at Jenks [a powerhouse high school football program in the Tulsa area]. He's a good player, but we're probably not going to offer him." That gave Cooper the green light to go after a guy he wouldn't have to battle OU for.

Gamesmanship

Although coaches are collegial, they still find themselves jockeying for position vis-à-vis one another. Conventional wisdom in football sales says that you want to be first. The young prospects remember who sees them first and tend to assume that coaches value most the guys they visit early in the process. That leads to a great deal of racing and positioning the first few days coaches are allowed to hit the road.

Gary Barnett got a taste of the first-week visiting frenzy during his first year as head coach at Northwestern. On the first night, he and one of his assistants were the third set of coaches queued up to hold an in-home visit with Marquis Mosley and his parents in Bloomington, Illinois.

Barnett and his assistant sat in the car outside Mosley's house for an incredibly long time. Illinois went first, followed by Miami and then Northwestern. Finally at 10:15 p.m., Barnett was opening the door letting Miami out as he was going in. By the looks on their faces, it was patently obvious that the parents were exhausted from the first two visits.

"You don't ever want to be in that position," Barnett said. "The parents can only take so much of that stuff in one night, so I knew we didn't have a very good chance." Sure enough, Mosley ended up playing in Champaign for the University of Illinois.

The backlog of coaches waiting to go into a player's house happens quite frequently the first two weeks of on-the-road football selling.

"When you talk to them on the phone, recruits will ask, 'Are you visiting me first?' 'Are you coming to see me the first day?'" Barnett said. "So there's a bunch of guys you promised to see that first week. Well, everybody else has made that same promise, so guys stack up and parents just don't know what to do."

Sometimes the stack-up of visiting coaches happens because players and parents do a poor job of planning their schedules.

A few years ago, University of California head coach Jeff Tedford and Louisiana State head coach Les Miles were chasing the same blue-chip player who inadvertently scheduled appointments with the two men at the exact same time. Tedford and Miles were waiting for the young man outside his school to talk to him after he returned from a basketball game. To complicate matters, the bus bringing the kids back from the game was running quite late.

Tedford and Miles chatted for some time until the bus finally arrived. As the two men walked to the locker room door, each started walking faster and faster trying to get there first. Knowing it would look rather weird if they broke into sprints, it became an odd-looking speed-walking race.

"I outran him that night," Tedford said, "but I'm not sure it was best to be first in that situation. It was late at night, so I tried to do my duty and then give Les some time. I found out later that he stayed up until one in the morning with the kid. Guess I should have been last that night." By the way, the kid went to LSU.

As coaches compete to gain prospects' attention, some rather creative methods of standing out tend to emerge. Coaches love playing one-upmanship with each other. A number of memorable stories come from the long battle between Nebraska and Oklahoma back in the 1970s and '80s.

Because the two teams ran similar offenses and defenses and were in the same Big 8 Conference, they often ended up going after the same high school players. One time a Nebraska assistant was attempting to make a big impression visiting a high school by arriving in a caravan of limos. Unfortunately for him, he was upstaged when Oklahoma coach Barry Switzer arrived via helicopter and landed right on the practice field.

Switzer and Nebraska coach Tom Osborne fought many spirited recruiting battles. Switzer was the laid-back, free-wheeling, shoot-from-the-hip kind of guy. Osborne was the businesslike, serious, professional type. Switzer loved to play with Osborne's idiosyncrasies.

In fact, Switzer would find out when Osborne had player visits in Dallas and then arrange to have an appointment with the same family an hour and a half before. Knowing how polite Osborne was and that he would never interrupt another coach, Switzer would stay inside two or three hours with Osborne sitting outside in the car waiting for his turn. Switzer would come out and feign surprise: "Geez, you guys been out here? Oh man, I'm sorry to keep you waiting."

It was a back-and-forth battle, and while Switzer used to push Osborne's buttons, Osborne won quite a few of the recruiting battles too.

Former Nebraska assistant coach George Darlington spent thirty years selling the Huskers to star West Coast players. During that time, he had a number of memorable on-the-road skirmishes with Pac-10 schools. Some of his more memorable stories seem to involve the University of California.

In the 1970s, after a spirited recruiting battle with Cal, Darlington received a verbal commitment from Frank Lockett, a junior college wide receiver from the Bay Area. The rules at the time made it possible for Locket to move to Lincoln, Nebraska, before actually signing.

Because the battle with Cal had been intense, Darlington was concerned. He wanted to make sure that Lockett actually arrived in Lincoln, so he booked himself a ticket on the same flight in the seat right next to Lockett. Furthermore, he booked their flight out of the San Francisco airport even though Oakland's airport was much closer.

"If Cal was going to pull any last-minute tricks, it would be easier for them to do it in Oakland," Darlington said.

Feeling on edge the whole time, Darlington finally got Locket to the airport and checked-in for the flight.

"His girlfriend was crying as if the whole family had died," Darlington said. "Never stopped crying, trying to get him to stay home with her. Well, I finally get him on the plane, sit down and breathe a sigh of relief. We'd finally got him on board and strapped into the seat."

All of a sudden, a flight attendant approached and said, "Mr. Lockett, there's an emergency at the gate." Darlington knew the family and girlfriend had kissed the guy goodbye, so something was up. He followed Lockett back out of the plane.

"Sure enough, there were two Cal coaches offering him all sorts of things to stay in California," Darlington said. "I told them they were nuts and walked Frank back on board."

Sometimes on-the-road encounters among competing football coaches can be downright comical. Former Tennessee coach Phillip Fulmer often beat the University of Arkansas for players who lived in Arkansas. Fulmer could tell this drove the Arkansas coaches crazy especially because Razorback fans put a lot of heat on them for allowing talented players to leave the state and go to Tennessee.

"Arkansas actually had assistant coaches follow us one time," Fulmer said about an encounter on the recruiting trail. "It looked like a movie with their black SUVs and Hummers chasing us around from visit to visit."

A Safe Hide-Out

If you can't have a world without competition, perhaps you can hide your best prospects from your competitors. Before it was banned by the NCAA, coaches would literally hide players so competitors would not have access to them. They called it "hiding out."

> If you can't have a world without competition, perhaps you can hide your best prospects from your competitors.
>
> FROM the PLAYBOOK

If a player was verbally committed to a particular team, the coaches would try to protect him for a couple days leading up to National Signing Day to prevent an opposing coach from trying to flip him at the last minute. Sometimes coaches would hide players in their hometown; other times they would be sent to far-off, out-of-state places. Sometimes a parent would go with them, or the player would spend a few days with an alumnus or a booster.

Donnan once had a young man who wanted to sign with him, but the kid had a hard time saying no to the other teams that were courting him. The other coaches were on him like bees to honey, so Donnan arranged for him to hide out at his high school guidance counselor's home the night before signing day. He thought nobody would bother to check there. It worked as the kid had a nice quiet night.

The next morning, however, the player's mom drove over to see her son at the guidance counselor's home. A couple competing coaches, who had been staking out the kid's house all night, followed her. Much to those coaches' chagrin when they arrived, they found Donnan waving out the window shouting that he was signing the kid right then and there.

Donnan had a similar situation in a different year with another prospect. Both the kid and the parents wanted to sign with Donnan's school, but the kid didn't want to turn down the other suitors. Every time Donnan would visit the house, coaches from the other school would be outside the house as they were staking out the place twenty-four hours a day.

To get around this situation, Donnan arranged for the kid and parents to meet him at a certain time inside a local grocery store. As the family drove to the store, the other coaches followed them but didn't bother to get out of their car when they saw it was just a grocery store visit.

Meanwhile, Donnan was waiting for the family at a prearranged spot right next to the meat counter. Both parents and the kid signed the documentation right there in the store and sealed the deal as customers purchased steaks and chops.

Similar to hiding out was the guarding concept. When it used to be allowed, coaches would spend the night at top prospects' homes to fend off any last-minute competitors intent on stealing commits at the eleventh hour.

In 1985, Pierce had successfully won a verbal commitment from Broderick Thomas, a blue-chip linebacker/defensive end who happened to be the nephew of the great Chicago Bears linebacker Mike Singletary. Pierce stayed overnight at Thomas's house so he could guard him during the twelve hours leading up to National Signing Day.

"I was so afraid somebody was going to try to steal him," Pierce said. "Broderick let me answer the phone all night. He got a ton of phone calls! I blocked several calls from Texas and Texas A&M alums who wanted to make a last-minute pitch."

The effort paid off as Thomas was a two-time All-American for the Huskers and had a successful pro career.

Poach the Competition

All is fair in love, war and college football. Because the business is so brutally competitive, some coaches look for ways not only to beat the competition but to weaken it preemptively.

Many of Sun Tzu's ancient Chinese theories on military strategy apply to the game of football, college football recruiting and competitive sales efforts in any industry. In sales, you sometimes need to outflank the competition, employ the element of surprise and weaken your competitors before you even begin the battle.

A dramatic way to strike a blow to a competing football team is to hire away one of their coaches especially if he happens to be an effective salesman.

YOUR COMPETITION

As North Division rivals in the Pac-12 Conference, California and Washington duke it out on the field as well as in living rooms and high school coaches' offices. In early 2012, Washington hired Tosh Lupoi who had been a defensive line coach at Cal. Not only did Washington head coach Steve Sarkisian pull away a good coach from a divisional rival, he also landed a skilled salesman.

Many college football experts believe Lupoi is one of the greatest recruiters in the game. In fact, recruiting guru Allen Wallace of SuperPrep called him the best recruiter on the West Coast. The move paid off quickly for Washington as one of 2012's bluest blue chippers followed Lupoi. Rivals.com's number-four player in the nation, Shaq Thomson, switched his commitment from Cal to Washington shortly after Lupoi was hired.

If you can't beat 'em, steal their best salesperson.

Even if you have the heart of a cut-throat competitor, be cordial when you run into the competition. You never know when you actually might need them.

A wily competitor might be gathering intel during casual conversations, so stick to pleasantries and superficial talk.

If you sell for a small organization, you may be able to grow quite wealthy living off the big guy's table scraps.

If you engage in one-upmanship with competitors, make sure you do it for valuable reasons and not simply to boost your ego or satisfy a constant craving for competition.

In highly competitive sales efforts, your personal presence may be necessary to ward off competitors looking to steal your client at the last minute.

As appropriate, find ways to hide your prospects from your competitors. Do what you can to keep them under the radar.

Chapter 18

PEOPLE BEFORE FOOTBALL
Staying Motivated in a Brutal Profession

In 2006, Bruce Feldman received a rare opportunity that surely made sports journalists nationwide turn green with envy. A *New York Times* best-selling author and writer for CBSSports.com, Feldman convinced Ed Orgeron, the then-head coach at Ole Miss, to allow him to be a fly on the wall inside the Rebels' football complex in order to do research for a book that became known as *Meat Market: Inside the Smash-Mouth World of College Football Recruiting*.

For parts of an entire year, Feldman observed first-hand exactly how Orgeron and his assistants strategized and carried out their efforts to attract blue-chip players to Oxford, Mississippi. Throughout that year, Feldman quietly observed the inner workings of a football sales machine and witnessed the emotional rollercoaster coaches ride from the joy of landing a top-100 player to the agony experienced when your prized target turns you down.

As it turned out, Ole Miss brought in an outstanding class that year, but there was one huge disappointment. Joe McKnight was a blue-chip running back from the New Orleans area considered to be the best player in the nation by some college football recruiting analysts. It was a stretch for

Ole Miss to land a player of McKnight's caliber, but Orgeron was a fearless, relentless recruiter who had a knack for reeling in big fish.

From all appearances, McKnight liked the Rebels' coaching staff, but he was also strongly considering two blueblood schools—University of Southern California and Louisiana State University. Most prognosticators said he would eventually choose his home state school LSU.

Despite the long odds, Orgeron and his staff forged ahead, pouring heart and soul into selling themselves to young Mr. McKnight. It was an all-out, totally committed, full-court press. Ole Miss was all in.

As time progressed, the Ole Miss coaches started growing more and more hopeful that they would pull off the stunning upset and land one of the biggest recruits in school history. McKnight officially visited Mississippi in January of his senior year of high school before taking two more visits to LSU and USC. As the date of McKnight's announcement approached, the story intensified with energy and excitement in the way a good novel builds toward the climax.

In the end, the novel was a classic tragedy at least from the Ole Miss coaches' perspectives. McKnight pulled a surprise and signed with USC. Upon hearing the news, coaches gathered at their office. Some of their spouses even came along to show support. In describing the scene, Feldman said it felt like somebody died.

When you put everything into a highly competitive selling situation, it's hard to handle rejection. It's especially hard when you have emotionally invested in the relationship depth chart concept, built a trusting relationship and developed genuine fondness for the prospective client. Making sales through intensive relationship building and trust establishment works better than any other sales approach in the world, but it comes with a risk. When it doesn't work, you feel it.

"It stings," said Cal head coach Jeff Tedford. "You build such great rapport, and you work so hard on a kid. There are guys that you really feel like it comes down to you and one other school. You've worked really, really hard to have a great relationship, and then they go away. You feel like you got kicked in the stomach."

> ## When you put everything into a highly competitive selling situation, it's hard to handle rejection.
>
> FROM the PLAYBOOK

Long before he became a head coach, Gary Barnett vividly remembers how hard it was to handle rejection the first year he hit the sales trail as an assistant to Colorado head coach Bill McCartney in 1984.

"I was recruiting a big tight end in St. Louis, and I just loved the kid," Barnett said. "Coach McCartney told me this guy's gonna break your heart. He went to Iowa, and it did break my heart. I lost three players to Iowa that year and that broke my heart too. That was early in my career, and I think you get hardened by it. You concentrate on the ones that you do get—your guys."

When Tennessee coach Phillip Fulmer thinks back to one of his biggest disappointments in recruiting, Chris Simms comes to mind. Simms was a blue-chip quarterback in 1998 from New Jersey and was named *USA Today*'s Offensive Player of the Year. He verbally committed to Tennessee several months in advance, but just a couple weeks before signing day, he flipped his commitment and signed with the Texas Longhorns. Tennessee wasn't planning to bring aboard any other quarterbacks that year, so Simms's sudden departure left the Volunteers in a bind.

Despite the massive salaries, the fame and the occasional glory, working as a college football coach is in many ways a hard-knock life.

Staying Motivated

With all the emotional, high-risk/high-reward scenarios playing out each year and with so much riding on their ability to bring in great players, how do they cope with the disappointment? How do they cope with the pressure?

For one thing, they need to know what they're getting into. For another, it helps to have a support structure at home. And sometimes they need to take a break no matter how busy they are and how much the competitor inside wants to win.

"It's not a job," Fulmer said. "Anybody who thinks it's a job is wrong. It's an absolute lifestyle. Your family has to understand that. You need a very understanding and supportive wife and children. Coaching is 24/7. That said, on occasion, you have to tell your staff even during the season, 'Let's go home tonight and be fresh and ready to go tomorrow.'"

One of the best ways to survive a brutally competitive profession is to enjoy it. If you don't enjoy working in sales or marketing, you probably should look for a different line of work. Despite the pressures of coaching and sixteen-hour workdays away from friends and family, Fulmer loved it and seldom viewed the long days as drudgery.

Former Georgia and Marshall head coach Jim Donnan agrees that if you love what you do, work won't feel so much like work.

"I don't think you can be a good football coach if you don't thrive on the competition and if you don't love recruiting," he said. "You gotta have all ten coaches working their butts off year round to be successful selling your program to the right players."

If you love your work and make a commitment to finding the joyful and positive within it, your ability to stay motivated and cope with pressure increases. If you are positive about what you do for a living, you will also be better prepared to handle unexpected interruptions and will be better equipped to wear your smiling game face when something bad happens.

Football coaches must cope with a certain sales challenge that few other sales professionals could imagine—hosting and entertaining prospects immediately after losing a football game.

Most teams invite a group of prospects to each of their home games. It's a great selling tool. The high school players are walked out onto the field, the fans are cheering and the marching band is playing. Few things in the world are more powerful and effective sales tools than a sold-out football game in a picturesque campus setting on a balmy Saturday afternoon in mid-October.

But what happens if you lose the game?

Think about that. Imagine strategizing and practicing all week to beat another team on the field. You work day and night getting ready for the game and dedicate every ounce of your being to the effort. Then you go out and lose.

Maybe it was a last-second heart breaker. Maybe you got blown out by a much better team. Either way, thousands of people in the stands and millions of fans watching on television are crushed, disappointed and perhaps angry about some in-game decision the coach made. Every game the team loses makes the coach at least a little bit worried that he could be fired from his $2-million-a-year dream job. He might even feel sick to his stomach.

But after all that, he has to suck it up, put on a happy face and go entertain a bunch of seventeen-year-old boys upon whom his professional future rests.

"That's just part of the deal," said Texas A&M's R.C. Slocum. "I would go across the field, see the visiting head coach, go into the locker room, talk to my team, go do the press conference, win or lose, and then walk into a room of recruits and visit with them. You might have lost that day, but go in there and put a positive spin on it."

The pressures are tough before the game as well. The coach probably wants to focus on his game plan, but he has to entertain prospects and make small talk with some of his supporters and champions, who expect him to give them personal attention.

Slocum counts among his friends former President George H.W. Bush, an enthusiastic fan of A&M athletics, who would sometimes stop by on the field before games and say hello. Of course, if a former President wants to say "hi" before the game, that's a distraction. Similarly, members of Congress, influential business leaders and powerful boosters often expected a little pre-game face time with the head coach as well.

"You have to enjoy the whole process," Slocum said. "Stop and be cordial and gracious to people. At kickoff, you then flip the mental switch and you're fully into the game. I'm a big enough person that I can flip that switch."

Former Minnesota coach Tim Brewster is known for his sales ability and was a star recruiter back when he was an assistant coach at Texas. He stayed motivated in both coaching and recruiting by savoring the competitive nature of everything.

"I loved going head-to-head, trying to figure out a way to win," Brewster said. "I loved finding out who the decision maker was and unlocking the secrets. I took every recruiting battle personally. I don't know how you couldn't because you dedicate your life. You work your tail off trying to make something happen, and, yeah, there's mourning when you lose, but there's exhilaration when you make something happen."

Similarly, Barnett overcame disappointments and pressure by thriving on the competitiveness in recruiting. "I like the competition, competing against other schools and coaches," he said. "Recruiting was like picking your family. I liked getting to know a youngster, bringing him in and watching him grow up."

Taking a little time to celebrate your victories also keeps a person going. One time during his tenure at Colorado, Barnett had one of the nation's top recruits commit to him right before National Signing Day. The football offices were like a party atmosphere for a while after all the staffers heard the good news. "In your own little way, you celebrate every recruit and appreciate them for making your hard work pay off," Barnett said.

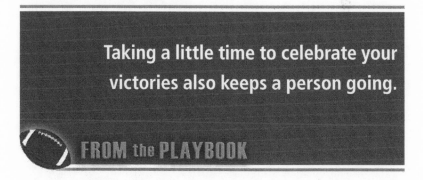

Taking a little time to celebrate your victories also keeps a person going.

FROM the PLAYBOOK

Much of a coach's source of continuing motivation comes from the people who surround him. Enjoy and appreciate the people who help make you successful. Put an emphasis on serving your clients and the staff that serve you. Valuing the people who influence your success does wonders for your motivation. Determine what really matters to you in your life, and when you see it, honor, acknowledge and savor it.

As Slocum would travel the state of Texas looking for blue-chip prospects, he saw the best and worst in people. In one day, he might find himself inside a humble home in a poverty-stricken part of south Dallas followed by a visit to a mansion in affluent Highland Park, Texas.

At each socioeconomic level, Slocum encountered some of the most wonderful human beings imaginable as well as some of the sorriest characters you would ever meet. He cherished the strong-willed characters who stood on solid foundations. As a man who came from a humble background, he particularly appreciated it when an uneducated poor family exhibited extraordinary character.

Years ago, Slocum visited a prospect and his mother in a severely impoverished area.

"Coach, I knew you was comin'," the player's mother said to Slocum. "You must be terribly tired as much as you run around, and I want to fix you a sandwich."

The mother tore a paper towel off the roll and carefully folded it around a perfectly made sandwich. She handed it to Slocum with a Dr. Pepper, making the lunch look as attractive as she could within her limited means as a single mom in a humble, little apartment.

"I almost cried," Slocum said. "She had gone to so much effort. It wasn't fancy by fancy standards, but in terms of what she had to offer, it was amazing."

Slocum and the player's mother had a great conversation and started to build a trusting relationship. As he walked out of the apartment, he said to the assistant coach who accompanied him, "'Man, there's all kinds of class. That lady right there is a perfect example. I bet her son is a success.' Sure enough, he came and he started for me for four years and was a great player, got his degree and is living a successful life. He grew up poor, but he grew up around a whole lot of class and a whole lot of character."

When you grow weary or when you're feeling burned out, draw inspiration from the people around you. They all have stories. Some of those stories illustrate why the products or services you sell are worth selling.

> When you grow weary or when you're feeling burned out, draw inspiration from the people around you.
>
> FROM the PLAYBOOK

Character Is King

Ultimately, success in sales or any other profession comes down to character. Just as some football coaches decide to cheat, a certain segment of professionals in any industry choose the illegitimate path. That might work for a while, but not long term. We are all in business to make money or garner whatever else we value, but part of our focus should be on serving others and making the world a better place. In the long run, it usually pays to lead an ethical career.

Former Nebraska coach Tom Osborne enjoyed tremendous success, winning three national championships, thirteen conference championships and more than 83 percent of his games over a twenty-five-year head coaching career. ESPN named him Coach of the Decade for the 1990s.

Despite all that success, when asked what mattered the most in his successful career, Osborne responded, "Character." When hiring assistant coaches, Osborne hired for character. When recruiting players, he wanted people with a strong work ethic and commitment to team values.

"Some players have a lot of talent but have skewed value systems or overly inflated opinions of their importance or are primarily interested in the National Football League," Osborne said. "If you have too many of those people, it's not going to work out very well. Character is critical."

While coaches are wise to seek character when prospecting, they need to exhibit it themselves. Osborne was careful to tell prospects the truth when recruiting them. Over the years, his teams had very high retention rates because he did not allow his staff to promise playing time or guarantee that a prospect would be a starter someday. Osborne lost some players over the years because he warned them that playing for Nebraska would be hard work.

One high school coach had a highly coveted blue chipper on his team. Nebraska was among the schools in contention. The high school coach liked Osborne and wanted the young man to play for him in college. Frustrated that the kid was leaning toward a different team, the high school coach said to Osborne, "Just tell him what he wants to hear, Coach. Everybody is coming in here and telling him he's going to start as a freshman. Just tell him what he wants to hear, because I'd like to see him go to Nebraska."

Osborne thanked the coach for his support but told him that was not going to happen. "I have other players in my program," Osborne responded. "I can't promise their playing time to a guy who has never played a game with us."

Those sales professionals who focus on character— improving their own while fostering it among their colleagues and clients—can rest assured that their careers will be meaningful when it's time to retire.

> Those sales professionals who focus on character can rest assured that their careers will be meaningful when it's time to retire.
>
> FROM the PLAYBOOK

Each year, Coach Slocum takes part in a golf tournament at Pebble Beach. Twenty-five football coaches participate, and each is allowed to bring three guests. Slocum normally brings three of his former Texas A&M players.

Referring to the three alumni he brought with him recently, Slocum said, "I was so proud. These guys were all grown, had families and careers. I have often said, if you really want to measure the worth of a coach, just look at his players five, ten years down the road and see what they're doing. See what kind of jobs they have. That'll be the best measure."

The wins were important to Slocum, but they all run together in his mind now that he's been out of coaching for quite a while.

"What really has lasting meaning is the influence you have on those young men that were placed under your leadership—the example you set, the values you taught them. That's the way I approached coaching," he said. "As a result, I can look all those guys in the eye. I didn't teach them to cheat or be abusive people. I taught them to be good, so I can live with that and feel good about it as I look back."

Hayden Fry, who coached the Iowa Hawkeyes to three Rose Bowl appearances, believed strongly in exhibiting character and putting others before himself. Though he was a strict disciplinarian, his players knew he loved them.

Whenever one of them would be injured, Fry was always one of the first to check on him.

Even today as an octogenarian living in retirement, Fry is busy spending time with his many former players in person, via phone and over the Internet.

Fry recently received the American Heart Association's Paul "Bear" Bryant Lifetime Achievement Award at a ceremony in Houston. "I had over a hundred players in attendance," he said. "Some of them traveled across the United States just to come to the banquet, and I had a whole bunch of my old coaches there too." The outpouring of support from those former players meant so much to the retired coach who always cared so much about them.

Men and women of character show respect to everyone, even to those people who can seemingly not do a thing for them. They are also loyal to the people in their lives. They remember those who have helped them and continue to appreciate them long after the working relationship has ended.

In 1977, college coaches from far and wide converged on Anniston, Alabama, a small city in the northeastern part of the state. The target was Andra Franklin, a blue-chip athlete with the physical size of a lineman and the speed of a running back. He played tight end until his junior year, during which he gained more than 500 yards rushing on end-around reverses alone. After reeling off so many long runs, it occurred to the coaches that Franklin might be better used at tail back. The long-overdue position switch was wildly successful as Franklin became a dominant, punishing running back.

Both Alabama and Auburn pulled out all the stops zealously trying to sign Franklin, especially Alabama. In fact, Franklin was leaning toward Alabama for much of his senior season. One day after visiting the Alabama campus, Franklin returned home and talked with Jack Pierce, an assistant coach on the high school football team.

"Geez, Coach, I just don't feel good about Alabama," Franklin confided in Pierce. "The racial stuff down there is still going on, and I just don't want to play football in that situation."

It was obvious Franklin was feeling a great deal of angst over the college-selection process. He felt trapped, so Pierce volunteered to help the kid out. Pierce sent copies of Franklin's game film to a few college coaches he happened to know. One of those guys was John Melton, linebackers coach at Nebraska. Immediately upon reviewing the film, Melton was impressed. He sent an airline ticket down to Anniston and told Pierce, "Get him on the plane. We want him to come up here."

Franklin talked to his mother and decided to take the trip up north. When the high school's head football coach found out, he was furious as he had a strong relationship with the University of Alabama coaching staff. In those days, Alabamans didn't tolerate star football players leaving the state especially if a local assistant high school football coach facilitated the defection.

During his visit to the University of Nebraska, Franklin fell in love with the place. He returned home and told Pierce he had made up his mind—he planned to sign with the Huskers. Knowing that the decision wasn't going to go over well in Alabama, Pierce took a deep breath and said, "Okay, let's get you ready."

Three days later, Pierce and his family were driving home from an appointment. As he pulled into his driveway, Pierce saw two men standing on the front porch waiting for him. One of them was the head coach of the high school team. The second one was none other than Paul "Bear" Bryant, legendary coach of the Alabama Crimson Tide.

"Bear made it clear in no uncertain terms that if Andra Franklin went to Nebraska, he would make it very, very difficult for me there," Pierce said. "Bill Farrell [the head high school football coach] told me, 'He'll make it difficult; I'll fire you.' Bear told me I'd never work in the state of Alabama the rest of my life."

Well, Franklin did sign with Nebraska, and, sure enough, Pierce never worked in Alabama again.

When Nebraska coach Tom Osborne learned of Pierce's fate, he felt bad. He called Pierce and told him he would be happy to find a high school coaching job for him in Nebraska. Pierce took him up on the offer. Osborne placed him at Lincoln High School, just minutes away from the University of Nebraska campus.

That summer, Andra Franklin and the Pierce family left Anniston together. Pierce drove the U-Haul truck while his wife drove one of the family cars and Franklin drove the other. The three vehicles caravanned together for the sixteen-hour drive to their new lives in Lincoln, Nebraska.

As it turned out, both Pierce and Franklin ended up having rewarding careers in Nebraska. Shortly after arriving, Osborne hired Pierce to work in the Huskers recruiting office. He eventually became an assistant coach at Nebraska and then the off-campus recruiting coordinator. He left the university in the 1990s when the NCAA banned the off-campus recruiter position, but he took a different job outside football and made a permanent home in Nebraska.

As for Franklin, he had a stellar career as a star fullback in Nebraska's vaunted I-formation offense. He was a bruising runner and a crushing blocker. Osborne considers him one of the best players he ever coached. He was drafted by the Miami Dolphins in 1981, earned All-Pro status and starred in the 1983 Super Bowl. He even got his picture on the cover of *Sports Illustrated.*

Unfortunately, a severe knee injury ended his NFL career prematurely. Eventually, Franklin moved back to Nebraska.

His health deteriorated, and he developed severe heart problems. Already a quiet, private fellow, Franklin withdrew from the world and became somewhat of a recluse. As his health worsened, he couldn't hold a job. In late 2006, at the age of forty-seven, Franklin died alone in a tiny apartment in Lincoln.

Franklin's family decided he would be buried next to his parents in a cemetery back in his hometown. Who do you suppose transported his body down to Alabama for the burial? Jack Pierce. The man who took him by the hand as an eighteen-year-old and led him to Nebraska was the same man who drove his body back to Anniston almost thirty years later for his final rest.

Pierce left the coaching profession more than a decade before Franklin passed away. There was no longer anything that Franklin could do to help Pierce's career, but that didn't matter. Pierce still cared about him. He was thankful for the time he had with Franklin. Death did not end the sense of loyalty Pierce had for his former player, a young man whose choice of colleges opened a world of opportunity for the former coach and ended up profoundly changing the lives of many.

To cope with the inevitable rejection in a sales career, concentrate on your victories. Celebrate each one of them in your own way.

Those who don't find ways to enjoy their work typically don't survive long in a brutally competitive industry.

Find the joyful and positive aspects of your work.

Be nimble, always ready to flip the switch between operational and selling activities.

Playing to win removes the drudgery of day-to-day work.

Draw inspiration and motivation from the people who surround you.

Long-term success depends directly on character.

Tell the truth even when it hurts. You will be rewarded with high levels of client retention.

As you sell today, imagine what your legacy will be years down the road.

ACKNOWLEDGMENTS

Although an author spends many late nights alone clicking keys on the laptop, the creation of a book is not a solitary endeavor. It takes a team of people to put together the finished product, and I couldn't have asked for a better team.

I would first like to thank my wife, Stephanie Beals, who always provides me great support and encouragement, and my children, Jack and Maddie, who too often had to hear, "I can't play tonight; daddy's too busy writing."

I love and appreciate my parents, Terry and Mary Beals, and my other supportive family members including Jill and Scott Graves; Greg and Maria Beals; Kacie and Nick Ferrazzo; Rollie and Shirley Winter; Manish Das and Lisa Winter-Das; and Jim and Jessica Matheson.

My colleagues at World Group Commercial Real Estate and Seldin Company are sources of inspiration and support. I would especially like to mention Trenton Magid, Kevin Rhodes, Ted Seldin, Randy Lenhoff, Tucker Magid, Jennifer Goaley, and Sarah Childers. There are so many others.

Mark Hunter, author of *High-Profit Selling: Win the Sale without Compromising on Price*, has been an adviser and mentor to me in my work as a professional speaker, and I greatly appreciate his support. Fellow authors such as Tom Becka, April Kelly and J.P. Hansen have allowed me to bounce ideas and talk shop.

A big thank you to my friends at Clear Channel radio in Omaha where I host a weekly talk show and produce a daily feature: Gary Sadlemeyer, Jim Rose, Roger Olson, Melissa Gerardy, Tom Stanton, Scott Voorhees, Erik Johnson and Michelle Filips.

A book cannot be successful without a dedicated publishing team. Mine was world-class and included Lisa Pelto, owner of Concierge Marketing, and my editor Sandra Wendel. Lisa and Sandy are absolutely top-notch publishing professionals, and it's a stroke of good fortune that we all live in the same city. A special thank you goes out to Katie Dittman, who painstakingly transcribed hours and hours of my interviews with coaches, journalists and players.

To research this book I interviewed far more people than I initially imagined. These people took time out of their busy schedules to provide me with valuable content. Thanks goes out to Sean Callahan, the late Bob Billings, Don Bryant, Jeff Lake, Jack Pierce, Gene Williams, Ryan Abraham, Adam Munsterteiger, Josh Helmholdt, Adam Gorney, Bryan Matthews, Mike Scarborough, Bruce Feldman, Jeff Ketron, Max Emfinger, Dr. Bernie Kish, John Talman, Tom Osborne, A.J. Tarpley, Austin Shepard, Alex Crosthwaite, Joey McGuire, Donn Landholm, Joe Moglia, Phillip Fulmer, Barry Switzer, John Cooper, Jim Donnan, Gary Barnett, George Darlington, Tim Brewster, R.C. Slocum, Marvin Sanders, Jeff Tedford, John Peterson and Hayden Fry.

Several people guided me to resources or helped me schedule interviews including Jim Grotrian, Randy Schmaizl, Max Olson, Jeff Beckman, Mike Schreurs, Anne Hackbart, Cyndi Fisher, Andy Seeley, Shelly Poe, Kenny Mossman, David Plati, Kyle McCrae and Tim Cassidy.

ACKNOWLEDGMENTS

Finally, several friends gave advice, feedback, ideas or other forms of assistance including Mitch Arnold, Ed Burns, Becky Gima, Jerry O'Doherty, Jacqueline Flynn, Doug Roesemann, Susan Baird, Scott Kennedy, and Bridgit Lynch.

ABOUT THE AUTHOR

Jeff Beals is an industry leader in sales and marketing. He is an award-winning author, keynote speaker and radio talk-show host.

He is an active member of the National Speakers Association and delivers hundreds of keynote speeches and workshops to diverse audiences worldwide each year.

As executive vice president at World Group Commercial Real Estate and Seldin Company, Beals supervises marketing for the companies' combined 10,000 apartment units and 3.7 million square feet of commercial real estate space in six states.

Beals is co-host of an award-winning weekly radio talk-show, Grow Omaha, on 1110 KFAB, a Fox News affiliate. In 2009, he served as host of a weekly television show on an NBC affiliate.

A frequent media guest, Beals has been featured in *Investors Business Daily, USA Today, Men's Health,* and *New York Times Online* and on a number of television and radio stations across the country.

Beals's award-winning first book, *Self Marketing Power: Branding Yourself as a Business of One,* is about personal branding and professional success. The book has won four major awards including the Bill Fisher Award for Best First Book (Ben Franklin Awards); *Foreword* magazine's Career Book of the Year, Silver Medal; National Indie Excellence Awards, Finalist; and *USA Book News*, First-Place Award for the business category.

More than 250 of his business articles have appeared in local, national and international periodicals. He writes the bi-weekly "Business Motivation Blast," which has more than 9,000 subscribers.

From 2003 to 2009, he served as an adjunct faculty member at the University of Nebraska at Omaha's College of Business Administration. Previously, he was Dean of Student Affairs at Clarkson College.

Beals holds a master's degree in political science and a bachelor's degree in journalism, both from the University of Nebraska–Lincoln. He and his wife, Stephanie, have two children, Jack and Maddie.

To contact the author about speaking to your company or organization, visit www.JeffBeals.com.

To order additional copies, related products or to book a speaking engagement, go to www.JeffBeals.com. Contact the author at Jeff@JeffBeals.com or Keynote Publishing, LLC, PO Box 540663, Omaha, NE 68154.

INDEX

INDEX

salary of, 39
as sales leader, 142–143
as salesmen, 9, 15, 49
sales strategies of, 114–116, 121, 133–137
as situational recruiters, 46–47
staff assistance to, 26
stress management by, 11, 14
success of, 53–54
time management of, 39
as traveling salesmen, 47
work ethic of, 44, 101
Coach prospecting
attention to detail and, 64–65
branding and, 85, 88–92, 94, 97–99, 107
client-contact management system and, 65
communication and, 27, 42–43, 65–69, 70–71
dealing-making process and, 78–79
for "diamond-in-the-rough" client, 169–170
division of labor and, 128–132
fiduciary responsibilities during, 70–71
geographical, 126–128
hiding prospects from others, 330–332
improvising, methods during, 48–49
in-home visits, 28, 47–48
Internet-based recruiting websites and, 33–34
leads for generating, 126
multiple, handling of, 44
on-campus visits, 27–28
private vs. public, 32–33
qualifying and, 75–78, 176
referrals and, 171–174
relationship, building of, 102
through camps, 167–168
Coach sales strategies
balancing games for, 136–137
goal setting and, 121
over-offering and, 136–137
relationship depth chart and, 115
southern, 114–115
tactics vs., 115–116
war room for presenting, 133–135
Coastal Carolina University Chanticleers, 14
Coca-Cola, 85, 86
Coffeyville Community College Red Ravens, 277–278
College football
as "caste system," 23
character in, 35
motivation inspired by, 35
purpose of, 34
as sales process, 3
College football coaches. See coaches
College Football Hall of Fame, 15, 37, 282
College football recruiting. See also recruiting/ recruitment
as business process, 12
commitment to, 187
communication and, 190
competition and, 9, 10–11, 53–54, 62, 71–72, 332–333
evaluation season for, 27
fiduciary-like selling and, 71
gamesmanship and, 326–330
group evaluation approach to, 324

honesty and, 59–61
importance of, 11, 20–21, 34, 40
landscapes of, keeping up with changing, 49–52, 188
as lifeblood of college football, 24, 39–40, 107
as marketing process, 12
of mother, importance of, 8
NCAA rules for, 28–29
process of, 13, 19–20
recruiting budget for, 11
as sales process, 12, 52–53
as second season, 12, 22
secrecy and, 324
strategic thinking during, 73–75
success and, 37, 115
as third season, 22
work ethics and, 38–39
year round, 24
Collins, Jim, 57
Commitment
to brand/branding, 93
closings and, 314–318
of coaches, 44, 53
to college football recruiting, 37, 187
motivations and, 339
to prospecting, 161
of salesmen, 38
verbal, 10, 28
Commitment-flipping stories, 315
Communication
coach prospecting and, 27
college football recruiting, use for, 190
empathy and, 69–71
influencers, establishing of good, 270
informative, 188
interpersonal, 233
listening and, 65–67, 237
personality and, 67–69
persuasive, 188
relationship building and, 42–43
sales, 188–189
Communication plan, 188–206
designing, 188
intelligence gathering and, 202–205
listening and, 237
for marketing process, 189
for mass media, 189–190
for message, 188
mixed-media approach to, 189
personal tactics of, 205–206
for salesmen, 189
for sales process, 189
steps to, 188
for targeted media, 191–197
for telephone, 197–199
for voice mail, 199–201
Competition
in business world, 49
of CEO's, 14
within college football recruiting, 9, 10–11, 53–54, 62, 71–72, 332–333
ego and, 155–156
gamesmanship and, 327–330
marketing process and, 323

INDEX

SELLING SATURDAYS

INDEX

INDEX

NEED A SPEAKER FOR YOUR CONFERENCE OR MEETING?

Jeff Beals is a proven, experienced speaker, who weaves together research, personal experience and humor. He's a storyteller who engages and motivates audience members, leaving them pondering the topic long after the presentation has ended.

Customized Presentations

Selling Saturdays is wildly popular with all types of groups. In this thought-provoking presentation, a Beals shares the sales-and-marketing secrets he learned by interviewing legendary college football coaches. You'll become more effective at marketing, selling and building interpersonal relationships by learning how famous coaches battle their competition in the brutally competitive race to sign the nation's most prized, blue-chip athletes. This mind-boggling presentation is part soap opera, part mystery novel and part action-suspense movie. When the presentation comes to a close, your attendees will be inspired and motivated to pick up the phone, hit the streets and close deals!

Self Marketing Power is based on his international-award-winning book of the same title. The material comes from Beals' experiences as a real estate executive, radio/television talk-show host, writer, college dean and part-time professor. He has delivered this speech more than 400 times in over 30 states. This presentation is offered as a keynote speech, break-out session and a workshop.

Jeff Beals delivers a superior return on investment at your meetings and events. Presentations are customized to meet your organization's unique needs. For information, call (402) 637-9300.

Made in the USA
Lexington, KY
14 April 2013